"The Babylon Project is a dream given form.

It is a community which we build to create a lasting peace in the galaxy:

a place where diverse populations can gather calmly without the threat of war

and discuss their differences with the hope of understanding each other

and settling their disagreements peacefully. Today we gather here in neutral space,

in the shadow of a war that nearly cost us our civilization, to dedicate a place

for all sentient beings to meet and interact openly. The Babylon Station

will be built here in this orbit as a monument to those

who have died in wars of misunderstandings; a place where

the differences of our past can be overcome and we can live in peace

with all inhabitants of the galaxy."

—Senator Calvin Natawe,
at the commencement of construction of Babylon Station

The Babylon Project

The Roleplaying Game Based on BABYLON 5,
the Warner Bros. Series Created by J. Michael Straczynski

Written by Joseph Cochran, with additional material by Ronald Jarrell,
Charles Ryan and Zeke Sparkes

Designed by Joseph Cochran and Charles Ryan, with additional design
by Ronald Jarrell and David Martin

Illustrated by Joe Bellofatto, Catherine Burnett, Bill H. Burt, Shane Colclough,
Audrey Corman, Jonathan Darkly, Chris Impink, Veronica V. Jones, Shane Magill,
Mark R. Poole, Charles Ryan, Theodor Schwartz, Douglas Shuler, and Christina Wald

Cover by Netter Digital Entertainment, Inc.

Edited by Charles Ryan, with additional editing by Ronald Jarrell
and Joseph Cochran

Graphic design by Charles Ryan

Art Coordination by Matthew Tice

Playtested by Jon Brage, John Morris, David Sisson, and Zeke Sparkes,
with additional playtesting by Bonnie Arroyo, Jesse Braxton, Amy Churchhill,
Josh Durham, Dwight Gibbs, Chris Libey, Michael O'Brien, Laura Pearce,
Paul Pearce, and the Virginia Beach gang

Thanks to David Martin and David Sisson for development assistance,
and to D. Todd Perry for catering and food service.

ISBN 1-887990-05-4
First Printing

Original illustrations in this book are not intended to represent specific characters
from BABYLON 5.

Chameleon Eclectic Entertainment, Inc.
P.O. Box 10262
Blacksburg, VA 24062-0262
800.435.9930
info@blackeagle.com
www.blackeagle.com

WireFrame Productions, Inc.
P.O. Box 431
Blacksburg, VA 24063-0431

Printed in Canada

Contents

Introduction

Hyperspace, near Epsilon 3. March 3, 2250

"Major, we are approaching the jump gate."

Major Johnston looked up from the manifest report and gave his aide a short nod. "What's the status on the station?" he asked.

"We're receiving the reports now," the junior officer responded.

Johnston moved across the busy command deck of the Earth Alliance Starship *Eisenhower* to the communications center, where Captain Rowe watched incoming data flash across a vid screen.

"Looks good, major," the captain said, turning to greet him with a nod. She handed a data pad to an officer standing nearby, waving him off as she turned back to the screen with the major. "The reports indicate that the non-rotating support framework is nearly complete." Rowe indicated the console, where a wireframe diagram of the station rotated end over end. "The fusion reactor is ready to go online once you arrive."

"That's only the beginning, Captain. I was just going over the numbers myself," the major said, nodding at the reports in his hand. "We've got a lot of work ahead of us."

Rowe watched the rotating diagram on the vid screen for a moment. "I think you'll enjoy the work," she said. "You love challenges like this. It's going to be a really amazing sight when it's done." She chuckled a moment. "Hell, it might even draw tourists." The two stood silent amid the bustle of the command deck for a moment more, watching the computer drawing of the finished station rotate slowly, a green outline waiting to be filled in.

"What did they call it?" the major finally asked, pausing to think a moment, "a community for peace between Humans and aliens..." His face soured for a moment.

"Don't worry about it, Paul," Rowe answered. "You get to supervise the building, but the aliens don't come aboard until after you leave."

"I suppose that's some small comfort." He sighed. "What have you heard about the command of the finished station—have they finalized a decision?"

"Not yet. I talked to General Hague last night, and he said that they're waiting for an approval from Earthdome on the list of candidates."

"That's always the way of it, isn't it?" the major chuckled. "No matter how far along we think we are, there's always another step in the approval process. Another form to fill out, and another government official who has to lay hands on it to claim the credit later."

"You're always so pessimistic, Paul. Lighten up. Tell you what, when I take my leave next month, I'll—"

The captain was cut off by a beep chiming from the communications officer's station nearby. Putting his hand to the receiver in his right ear, the young technician listened a moment. "We've arrived, captain."

"Very good," she replied. "Begin the jumpgate sequence."

"Aye, captain. Jumpgate activated."

There was little indication of the ship's transfer back into normal space—a slight rearward tug as the ship accelerated, and in a moment the ship was through. The two officers watched the diminishing glow of the jumpgate on the main screen.

"Sequence completed, Captain," the tech said when the vortex closed. "We've arrived."

The captain turned back to the major. "Welcome to Babylon Station, Major Johnston."

What is The Babylon Project?

Welcome to *The Babylon Project*, the roleplaying game based on the television series BABYLON 5. A roleplaying game is a game for a group of two or more players and a gamemaster, in which they interactively tell a story. There is no board and there are no pieces, and the goal of the game is to experience the story that you create together. This book is a guide to the rules of play for *The Babylon Project*, as well as a reference for information about the BABYLON 5 setting. If you are not familiar with roleplaying games, the rest of this introduction helps explain them.

Roleplaying and The Babylon Project

Humans are social creatures, and we interact with each other on many levels all the time. Roleplaying is the art of taking on a new role, a new perspective, position, or personality. It can allow us to see the other side of an issue, or to look at things from a new perspective. It gives us a chance to escape from the limitations of our own point of view. Roleplaying games let us play those other roles for fun. The characters in the game are the alter egos through which players experience the alternate world of the game.

There are three things that bring the world of a roleplaying game to life. The first is the book you hold in your hands; the setting of the game and its rules. The second element is the character, each one brought to life by a player. The final component is the gamemaster (or GM), who plans the story and guides the game.

For this game, the setting is the rich and varied universe of the BABYLON 5 television series. This book contains a guide to the races, history, technology and flavor of the award-winning show. It also provides a guide to telling a story in that world, in the form of rules that help shape the story and allow the players to interact with the multitude of characters and settings in the galaxy.

The player characters are the fictional protagonists who inhabit the setting. They are much more than the characters that you might find in a novel, though, because they are brought to life and live in the minds of the players, who control their actions and affect the destinies that they will hopefully fulfill. The heart of the game is the life that players give to the characters.

The final part of a roleplaying game is the gamemaster. The GM plans out an overall storyline for the characters to experience and acts as arbiter of events that occur in the world. While the game itself provides a background and a setting, the GM provides the interface between the players and the events that happen to the characters.

The rules and background information in this book are tools. Alone, they provide additional information about the setting of BABYLON 5, a peek into the world that provides a backdrop to the story. But when combined with the imagination of, and a spark of life from, the players and a gamemaster, the tools herein go beyond a mere glimpse to bring the players an experience in the world where their own actions define their characters' compelling lives and stories.

The Babylon Project and Babylon 5

The story told in the BABYLON 5 television series is the story of the struggle of Humans to become more than we are, to achieve a destiny nobler than we know. Set at the dawn of the third age of mankind, it is the story of Humanity's quest to live up to its full potential. In many ways, it is the story of Human history, where fallible and real characters plot and scheme, live and die, and try to leave their mark on the world. In other ways, BABYLON 5 is a modern-day myth; an epic tale where heroes, born to fate and forged of necessity, overcome their own fears and limitations to fulfill a great and valorous destiny despite the overwhelming odds arrayed against them. It is a world that blends epic tales from our past, hopeful expectations of our future, and characters who remind us very much of our present, to captivate us in its scope and form. It is a tale of a world close to our own, told on an epic scale, a world where one or a few people can change the course of destiny.

Playing *The Babylon Project* is not about telling the same story as the television show—rather, it is used to tell the same types of epic stories against the same broad

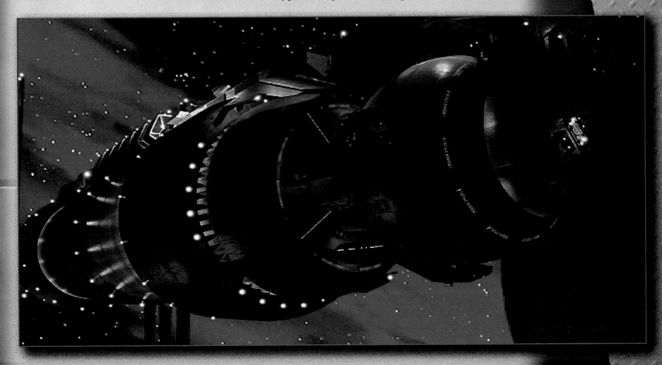

setting. While the main characters of the television series are epic heroes whose deeds shape the future of the galaxy, their story is not the only one that might occur in the universe behind the show. Events happen all over known space that affect the course of history, both to heroes and to normal people alike. Some of these dramatic events go unnoticed, and sometimes the repercussions echo over an entire galaxy. The characters created for and played in this game are not the main characters in the show, and their part in the overall events of the setting are different than those of characters such as Captain Sheridan, Commander Sinclair or Delenn.

So if players don't follow the story from the television series, what might their stories be about? The potential is infinite: in an outpost on the edge of Human space, characters may bravely repel an attack from a new alien race, then struggle to convince their leaders to sign a treaty with Humanity. The pilots and escorts of a freighter of medical supplies might drive off a raiding party, saving a Centauri colony from certain death. Whatever the story, it is a part of the tapestry of events that fill out the universe behind the show. The characters in the game are realistic people, complete with friends and families, interests of their own and personal quirks, who are thrust into the events around them and whose destiny is to defeat their enemies and live up to their own unique potential. Their fate plays a part, but it is ultimately up to them to use teamwork and their personal strengths to overcome their limitations and prevail over the obstacles in front of them.

The Babylon 5 station is the central setting of the television series, which concentrates mainly on the characters who inhabit and affect that station. But it's a big galaxy, and events all over known space affect the lives of millions. This game allows you to tell your own story in this future of mankind, and although Babylon 5 is an important crossroads to interstellar commerce and travel, most likely you and your play group will want to center your campaign of stories in another place or another time, where the exploits of your characters affect the galaxy in other ways than those of the show's featured characters. The adventure scenario at the back of this book provides one alternative setting—others are discussed elsewhere in the book.

Playing The Babylon Project

To play this game, you don't need a board or pieces, but you do need a few things other than this book. Each player will need paper and pencil to keep track of notes that his character, and the gamemaster will need paper and pencil to keep track of many of the details of the story. In the back of this book are three references that you may photocopy for your personal use: the Character Worksheet (used in creating characters—each player will need one); the Character Record (used throughout play—again, one per player); and the GM Reference Sheet (for the convenience of the gamemaster). Finally, you will need at least two standard six-sided dice in different colors (green and red, preferably, plus a third die in black, grey or blue).

As mentioned above, both players and gamemasters add a unique piece to the experience. The first section of the book, the introduction which you are now reading and

---

Game Terminology

BAB/COM

Roleplaying games have their own unique concepts and terms to describe them, many of which are used throughout this book. Here are some of the more common terms:

Gamemaster (or GM): The player who creates and guides the story, controls the non-player characters, and keeps track of other game setting details.

Player Character (or PC): A character created, and controlled throughout the game, by a player other than the GM.

Non-Player Character (or NPC): A character controlled by the gamemaster. Most are not as central to the story as the player characters; most in fact play very minor roles.

Game Session: A few hours of game play. Most groups of players meet regularly one afternoon or evening a week.

Story Arc (or Campaign): The overall plot of the ongoing game, created by the GM. It generally takes many game sessions to complete a story arc.

Adventure: One "episode" of the story arc, a smaller tale that spans a shorter period of time. Adventures usually take only one or a few game sessions to complete.

chapter 1, is a resource for the game—useful no matter how familiar you are with role-playing games and with BABYLON 5. The introduction details some history of the setting and Humanity's expanding role in the galactic community. Chapter 1 covers the rules for creating characters, along with enough background on each of the races for players to come to know the world in which those characters live.

The material from chapter 2 onward is best read only by gamemasters, as it contains the rules for determining how the characters' actions affect the world around them, as well as more information on drafting compelling story arcs for the players. Chapter 3 gives more information on the background of the game setting, including detailed histories of the different races and technologies (which might include details not generally known by the player characters at the outset of the game). Finally, chapter 4 introduces a fully fleshed-out sample story with both plot and character information, ready for any gamemaster. Reading any of this information may ruin some of the suspense in the story for the players, which is why it's suggested for only the GM.

History of The Babylon Project

The Babylon Project is set in our own universe, about two hundred and fifty years into the future. Its roots, however, are in the present, and it explores Humanity's future as a member of the galactic community. By the year 2248, the beginning of the time setting for this game, Humans, banded together under the Earth Alliance, have become an influential species in a galaxy inhabited by scores of known alien races.

Among over a hundred non-aligned species on various worlds are several larger spheres of influence. The Earth Alliance is the youngest of these, having explored and expanded their number of worlds rapidly. The Centauri are a race of Human-like beings whose mighty Centauri Republic ruled this area of the galaxy in its prime hundreds of years ago. The Narns, also humanoid, are a reptilian race once subjugated by the Centauri who have, through sheer determination, not only won their independence but also carved out a rapidly growing empire of their own, the Narn Regime.

In addition to the many "younger" races, there are two races older than all others whose influence reaches into this area of the galaxy. The first is the Minbari, a powerful humanoid race with a long and complex tradition of honor. This game takes place just after the Earth-Minbari War, a conflict that arose following a misunderstanding during Humankind's first contact with the Minbari and which almost resulted in the genocide of the Human race. The second "older" race is the Vorlon, an ancient, powerful and enigmatic race who do as they please. Those who cross the Vorlons never live to tell about it.

The story of the Human expansion from a lone planet to an alliance that spans over two dozen star systems is the tale of two hundred and fifty years of struggle, exploration and diplomacy. A testament to a race

Telepaths and the Psi-Corps

Shortly before the founding of the Mars Colony, a phenomenon that had been the object of joke, scorn and ridicule began to gain a measure of solid respect. Psychic abilities in Human beings had been an unproved oddity for centuries—but in February 2081, an amazing study from the Johns Hopkins Medical Center proved the existence of people with psychic abilities. The standard Rhine Card Reading test began to show, for some people, consistent and accurate results. Despite its amazing results, the study was accidentally overlooked, and did not come into the public eye until the turn of the century.

At first, only a few individuals proved able to read minds, and then only with a great deal of effort. But in the early 2200's it became evident that more and more people were being born with stronger talents. While this was hailed as a new step of evolution in scientific circles, in political and business circles, some powerful people became worried. This, combined with natural paranoia of the unknown, caused telepaths to be treated with fear and suspicion. Legislation was passed prohibiting mind-scans as an invasion of privacy, and strict prohibitions on the use of telepathy were enacted in all developed nations.

The research into psychic phenomena continued over the next ten years despite the public perception. An Earth Alliance governmental committee was set up to monitor this new talent. Telepaths of varying strength were identified, although none exhibited other paranormal abilities such as telekinesis. To classify the various strengths of different telepaths, the Psi Scale was created, quantifying the abilities of weaker and stronger telepaths. The Psi Scale was a useful scientific tool for research into telepathy, but in the absence of large numbers of telepaths, it had little practical application.

Children and teens whose ability began to manifest itself often hid their talent from the world to avoid persecution. Those who did tell others of their abilities were harassed and assaulted, not only by physical threats, but also by the hatred and fear of those around them. Telepaths were forced underground. They lived lives of quiet fear. They could not use their abilities for more than the lightest of scans without being discovered—yet they could not help but use them whenever they came into contact with others. They were a silent, lonely minority. But with the advantage of being able to read the thoughts of others, some of them did manage to rise to positions of power.

This changed in 2152. In September of that year, with tempers still running high from the bombing of San Diego, an assassination attempt on the life of Earth Alliance president Marion Robinson was thwarted by the actions of one of her security escort officers. It was later discovered that he was a secret telepath—and that his capabilities had played a major part in uncovering the assassin. President Robinson, realizing that telepaths were everywhere and recognized or not were going to be a part of society, decided to found an organization where they could exist without prosecution. The Committee on Psychic Phenomena that had been keeping track of these abilities since that first astounding study became the Psi-Corps, an organization devoted to finding ways to allow everyone, telepath or not, live together.

The young Psi-Corps drew telepaths from all over the world. No longer alone and no longer persecuted, telepaths could learn to use their powers. At the same time, study of telepaths moved forward at an accelerated rate. Setting up training and experimentation centers, the Corps provided a level of security that no telepath had ever known before.

Likewise, the Corps provided security for those without psychic abilities. With telepaths known and identifiable, paranoia decreased. A PR campaign further eased public concern. In a matter of a few short years, the Psi-Corps became one of Earth's most valued resources.

that thrives on challenge and that loves the unknown, it is a story that begins just around the corner...

Early space travel

Early in the twenty-first century, technical problems resulted in the abandonment of Space Station Freedom. However, the completion of the first truly permanent space station, Station Prime, in the mid twenty-first century signaled a new enthusiasm for space travel among the nations of the world. This inspired an unprecedented cooperation in efforts to create a permanent colony on another world. The efforts of new visionaries gave the nations of the world a renewed sense of wonder. The moon again became Humankind's bold frontier, with several exploration missions that heralded the return of Human footsteps on the lunar surface. The Earth's first permanent outworld colony was established on the Sea of Tranquillity in late 2064. With the excitement of the founding of Armstrong Colony, the perennial movement to colonize Mars gained considerable momentum, and a new alliance of nations signed economic and political treaties with the goal of a self-sufficient colony on Mars. Under the banner of this new Earth Alliance, the world had a united goal of settling Mars by the end of the century.

"The stars are our future, and we take the journey there as a united Earth for the first time in history," said Earth Alliance president Daniel Piezanni on the eve of the launch of the first family ship to settle the red planet. True to the goal, a permanent colony was founded in early 2090. It was plagued by problems in the early years, not the least of which was a attack by radical anti-colonist terrorists which destroyed the main dome, killing all of the colony's civilian population. A truly stable, self-sufficient colony was not established until 2105.

Following the eventual success of its Mars Colony, the Earth Alliance became the dominant government on Earth, catalyzing the failure of the United Nations. The more successful Alliance's government and military went farther than ever before in breaking the bonds of racial, social and cultural tension that had long kept many of the nations of the world at war. It was not the ideal model of peace, but the Alliance's programs of exploration and settlement galvanized the world.

The colonization of the Moon and Mars allowed Humans to look further out into the unknown, and early in the twenty-second century scientists began to seriously suspect something that had long been a subject of speculation and fancy; that we were not alone in the galaxy. Weak radio transmissions had always been thought to be simple background radiation from the galaxy, but the actual discovery of faster-than-light particles called tachyons led to the detection of real signals that indicated intelligent life.

Limited by the vast distances between stars, Humanity's main thrust of exploration was confined to the solar system. Orbital stations were built near Jupiter and Saturn, and Station Prime in orbit of Earth was constantly expanding. A new breed of frontier people began to form, whose needs and concerns differed from those back

home. The Alliance, although generally responsive to their needs, was sometimes at odds with factions on one colony or another, but the common purpose of exploration and growth generally kept the peace.

Despite these shared goals, the Earth Alliance was in danger of fracturing. The economy of Earth had irrevocably shifted during the fifty years of the solar system expansion. By the time the last feasible planets and moons in the solar system had been colonized, as in ancient Rome, the lack of future habitable sites caused economic unrest and strife among the colonies and nations of the Alliance. The epitome of this unrest was a terrorist nuclear bombing of San Diego in 2150. To keep the economy stable while quelling the unrest, the next logical step the Alliance could take was to explore other stars.

Unfortunately, despite much speculation from fiction writers, Humanity had never managed to discover a way to travel faster than light, and as such, trips to other stars in one lifetime were impossible. However, with the discoveries of tachyon emissions and with new advances in medical technology, a few brave souls set out on centuries-long journeys in cryogenic suspension to attempt to reach far-flung stars and perhaps contact any unknown alien races that might exist among them. These deep space exploration ships were the first serious attempt to find others, and as circumstance turned out, also the last. Because after centuries of outreach and speculation, it was not Humanity that contacted other races, but one of them that contacted us.

Alien Races

All speculation as to the existence of alien races was put to rest in the spring of 2155. In that year, Humanity had first contact with sentient alien life. A passing patrol ship from another race detected the signals from Humanity's colonization efforts, and reported back to its command via tachyon link, an instant form of interstellar communication. Days later, on April 7, the crew of a freighter passing cargo from Earth to Mars were the first Human witnesses of a jump point as a cruiser from this new race arrived in the Sol system with its escort.

In the initial confusion of this momentous event, members of the media assumed that the aliens were from Alpha Centauri, Sol's nearest neighbor, and took to calling this new race the Centauri. As each race began to learn the other's language, it was found that this was not true. The Centauri told Humanity of their glorious Republic, a vast empire that dominated hundreds of planets in this sector of space.

The physical similarities between Humans and Centauri were amazing, and the Centauri were happy to help their "long-lost cousins" learn to travel the stars. In exchange for some artifacts of "native" culture, the Centauri allowed Humankind to use faster than light travel and communication, and constructed a jump gate for Human use in orbit of Earth. This gate served as Humanity's primary conduit to other stars until the Alliance built its own gate in orbit of Jupiter several decades later. Under this leased use of the Centauri's jump gate, Earth finally began its full scale expansion of the stars.

The suspicion that the galaxy was home to other intelligent life was more than proven, and in those first few years Humans visited dozens of races in their galactic vicinity and made many fascinating discoveries. The major powers near Earth's solar system were the Centauri Republic and the Narn Regime who each spanned dozens of worlds, but there were also several cultures of only one or two worlds each, not aligned with these two major powers.

With contact opened to all of these races, Human scientists finally got a sample of Centauri DNA. Despite their claim, it turned out that aside from the physical similarities that the Centauri played up, they were in no way related to Humans. The Centauri were also a republic of only about a dozen worlds, far from the height of their power. As this information became public, the Centauri found their relationship with Humanity shifting. They agreed to sell outright the secrets of constructing jump gates and tachyon transmitters to Humans.

Interstellar Travel

With the secrets of interstellar travel and a system-wide economy geared toward expansion, Humanity reached for the stars with vigor. The Centauri contact occurred at the peak of Human expansion within the Sol system, and jumpgates allowed existing Earth ships to travel the stars with very little modification. From the acquisition of jumpgate technology in 2161 to the end of the century, Humans established twelve colonies on worlds at nearby stars, with six more outposts in systems with no remotely habitable planets. The young race's star began to rise as it left the Sol system, its home.

The era of interstellar travel brought new challenges to the Human race. Possessing the designs for jumpgates and tachyon transmitters was not the same as having the finished product, and a new field of exploration and manufacturing opened up based on implementing these new technologies. The key compound in constructing jumpgates was a rare metal known as quantium-40, which was found in very small amounts in Sol's asteroid belt, but not in any significant amount anywhere else in the

system. As a result, the first priority of Earth's new technology in the 2160's was to build ships capable of navigating the hazardous expanses of unexplored hyperspace, to find new star systems with more deposits of the valuable Q-40. This was no easy task, nor was it inexpensive.

Established links and beacons already in hyperspace were not difficult to follow, even for pilots and crews new to the experience. However, they led only to stars that had been explored and settled by other races. In order to explore and claim stars of its own, Humanity had to use the technology it had learned to build jump engines of its own.

A ship attempting to reach new stars had to navigate the quickly shifting eddies and unpredictable gravity inclines of hyperspace to a spot where a star was believed to be and open a jump point into the system using its own jump engines. Jump engines required enormous amounts of power, and any ship large enough to house its own jump engine and the power generators to support it was expensive and hard to build. Once a system was entered, the first ship would build a jumpgate and beacon for later ships, and continue on to another system. Unfortunately, even these behemoth ships were not immune to the ravages of hyperspace, and some were lost there, never to be seen again.

The first presence Humans established outside the Sol system was an orbital station in the Proxima Centauri system, a system that was not inhabited despite the similarity

in name to mankind's beneficiaries. Compared to Sol, the Proxima system was rich in Q-40, and enough was found to supply the Alliance with the materials for jumpgates for most of the nearby systems. The Proxima system also provided Humanity's first chance to settle an outsystem world. On June 10, 2165, Proxima III became the Alliance's first frontier world.

Even after a jumpgate was opened, settling a system was a difficult process at best—and a dangerous prospect at worst. Flush off of the success in the Proxima system, the next attempts at settlement included the Barnard's Star, Sirius B and Procyon A systems. The Barnard system provided small amounts of Q-40 and an excellent planet for colonization. Within months, a colony was established without problem. In the Sirius B system there were no suitable planets, but a station was established near the third planet, which was rich with all manner of metals and minerals. At Procyon A, there was no detectable Q-40 in the system, but the second planet seemed habitable. Scouting missions to the planet provided a perfect location, and a colonization team went to the planet. Two days after they arrived, all communication from the fledgling colony suddenly stopped, and the jumpgate stopped responding to ships in hyperspace—resulting in the loss of several ships. When a ship finally jumped into the system, the jumpgate apparatus was there but non-functional, and the colony had been abandoned. Not a soul remained, although there was no sign of attack or disaster. The Procyon A system was a deadly reminder that space exploration could be a great risk.

Despite the hazards and losses of life such as those on Procyon A II, Human expansion continued. With the jumpgate at home now available to all Humans and new jumpgates being built at stars nearby, all sorts of groups and ventures sent ships outward into the galaxy. As is often the way with exploration, claim jumping and small squabbles, as well as the occasional bad encounter with an alien ship, made the Human frontier a dangerous place to live. It quickly became clear that some control and organization was needed if the Human race was to survive in space.

The Earth Alliance was to be that organization. The EA headquarters in Geneva became the coordination center for all off-planet operations. From Earthdome, the Alliance maintained the definitive records of off-planet holdings, from privately owned mining settlements and resort stations to independent nation-colonies and Earth Alliance stations. As the Earth Alliance began smoothing out the colonization process and establishing borders with aliens, more colonies and stations were founded. The larger colonies were those only one jump away from alien space, where trade of materials, technologies and cultures became very popular and, for many people, profitable. Of these, the largest colonies were Orion VII and Proxima III. These two colony worlds became Earth's chief outsystem trade centers, with ever growing domed cities being built and settled as people arrived and prospered.

Earthforce and Military History

As the Earth Alliance took on the roles of administration of colonial claims, it be-

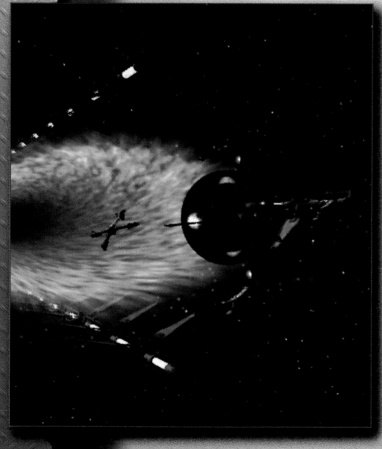

came evident that some sort of peacekeeping force was needed to enforce this authority. This peacekeeping militia, called Earthforce, had a very large defense charter and required more manpower than any single nation could provide alone, becoming a multinational organization. Earthforce became guardian of and peacekeeper between the various Human settlements in many different systems.

As Earth's sphere of influence gradually expanded, more and more people began to travel among the stars, and the Earth Alliance became not only a noticeable political influence in the galactic community but also a protector of the Human race. Earthforce became one of the most important organizations in the Earth Alliance, protecting Human interests and defending Human lives from those that would harm them. Individual nations' military forces were downsized even further as the need for more defense on various colony worlds and in Earth-claimed systems increased. Even so, Earthforce was spread dangerously thin over the new stars.

This need for more defense forces outsystem prompted Earthdome to reexamine the Sol system. The old Centauri gate in orbit of Earth was deactivated (eventually to become part of a living museum of space travel history), and the first of a new Human-designed model of jumpgates was built in orbit of Io, one of Jupiter's moons. This became the primary transfer point into the system.

Ship production also became a high priority, as Earth's space fleet proved very small in relation to the space it needed to cover. The heavy weapons developed by Human engineers were not as effective as those available through trade, but new ships were needed to effectively deploy such weapons. Bid requests went out to major contractors for all classes of ships, from frigates, cruisers and carriers to fighters and gunboats.

Despite the best speed that Humans could make on construction and recruitment of new fleets, it was not enough to protect all life at first. This fact became clear in 2169 when the outpost in orbit of 61 Cygnus A II was raided by the Koulani, a race from a non-aligned world in the neighboring system. The race took the outpost as a sign of aggression despite the fact that they had disavowed any claim on the system. Their attack was far too powerful for the meager defenses of the station, and half of the two thousand residents were killed before the Earthforce cruiser Asia arrived to even out the battle. All told the Koulani attackers, mostly fighters and a light cruiser, killed three quarters of the residents of the outpost and critically damaged the Asia, which was scuttled after the battle.

This loss of life fueled the Earth Alliance military buildup. The following year saw the successful debut of Earth's own fighter force. An attack by the Ch'lonas (another non-aligned race) on a colony settlement on Ross 128 IV threatened Human life and safety. This time, the EA was ready, and the Earthforce carrier *Avenger* met the attack, driving off the invaders. The key to this success was a new, maneuverable fighter, the Mitchell-Hyundyne SA-10 Starfury Aries, designed specifically for space combat. While the Ch'lonas fighters were designed to operated both in atmosphere and space, the new starfuries were able to outmaneuver the enemy with ease.

The success of the Starfury Aries gave the EA a distinct advantage over many of the non-aligned races, whose space fleets were not as capable as the new Earthforce fleet. This space superiority gave the Alliance a reputation among the alien worlds, and by 2200 most of the attacks from them on Earth territories had stopped. Representatives from those worlds began approaching the EA with respect, and embassies on some of the newer alien worlds opened to build stable, peaceful trade.

The Starfury, along with new weapons and ships built from Human and alien technology also drew the attention of the two major empires in the area, the Narns and the Centauri. While both races originally dismissed Humans as just another non-aligned world, unimportant to their own feud, the rapid expansion of Human territory gave them both cause to notice this new race, as Human space grew until it abutted both races' territories. First the Centauri, and later the Narn had border skirmishes with Humans. Eventually, the EA signed treaties with both races.

By 2220, the Earth Alliance had established a strong military presence in the area. Earth and its fourteen colony worlds and seven outpost systems were regularly patrolled by Earthforce ships. In addition, garrisons of Earthforce ground forces were

Alien History

The initial contact with the other alien life out in the cosmos generated enormous excitement on Earth—a sentiment not shared by all of that life. The Centauri Republic first leased and then sold jumpgate technology to Earth and sent an ambassador, but otherwise ignored the young race. Despite Humanity's excitement at finding out that they were not alone, to the older Centauri race Humans were just another non-aligned world. The Centauri had more pressing issues to deal with.

With a rich political tradition and a long history, the mighty Centauri Republic at its height spanned a over hundred systems. The Centauri encountered new worlds and races, almost all of which were technologically inferior, and subsumed them into their culture. Most were "willing" servants. Sometimes, however, planets objected to the gifts that the Centauri offered, and the populace was conquered as unwilling slaves. With their technological advantages, few races resisted for long. The Centauri had little trouble subjugating populations and removing troublemakers to become "honored servants" to the Centauri military on other worlds.

The Republic was ruled from Centauri Prime, a scenic blue planet with two major continents. The capital city was home to the Emperor and his advisory council, the Centaurum, a body of senators from all of the noble houses of the empire. The Emperor was given his title for life. When one Emperor died his next of kin would rise to the throne, if there was a clear line of succession. If no clear heir was apparent, the Centaurum would choose one of their number to assume the title and rule the Republic. Frequently, the term of rule of a Centauri Emperor was short, and it was always filled with suspicion and intrigue.

Over time, many of the senators became more concerned with their status in the Republic and less concerned with the planets that they were charged with governing. While Humans were first shooting rockets out of their atmosphere, whole worlds that had been subjugated by the Centauri were fighting for their lives, determined to never be slaves again. At first, many of these worlds were unsuccessful. The Centauri were powerful, and the only potential allies to Centauri-controlled worlds were the reclusive Minbari and the enigmatic Vorlons, much older races who were very far away. But as time went on, one by one some Centauri-held worlds were able to win their independence on their own.

By the time Humans were exploring Mars for the first time, the Centauri Republic had dwindled to an empire of only fifteen worlds, most of which were planets settled originally by the Centauri. None of the noble houses who had so badly mismanaged the colonies remained intact. The Centauri had gone from the Lion of the Galaxy to a fading shadow, but they were not a dead race by any means. Despite the long loss of their alien worlds, they were still the oldest and most advanced race in their region of space, and the pride and honor of the old

(continues)

(continued from previous page)

republic stirred the blood of young warriors and explorers. In a last effort to rebuild their grand dominance, the Centauri again began to explore the galaxy.

It was then, in the Earth year 2107, that the Centauri began exploring in new directions and discovered the Narn. The Narn were a reptilian race whose culture was largely agrarian, based on a familial ruling council, the Kha'ri. Offering gifts of advanced technology that would increase crop production and better the quality of life, the Centauri were welcomed by the Narn Kha'ri. This welcome soon turned to hatred, though, as the Centauri began to subjugate the Narn population. Within five years, the Centauri had mastered the Narn homeworld, and the Narn race was the first of a new generation of Centauri subjects.

The Narn began to change under Centauri rule. As conditions grew worse, their hatred and anger for their Centauri masters was refined and focused. The once peaceful people became a culture of guerrillas with a hatred for authority. Narns who were removed from the homeworld often allied with other races who used to be under Centauri control to engineer attacks on Centauri supply lines, to steal Centauri technology bit by bit. The new generations of Centauri subjects proved to be more a thorn in the lion's paw than a path to greatness.

During this period, the Centauri discovered Earth. Partially because of the situation with the Narn race and partially because Humans had a fairly high level of technology compared to most races that they encountered, the Centauri dealt with the Humans on a much more level footing, choosing to lease technology to the Humans in exchange for goods and services. This relationship proved profitable for both races, although it did earn the enmity of the Narn, whose motto had become "the friend of my enemy is my enemy."

While the Humans were busy exploring and expanding their tiny sphere of influence, the conflict between the Narn and the Centauri reached a turning point. After years of slavery, the Narn finally cut into the Centauri resource and supply lines to the point that the Republic itself was threatened. Finally acknowledging that "the Narn no longer desired their assistance," the Centauri withdrew from the Narn homeworld, but not before inflicting heavy damage on anything left behind.

The Narn, freed from Centauri rule, rapidly exploited all of the contacts their agents.

(continues)

stationed on all Earth territories, and all orbital stations were equipped with powerful defense grids capable of holding off all but the largest of enemy forces until backup could arrive from hyperspace.

Alien Wars

While the young Earth Alliance had participated in scores of border skirmishes with different alien races, they had not yet had any prolonged war with other races. This allowed them to build their fleet substantially. By the late 2220's the Earth Alliance had a fleet rivaling the Centauri.

The Earth Alliance, still in its early years, followed the philosophy that with great power comes great responsibility. As the EA fleet grew, its charter grew, keeping the peace in all sectors in which Earth had a presence. It also began to keep the peace in neighboring sectors, stepping in to help settle differences between races in conflict.

The stage was set for Earth to become a major power.

The turning point came in 2230, when the EA became aware of the actions of a race known as the Dilgar. Through the rumors of a dozen different races, Earth learned that the Dilgar were ruthless beings. Led by their War Masters, the Dilgar conquered and used worlds as they pleased, often as subjects genocide or cruel forms of experimentation. Prior to this time, the Dilgar had mainly confined themselves to worlds near their own, which was on the far side of the non-aligned worlds from Earth. But in 2230, the Dilgar began to strike out and invade many of the worlds with whom the EA had established trade relations.

Chief among the War Masters of the Dilgar was Jha'Dur, a brilliant tactical genius who also specialized in biological and chemical warfare. She alone was responsible for the deaths of whole worlds, many of whom perished as guinea pigs in her "research" into weapons of mass destruction.

Her legacy of blood and death earned her the appellation "Deathwalker," and among many races the mere mention of her true name was a capital offense.

With biological and chemical weapons developed through years of experimentation, the Dilgar had little regard for other species. Ambassadors to the Dilgar were met with disdain, and some were mutilated or dissected before whatever was left of them was returned to the EA. As the Dilgar expansion progressed toward Human space, the Earth Alliance felt that there was no other option than to stop the deadly advance of the Dilgar. In late 2231, the Earth Alliance formally declared war on the Dilgar.

The combined forces of the EA and the League of Non-Aligned worlds stopped the Dilgar invasions, and eventually began to drive them back toward their homeworld. The worlds that they were forced to evacuate, though, were no longer habitable. The testament of the Dilgar were dead worlds—plagued, poisoned, or contaminated with no concern for the billions who had perished on them in agony.

The campaign against the Dilgar was intense, but finally they were driven back to their homeworld. During the final charge, many of the War Masters were hunted and killed. Even Jha'Dur's ship was blown from the sky. All Dilgar found outsystem were either returned to the homeworld or summarily executed, depending on who found them.

Once the Dilgar threat was neutralized, the Earth Alliance left the system under the guard of some of the more peaceful non-aligned worlds. Only then was the true reason for the Dilgar invasion learned. Three years after the end of the Dilgar War, their sun went supernova, killing everyone on the homeworld—virtually every remaining member of the Dilgar race. Many worlds rejoiced at the end of the tyrants, but some mourned the inadvertent genocide caused by the Dilgar's own ruthlessness.

Through all of this bloodshed, the mysterious Minbari remained uninvolved, removed from the affairs of the younger races. Neither the bloody advance of the Dilgar nor the requests of aid from the non-

(continued from previous page)

Combining traded technology with that they had stolen during their subjugation, they were able to quickly establish an interstellar presense and build colonies on several worlds near Narn. But, like abused children free to do as they pleased, they began to do to others what was done to them. Their expansion was rapid and fierce and they cared little for the fates of the races that they met. Filled with the fire of their vow to never again be subjects, they conquered other worlds with an almost maniacal devotion. But their feud ran deepest and hottest against their old masters, the Centauri.

The Narn-Centauri feud was at its most intense immediately following the evacuation of the Centauri from the Narn homeworld. Neither race had the resources, however, to pursue a prolonged war, and after only two years of open combat the rivalry cooled to a series of colonial skirmishes and secret campaigns.

When the Narn first encountered the Humans, they regarded them with the same hatred as the Centauri, viewing the peaceful relationship between the two (and the physical resemblance) as a sign that the Humans had allied with their old masters. They attacked Human ships and invaded the Earth Alliance colony on Epsilon Indi V. But unlike the Narns, the Human fleet was not engaged in a war elsewhere, and Earthforce drove them back and eventually established a border treaty with them.

During this time, the Minbari watched the events of the Narn-Centauri conflict with concern. From their lead cruiser moving through the void of space the Grey Council, the enigmatic ruling circle of the Minbari and their leader kept an eye on the fierce conflict. But the older race was less inclined to interfere with events than the younger pawns in the ongoing struggle. Ambassadors to the Minbari were met with a sympathetic ear, but they always left with no promise of aid.

Though the Minbari had not yet met the Humans, they also watched the ambitious rise of the Earth Alliance. Their agents kept an eye on the young race, reporting to the Grey Council. This conduit of information went only one way, though. Although the Humans had heard of the Minbari, they had never actually met them, and their data on the Minbari race was largely second- and third-hand.

aligned worlds drew them from their own affairs. Despite rumors of their power, they did not interfere. To many of the younger races, including the Humans, they appeared dispassionate and aloof.

After the success of the Dilgar War, Humanity took on more responsibility as a peacemaker among the galactic community. With the ongoing feud between the Centauri and Narn, the Earth Alliance became the leading race in the area. With a vision unique among the races, the EA began to aid other worlds in building treaties and forming communities among neighboring systems.

During this time, a dream began to take form in the Earth Alliance. With all of the wars and squabbles that constantly occurred between the races, EA Senator Calvin Natawe proposed in late 2244 to form a place where understanding could be fostered and races could learn to settle their differences in a manner other than war. It was only a glimmer of an idea, though, and due to other concerns brewing at home it fell by the wayside. In the aftermath of the Dilgar war, many at home worried about Earth's vulnerability. They argued for a defensive, protected, even isolationist policy. This community of peace, while endearing rhetoric, was not a dream shared by all Humans.

All thoughts of expansion and peace were soon put on hold, though. On July 12, 2245 the Human race finally met the Minbari. But unlike their happy meeting with the Centauri, this first contact went tragically wrong. Its consequences altered the course of galactic events forever.

The first Humans to meet the Minbari were aboard the Earthforce cruiser *Prometheus*, escorting a light transport through one of the further sectors. As the Earthforce convoy entered the Altair system, they were greeted by the amazing sight of three Minbari cruisers. The Minbari, seeking to begin amicable relations with the new Human race that they had been following, decided to greet the Humans with honor.

As a gesture of respect for the Human race, the Minbari cruisers opened their gun ports to the Humans. The edgy Earthforce officers, however, mistook the salute, and fired on the Minbari ships that they thought were preparing to fire on them. Unfortu-

nately, the lead ship was the flagship of the Grey Council. Before the fight was over, one of the Minbari escort cruisers had been destroyed and the other two, badly damaged, escaped into hyperspace. The leader of the Grey Council, Dukhat, was killed aboard the Minbari flagship.

With their leader dying in the Grey Council's arms at the hands of the ignorant, savage Humans, the Minbari were enraged. A passion they had not experienced for centuries consumed them, and they quickly declared war on Humanity. While their main forces gathered, cruisers from their Warrior Caste began to strike hard at Earth Alliance targets. The younger race was no match for the Minbari crusade.

In a few short years, the Minbari changed from a peaceful culture to a warlike race, bent on avenging the death of their revered leader. All three of its castes, the Warrior, Worker and Religious, were of one mind for the first time in memory. With no dissent between them—no force of balance and no thought to reason—they ignored the

Humans' attempts at apologies, eradicating any and all Humans in their path.

Humans were faring poorly in the war. The best technology that the EA could muster was ineffectual against the Minbari ships. Even weapons and technology bought from the Narns and other races did no good as the Minbari continued their jihad against the Alliance.

In September 2248, the Minbari began their main offensive. On the theory that cutting off the head would disable the body and make the rest easy to clean up, they began a charge straight to Earth. All obstacles to their course were destroyed without mercy. Damaged ships were obliterated, leaving no survivors. The Minbari were poised to wipe Humanity out of existence.

All of the Alliance's remaining forces were gathered to summon a last line of defense between the Minbari and Earth in what became the largest and bloodiest battle of the war; the Battle of the Line. This desperate last ditch defense was a line of ships protecting the Earth from the Minbari, and the Minbari met it with unparalleled ferocity. They seemed poised to finish the war with the obliteration of the Human race.

And then, the Minbari issued a surrender.

Withdrawing their war fleet, the Grey Council offered terms of their surrender to the Earth Alliance. The Alliance accepted the terms without hesitation, desperately claiming the victory that the Minbari handed them. On the edge of defeat, Earth was given a new lease on life.

After the Dilgar War, Humankind saw itself as one of the dominant races in the galaxy. After the Minbari War, Humanity was under no such illusion. The war showed that the Minbari were centuries ahead of all of the younger races in technology, and they easily destroyed most of Earth's spacegoing ships, suffering only one real loss during the entire war. Over twenty thousand men and women formed the Line, yet only about two hundred survived.

For the Minbari part, they realized how close they had come to genocide. Once their bloodlust had cooled, they were willing to listen to Earth's appeals. In order to prevent further misunderstandings, the Minbari sent representatives to Earth.

The Birth of The Babylon Project

With the devastation of Earthforce's fleet and the fury of war turning to the tragedy of aftermath, people all over the Alliance were in the mood to support efforts to forestall future wars. In the Earth Senate, a project that had been suggested years before began to take on its own life. During the war, Senator Natawe, leader of the Nigerian nation, became an outspoken advocate of peace. His words, broadcast to far flung colonies and outposts, rallied the forlorn and gave the hope of peace to billions. In the surge of euphoria following the end of the war, the proposal by Senator Natawe for a neutral station devoted to the pursuit of peace became a funded project by unanimous vote of the Earth Alliance Senate. Despite those who still preferred to isolate themselves from other races, the project was begun to build Babylon Station, a monument to those who had died and a great hope for peace.

Funding for Babylon Station was quickly approved, and a suitable location was chosen over a lifeless world in neutral space.

Time Sense — BAB/COM

As different races from different planets communicate, one of the most confusing things to deal with is time. Most races base their measurement of time on the rotation of their home planets—a period which can vary from a few hours' Earth time to days or more. Trade and diplomatic contact forced interacting races to compensate for one anothers' time systems, but though the task of conversion was simple for computers, it often remained confusing for people. When the Babylon Project was formed, the diverse community that humans purported to build meant that dozens of different time scales would have to be integrated. The Earth Alliance's answer to this was to create a system called "standard time," corresponding to Earth's system of hours, days and years, that would give all of the participating races a common frame of reference. Although some races resisted at first, most found an integrated system more convenient than learning the time difference for every race with which they interacted. By the time Babylon 5 is founded in 2256, Earth's standard time specification is in wide use.

In 2249, the Babylon Project was begun. Construction began early that year on the largest and most ambitious project the Earth Alliance had ever undertaken. Babylon Station was built to house many different species, and to be a waystation for as many of those races as cared to travel there. Housing would be provided for half a million beings.

The station would also house the Babylon Council. This advisory council would allow the different races to peacefully settle their differences in a body of their peers. The Minbari and Centauri were quick to join, and even the Narn finally agreed to send representatives.

Before the station could be built, however, tragedy struck. During the assembly of the station's rotating habitation sections, the structure collapsed. It was later determined that substandard materials were responsible—materials that had apparently been delivered in error.

The dream of peace was still strong, however. The budget for the effort was increased, and many components of the original construction were salvaged. Work was resumed on what was now called Babylon 2. But again, tragedy was not far behind the effort. As the fusion reactor went online during superstructure construction, an explosion ripped through the station, destroying it.

Official reports called the reactor explosion an accident. Human error was the stated cause, and the matter was dropped. But some among the Alliance began to speak of other reasons for the destruction of the station. Many spoke of sabotage by separatist factions within the colonies.

The rumor of sabotage only shored up support for the effort, however, and rapid funding and approval for Babylon 3 was testament to the Senate's refusal to bow to the will of terrorists. Under heavy scrutiny and the watchful eye of the Senate, construction of Babylon 3 was begun. The infrastructure was completed this time, with no threat of collapse. However, soon after the next phase of construction had begun, the hull was damaged beyond repair by a series of strategically-placed bombs.

This more vicious attack and its terrible cost in lives prompted many within the Alliance to call for the abandonment of the Babylon Project. Despite the clear evidence of terrorist action, the Senate was by this point dubious of another attempt. But Senator Natawe's words—and the tragedies of the Dilgar and Minbari wars—still held great power in Earthgov. Full backing and funding—and a guarantee of security—was given to the Babylon Project by the Earthforce top brass. Under heavy guard, what could be salvaged of the previous stations was gathered, and construction of Babylon 4 began.

Babylon 4 was begun in late 2252. Under full military escort every step of the way, two years of round the clock construction began. Despite several attempts at sabotage, the construction was completed. After long years of effort and trial, Babylon 4 officially went online under the temporary command of its construction supervisor, Major Gerald Krantz.

But even this effort was doomed to tragedy. Twenty four hours after the station went online, it vanished without a trace with all hands aboard. Observers on a shuttle leaving the station at the time reported seeing a bright flash, then nothing. No debris was found, no energy traces, no signs of destruction. The station just vanished.

The Building of Babylon 5

Admitting defeat, the Earth Alliance Senate was prepared to give up on the project. Senator Natawe refused to give up on his dream, however. He approached the other alien races to try and get the necessary funding to convince the Senate that the project was a good idea. Initial proposals for Babylon Station had been met with no response. Surprisingly, however, this time the Minbari readily agreed to help, offering a large portion of the budget necessary to construct a new station. The Centauri and Narn followed the lead of the older race, offering just enough to convince the rest of the Senate to approve the project.

With a smaller budget, Babylon 5 was redesigned. With the history of sabotage, the military again offered escorts and support. Eventually, despite objections from civilian leaders, it was put fully under the command of the military, giving it more protection from those who would destroy it. The station was not as large as its predecessor, but the funding was still sufficient to allow a station housing a quarter of a million beings, with plenty of room for representatives from all of the known races. With what little could be scraped together, Babylon 5 was finished, and officially went online late in 2256 under the command of Commander Jeffrey Sinclair, one of the few survivors of the Battle of the Line.

The Babylon Council was formed, giving voice to the Humans, Centauri, Narns, Minbari and League of Non-Aligned Worlds. To the surprise of many, the ancient and powerful Vorlons also agreed to send a representative, who was also given a voice on the Council. Ambassador Kosh Naranek of the Vorlon Empire arrived on the station in September of 2257. The Babylon Project had taken form, and Babylon 5 was finally, as hoped, a beacon of peace.

Chapter 1: Characters

Roleplaying games are about the characters that star in them, and creating a good character and then developing it during play is one of the most rewarding aspects of this or any other roleplaying game. This chapter covers the creation and development of characters for *The Babylon Project*, providing game rules, techniques and tips, and background information for game characters.

The Role of the Player, The Role of the Character

The aim of a roleplaying game is unlike that of any other type of game. In many games, players strive toward a stated goal and victory, using cards, pieces, boards or other abstract icons as the playing pieces. This is not usually true of roleplaying games. The aim in a roleplaying game is to take on the guise of another character. While the character will often be trying to reach a definite goal (which usually involves winning some sort of conflict), the ultimate goal of the game is to experience the life of the character rather than to simply win. You use a character to accomplish this; instead of an abstract icon, you control the life of a realistic person.

The experience of this character is different from what you, the player, experience. You control the actions and thoughts of the character, although the character will like different things than you and will re-

The Babylon Project can be played in an episodic string of unrelated adventures like conventional roleplaying games, but it's really designed for epic stories like the one unfolding in the television series. In creating an epic story, there are a few decisions the GM will want to make before the players start generating their characters. If you are a GM, please read the section on building epic campaigns in chapter 2 before sitting down with your players to create the characters.

act differently than you do to different situations. Part of your job is to get inside the character's mind and act as the character would, regardless of what you might do in a similar situation. While you know it's all a game and that the character is completely fictional, the character would probably be quite depressed to learn that he's merely a figment of someone's imagination based on a television show. So you shouldn't let the character know things that you the player know. Keep in mind as you play that out of character, you will learn things about the game plot that your character won't know. This is called "out of character" knowledge,

and you need to keep this separate from what you have learned "in character." The GM and the other players will try to minimize out of character knowledge, but when you do learn something that the character doesn't know, try and make sure that you don't spill the beans to the character, either. Keeping what you know versus what the character knows separate will go a long way toward helping you feel like the game is a more realistic tale.

Section 1: The Character in Play

In any roleplaying game, the player characters are the centerpiece. The process of generating a well-defined character, and then developing that character through play, is the foundation on which all other aspects of the game—from compelling mysteries to edge-of-your-seat action—are built.

Character Creation

Creating a character for The Babylon Project is not a difficult process, but it does take a little time and involve some thought about who your character will be. Before the first game session, you may want to think a bit about the different types of people who inhabit the setting of the BABYLON 5 television series and about which of those types you'd like to portray. Your GM, who is putting together an overall story for the player characters, may have some suggestions or may be able to help you decide on a character idea.

Some players start with a specific concept for a character even before they open the book, complete with background, skills and 8" x 10" glossies of the grandkids. Most people, however, start with only a vague idea—a phrase or two describing the character's basics, such as an "Earthforce intelligence officer." If you don't know what you'd like to play even after reading the intro to the BABYLON 5 setting, don't worry. There are plenty of guidelines and sugges-

Examples   BAB/COM

The Babylon Project is a fun and simple system to play, for both you and the players. However, sometimes it can be difficult to see how things play out from a dry set of rules. With that in mind, examples of most of the rules are provided immediately after they are described. Refer to these italicized sections for examples of the rules in play.

tions below to help you build your character.

However you develop your character concept, there will always be some unanswered questions about your character, even after the character creation process is finished. That's okay, because the character will need some room to develop and to become more realistic in your imagination. These questions will be answered during play, and your GM can help you figure out how to fill in the gaps. If you don't have a concept in mind for your character, talk to the GM and see if there is a necessary role in the group that nobody else has filled, or a role that the GM would be interested in having you play.

When creating your character, keep in mind that you are describing someone who will be an integral part of a story. As such, it is essential that the gamemaster, who will be telling the story, is able to put these characters together into a group. Make sure that the GM knows what you're doing, so that the end result works best for everyone.

The next few sections detail how to build your character. First, you must set out a character concept. Next, you'll assign your character's Attribute levels in game terms. Then you'll build upon your character concept to create a list of Learned Skills and Characteristics. Finally, you'll fully define those skills and Characteristics, which you'll use in game play to determine how the character behaves and what he or she is capable of doing.

There are two important tools necessary to record your character in game terms. The first is the Character Worksheet, and the second is the Character Record. There is a blank copy of each sheet in the back of the book that you can duplicate and use for your own characters. The Character Worksheet is a temporary tool that you will use to build your character during the creation process. The Character Record is the permanent sheet that keeps track of all of the information about the character during play, once you have finished the character creation process. While some information will change very rarely once you have finished generating your character, other information, such as Fortune Points and wounds, can change frequently, so it is recommended that you use a pencil rather than

A character can begin the adventures chronicled in the game at any point in his or her life, from a young student to a grizzled veteran. However, upon creation a character is considered to be a "starting character" for the purposes of the game, regardless of actual age or background experiences. Starting characters have widely differing histories and specialties, but they are all roughly equivalent in terms of how capable they are in the game. There are no limits on what you can create, but if you want a character that is different from the guidelines presented for starting characters, talk with your gamemaster, as you and the GM have to be in full agreement on any decisions about your character.

Starting characters are no different qualitatively than most of the rest of the population of the galaxy. What makes them special is their destiny; the fact that your characters play lead roles in their adventures makes them special. Fate tends to be on their side. In game terms, this is represented through the use of Fortune Points, which allows characters to exceed their limitations or better their luck. The GM will give you these Fortune Points during the course of play, and you can use them to improve your character's chances at task attempts or to help your character out in a desperate situation. Fortune Points are discussed in detail for GMs in chapter 2.

a pen to keep track of the information on your Character Record.

Throughout this chapter, we'll follow Dana as she puts together her first character for The Babylon Project. Like most players, Dana has a very rough idea of what type of character she'd like to play, but she'll find that the character generation system helps her refine that concept into a sharply-focused and playable character.

Character Concept and Basic History

The first step in designing your character is to sketch out an initial concept, a

BAB/COM

The first step in developing a character concept is to come up with an identity—the core seed of your character idea. You can play almost any type of person in the BABYLON 5 world, so long as your GM feels that the character can be integrated into the events of your story. Some ideas include:

- Human ISN journalist.
- Narn war veteran.
- Centauri black marketeer.
- Human expeditionary geologist.
- Minbari diplomatic courier.
- Human business executive.

The first step is to establish your character's identity. Come up with a brief description or catchphrase that describes your first thoughts about the character—anything from "dedicated Earthforce space jock" or "itinerant construction worker" to "passionate Mars separatist" or "cynical Centauri diplomat." This identity is merely a convenient way to get a handle on the character (not necessarily what others see when they look at him or her), and describes the facet of the character most central to its concept. You'll build upon this facet, and develop others, in the steps that follow.

If you're completely stumped for a character concept and can't even come up with a compelling character identity, have a look at the sidebar for a few examples. In any event, when you've settled on an identity, write it down in the space provided on your Character Worksheet.

foundation on which the rest of the character will be built, and which will help you visualize what the character is like when you are adding to the detail of the character later on. There are three parts of this initial concept: the "character identity;" the "archetype;" and the "basic history." As you follow the steps below to develop these three parts, you will begin to fill in some of the sections of your Character Worksheet.

Note that the initial concept always includes the character's race. In the majority of campaigns, most characters should be Human, as both BABYLON 5 and *The Babylon Project* are mainly stories about Humanity's struggle to take its place in the stars. However, you can also choose to play a character who is a Narn, Centauri or Minbari. More information on each of the races is presented starting on page 138. If you

are considering playing a non-Human character, discuss your character with the GM before you get too far into the creation process, as it will be difficult to have characters from enemy races (such as the Narn and Centauri) cooperating or even being near each other without resorting to blows during the tense period in which the game is set. Ultimately your GM has to create a story that brings together all of the characters the players create, and it may not be possible to include characters from every race in every story.

If you're thinking about creating a telepathic character, talk with your GM before you go any further. Telepathy exists in the world of *The Babylon Project*, but it's very rare, and will have a profound effect both on your character and on your GM's story. If your GM agrees to allow your telepathic character concept, read the Psionics section later in this chapter. Then remember to account for the profound psychological and lifestyle effects telepathy has on characters when fleshing out yours.

You may also want to look at some of the Characteristics that relate to telepathy (the use of Characteristics will be explained below). They provide some options to straight Psi-Corps telepath characters, such as latent telepaths (those in whom telepathy hasn't manifested, and who might not even realize that they are telepaths).

As mentioned above, Dana already has a very rough idea of the character she wants to play, so this step is easy. On her Character Worksheet, Dana writes "Human transport pilot" in the Character Identity space.

Telepath or not, the next part of your initial concept is the archetype. The archetype is a short descriptor that conveys a bit about the impression the character makes on others. It can be anything from a job description to a personality type—anything that gives other people a handle on the character—but should at least include your character's gender, age (specific or general), and a couple of adjectives that reveal a little bit of personality or conjure a visual image. Your character's archetype may or may not be similar to its identity, depending on how obvious the central facet

Humans and Aliens

Most characters in this game should be Human. *The Babylon Project* is a Human endeavor and most of the events during the time period of the game are focused on Humanity. Don't play a non-Human without consulting your gamemaster to find out if an alien works with the story.

All four of the races that you can play are humanoids, but the similarities are only superficial. Each race has its own strengths and weaknesses, and each is unique in its history and traditions. In a nutshell, Humans tend to be community builders, and tend to be best at interacting with other races. We also tend to have the most eclectic mix of talents. Narns are physically the most powerful of the races, coming from a higher gravity planet, but tend to distrust other races. Centauri come from a culture with a high regard for society, and tend to be highly political. Minbari are an older race who tend to think before acting, and have a long honorable history. There's more detail on each race later in this chapter. Remember that most characters in the game at this time in the setting should be Human, so if you are not very familiar with the other races, you should probably play a Human.

is to others. Some example archetypes include "a cocky young woman, in a sharp, crisply-ironed Earthforce fighter pilot's uniform" (an archetype for the "dedicated Earthforce space jock" identity); "a bear of a man, middle-aged, with a thick mustache, hairy knuckles, and a mean scowl" (one for the "itinerate construction worker"); "energetic guy in his twenties" ("passionate Mars separatist"—note that not every descriptor has to have a lot of detail, but if you don't come up with something, your character will seem rather nondescript); and "a handsome but somewhat shabby older Centauri man, with a quick wit but something of a laisez-faire attitude" (the "cynical Centauri diplomat").

Don't worry about being too artistic with your archetype. And don't worry about being stereotypical, either. Remember that the archetype is just an initial impression, a starting point. Once you've settled on your idea, write the archetype down in the space provided on your Character Worksheet.

Dana builds on the identity she's started out with. The character she's contemplating is brash but earthy, good-

23

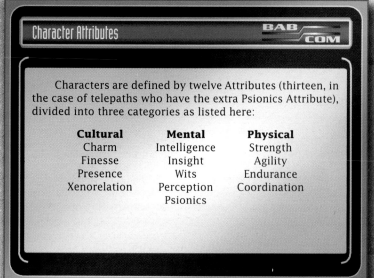

Character Attributes

Characters are defined by twelve Attributes (thirteen, in the case of telepaths who have the extra Psionics Attribute), divided into three categories as listed here:

Cultural	Mental	Physical
Charm	Intelligence	Strength
Finesse	Insight	Agility
Presence	Wits	Endurance
Xenorelation	Perception	Coordination
	Psionics	

looking, fairly sharp, mature but the type that was a tom-boy at a younger age. She's not Earthforce or a corporate pilot, but an independent, the type for whom being a pilot is a real hands-on job. After a bit of thought, she writes, "a small-framed thirty-ish woman with a coarse but friendly manner in a well-worn flight suit."

The final step to the initial concept is your character's basic history. While the identity, race and archetype give short stereotypes of the character, the basic history lets you tell a little more about what's gone on in your character's life.

Think of your character's life in terms of three phases: Childhood; Development; and Adulthood. You'll see these three areas in the Initial Concept area of your Character Worksheet (ignore the Detailed History area for now—you'll come back to it later). Fill in a sentence or two on each. For Childhood, specify where your character was born and spent the years of his or her youth. If there was anything particularly noteworthy about this childhood (if your character was raised in an orphanage, for example), make a brief note of it. Move on to Development, which covers your character's education and coming of age. What was noteworthy about his or her formal education, or youthful interests? What level of education did your character attain, and what was the course of study? Finally, Adulthood. Write down your character's career and major interests, and any major events of his or her adult life to date.

Picking a Name

Interstellar society in the BABYLON 5 setting is a bit more conservative than today's society. Humans and aliens tend to dress a little bit more formally than today, and address each other in a more formal manner. If you are playing a Human, take this into account when you choose your character's name. Names from many cultures are used, so if you have an ethnic background for your character, you may wish to use a name unique to that culture. Humans tend to go by slightly more formal names than nicknames. Instead of Charlie, you might choose Charles. Or Susan instead of Susie. Your character will probably be addressed by his or her last name, especially early in the story, so make sure that you tell the other players how to pronounce it if necessary.

Narns have only one name of two syllables, separated by an apostrophe (the emphasis is almost always on the second syllable). The first syllable is given from the hereditary family name, with the second being granted by the child's father when he or she is a pouchling. Typical Narn names include G'tak, Na'teen, So'ston and Ta'mar.

Centauri have a given first name and a surname just as Humans do, although they frequently go by only their given names. There are few naming conventions, as original and unique names are preferred, so that those who choose to go by only one name can be identified easily. Some typical given names include Reez, Mal, Dalleer, Kiron and Dira.

Minbari have two names over the course of their lives. When they are born, they are given names by their clan elders which they use during childhood. When they reach the age of majority, each Minbari chooses a new name to match the life he or she has chosen. A Minbari's name frequently has a significant alternate meaning in the dialect of the Minbari language that the character studied during his or her education.

You don't have to be too specific on any of this information just yet. It's probably sufficient to say that your character grew up on "a backwater colony world," rather than working out the specific details, dates, or place names.

You should decide your character's name during this step. However, if you can't think of one, or if you would prefer to name the character later, don't feel forced to pick one now. Just come back to this as soon as you do think of a name.

Dana decides that her character was born on Proxima III. She always wanted to travel as a kid, but her parents were homebodies, and even though she was an only child they didn't travel with her very much. When she was 18 she got a job with a cargo company that made Proxima-Earth shuttle runs, learning to be a pilot on the job. She made friends with several coworkers, with whom she regularly played pool at the local bars. The company trained her in all aspects of piloting cargo runs, from the actual technical stuff to a few tips on how to deal with hostile aliens or raiders. She got her solo license only recently, and is itching to explore the stars.

After a little thought, Dana names her character Jessica Moore.

Attributes

Having established an initial concept in a loose, broad manner, the next step is to define some of your character's specific capabilities in game terms. The most basic of these capabilities are the character's Attributes and Derived Values.

Attributes represent the natural, inherent aptitudes that characters have for certain different types of interaction with the world around them. They are measured on a 1 to 9 scale and are divided into three general categories: Cultural, Mental and Physical. Cultural Attributes are those qualities that the character uses to interact with other sentient beings. Mental Attributes are those qualities of the mind which the character uses to solve problems, think, and react to his or her surroundings in a measured manner. Physical Attributes are those

which allow the character to physically interact with the world around him or her.

The Cultural abilities are: Charm (a measure of a character's innate "likableness;" the ability of the character to engender a friendly response from other members of the same race); Finesse (the overall rating of a character's ability to manipulate others of his or her own race); Presence (an overall measure of a character's force of personality and the first impression that character makes on others of his or her own race); and Xenorelation (an overall measure of how well the character relates to other races). When a character is dealing with individuals of another race using a cultural Attribute, use the lower of Xenorelation or the cultural Attribute normally used in that situation.

The Mental Attributes are: Intelligence (the overall rating of a character's ability to apply logic, knowledge and scientific principles to problems and synthesize solutions); Insight (the overall measure of a character's innate understanding of "how

Human		Narn		Centauri		Minbari	
Charm	6	Charm	4	Charm	4	Charm	5
Finesse	6	Finesse	4	Finesse	6	Finesse	4
Presence	4	Presence	6	Presence	5	Presence	4
Xeno.	5	Xeno.	3	Xeno.	4	Xeno.	3
Intel.	5	Intel.	5	Intel.	6	Intel.	6
Insight	5	Insight	5	Insight	4	Insight	5
Wits	4	Wits	4	Wits	6	Wits	5
Percep.	4	Percep.	4	Percep.	4	Percep.	6
Strength	4	Strength	6	Strength	4	Strength	5
Agility	5	Agility	5	Agility	5	Agility	5
Endur.	4	Endur.	6	Endur.	5	Endur.	4
Coord.	5	Coord.	5	Coord.	4	Coord.	5

things work;" a measure of the intuition and common sense of the character); Wits (the ability of a character to think on his or her feet and come up with quick responses to problems); Perception (the overall measure of how well a character notices things and of his or her general awareness of the surroundings); and Psionics (the *very* rare measure of a character's ability to directly interact with the minds of others).

The Physical Attributes are: Strength (the overall rating of a character's physical brute force); Agility (the overall measure of the quickness and flexibility of the character; how well he or she moves); Endurance (the "lasting power" of a character, a measure of the ability to push physical limits over time); and Coordination (the overall measure of a character's fine motor skills and hand-eye coordination).

To determine your character's Attributes, start by rating them relative to the typical member of his or her race. On the Character Worksheet, under Attributes, the middle column is labelled "Variation." Rate each Attribute on a scale of -2 to +2, with -2 indicating that the character is well below average in the attribute, -1 meaning that he or she is somewhat below average, 0 meaning that he or she is about average, and +1 and +2 indicating that the character is somewhat or well above average in the Attribute, respectively. Your results must balance—that is, for every point above average you assign, you must assign a point below average in another Attribute.

Starting characters should have attributes that vary no more than 2 from the typical—however, you may have a specific story or character reason for more extreme values. If your GM agrees (and this should be fairly rare), you may choose a variation of +3 or -3 in one or two Attributes.

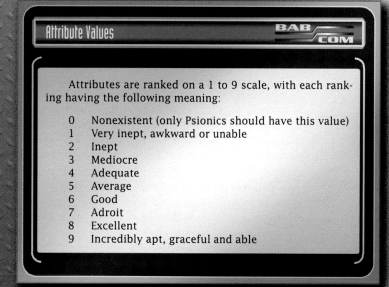

Attribute Values

BAB/COM

Attributes are ranked on a 1 to 9 scale, with each ranking having the following meaning:

0	Nonexistent (only Psionics should have this value)
1	Very inept, awkward or unable
2	Inept
3	Mediocre
4	Adequate
5	Average
6	Good
7	Adroit
8	Excellent
9	Incredibly apt, graceful and able

Dana decides that her pilot, Jessica, is much better in Coordination than the typical Human, but a little less strong, and a bit guileless. Thus, she writes +2 in the Variation column next to Coordination, and -1 by both Strength and Finesse. She writes "0" next to the other Attributes, indicating that Jessica is more or less average in these areas. Upon a little more reflection, Dana goes back and changes Jessica's Wits to +1, balancing that by reducing Xenorelation to -1. She has now defined a character who is very coordinated and quick on her mental feet, but who is slightly less strong and cunning, and less comfortable dealing with aliens than the typical Human.

Once you're satisfied with your character's relative values, copy the typical Attributes for your character's race from the Typical Attributes Value Table into the "Typical Value" column to the left of the variations you just assigned. Then add or subtract the variation as necessary, writing the results down in the "final value" column. Obviously, these results are the actual final values of your character's Attributes. If you'd like to double check your results when you're done, add up all of your Attributes (excluding Psionics). The total should be 57.

Dana copies the typical values for Humans from Typical Attributes Value Table onto her Character Worksheet. She then adds across, figuring in the variations she wrote down a moment ago. Her Charm is 6; Finesse 5 (a typical value of 6, -1 variation); Presence 4; Xenorelation 4 (typical value 5, -1 variation); Intelligence 5; Insight 5; Wits 5 (typical value 4, +1 variation); Perception 4; Strength 3 (typical value 4, -1 variation); Agility 5; Endurance 4; and Coordination 7 (typical value 5, +2 variation).

The next step is to calculate three Derived Values: Toughness; Initiative; and Resolve. These values are simply numbers that the GM will employ during gameplay to decide a few specific details when necessary. The formulas for each are listed on the Character Worksheet—simply copy in the appropriate final Attribute levels and do the math.

The most complicated Derived Value is Toughness. To determine your character's Toughness, add together the Strength and Endurance Attribute values. Then subtract 9 from that number (which may produce a negative result) and divide the result by 2, dropping any remainder. The others are simpler: Initiative is the average of the character's Agility and Wits, rounding down;

while Resolve is the average of the character's Insight and Intelligence.

Jessica's Strength of 3 and Endurance of 4 result in a Toughness of -1 (3 + 4 = 7; subtracting 9 yields a -2, which is divided by 2 to get -1). Her Initiative is 5, the average of her 5 Agility and 5 Wits scores. Finally, her Resolve is also 5, the average of her 5 Intelligence and 5 Insight.

If your character is a telepath, you will need a Psionic Attribute level (which is automatically 0 for non-telepathic characters). See the section on Psionics, below.

Detailed History

Now that your character's Attributes have been established, the next step is to determine Learned Skills, which reflect what the character has learned and done over his or her life, and Characteristics, the details, quirks and idiosyncrasies that make your character a bit more unique. To do this, we'll look back to the basic history you established earlier and build upon it.

Your Character Worksheet has a large section for Detailed History notes, broken into the same three general periods (Childhood, Development, and Adulthood) that you addressed when coming up with your initial concept. To the right of that area is a space for listing Learned Skills and another for Characteristics. You'll fill in those lists of skills and Characteristics as you work out details for each general period of your character's history.

The first section of the history is Childhood. Write down some details about your character's childhood years, answering some or all of the questions on the list below. You need not answer all of them, and you certainly don't have to write out your answers for each. Instead, answer the questions that seem most relevant to you or that catch your attention first, and then answer

any others that you or the GM see as important. Jot your notes down on the space provided on the worksheet.

- Where was your character born?
- Where did he or she live?
- What type of environment was it? Urban? Rural? Station-board? A colony dome?
- Was his or her family rich? Poor? Middle-class?
- What kind of relationship did your character have with his or her parents?
- What kind of relationship did the parents have with each other?
- What were their occupations?
- Did the character ever go to work with them?
- Did the character have any siblings? How many? How close in age are they?
- What were their names?
- Which member of the family was the character closest to?
- What were your character's childhood interests?
- Was he or she precocious? A late bloomer?
- In what way was your character's childhood unique?

After you've given a few moments' thought to these issues and maybe written down a couple of important points, it's time to choose a few Learned Skills and Characteristics. Look at the Skill List on the back of your Character Worksheet. Choose four skills that represent the sorts of things your character might have picked up as a child—skills related to his or her interests, early education, or general childhood experiences (you might refer to the skill descriptions later in this chapter if you have questions about any of the skills listed). A skill like Engineering, Aeronautical is a pretty unlikely unless your character was something of a prodigy (which you should have already noted), but Athletics or Diplomacy or History might not be, or even Survival if your character spent a lot of time tramping through the woods around her rural hometown. Don't worry yet about how much of an expert your character was at that age, nor about how good he or she is at these skills as an adult—just write down the names of the skills that fit.

When you've chosen your skills, move on to Characteristics. Again, they are listed on the back of your Character Worksheet, with detailed descriptions towards the end of this chapter. Choose one or two Characteristics that your character might have acquired during his or her childhood. Just write down the name of the Characteristics for now—you'll come back for the details later on.

Dana has already decided that Jessica grew up on Proxima III, which is a world with a domed colony, and that she grew up close to home. Her parents, she decides, were both blue-collar colony workers, who passed on to their tomboy daughter an appreciation for hands-on work—especially her dad, a Life Support Technician, who often took Jessica with him into the bowels of the colony's substructure. But she dreamed from an early age of being a pilot, and had a fascination with the stars and astronomy. She also enjoyed art, and wasn't half bad at it. She had a little brother, but he was killed in an accident when Jessica was 9.

Dana jots down a few notes on this history, then chooses four skills: Geography (which includes interstellar geography); Art; Engineering, Mechanical; and Hiding. She then looks over the Characteristic list, selecting Curious and Attractive.

If your character is a telepath, he or she may have family members who are also telepaths. Other than that, it is unlikely that his or her telepathy would impact upon your character's childhood, as it rarely manifests before adolescence.

Now you've described your character's childhood—next comes his or her Development. Write down the level of education your character attained, and maybe make a few notes on where he or she studied and any degrees attained. Some characters may have come of age through the school of hard knocks—if that's the case, think of these questions in terms of your character's experiences and what he or she might have learned from them. In any event, all char-

acters are assumed to have at least a high-school education (if yours doesn't, you should probably take the Missing Basic Skills Characteristic). Once you've decided on education level, as you did for your character's childhood, answer some or all of the following questions:

- What was your character's major course of study in school?
- Was that also his or her favorite subject? If not, what was?
- Did he or she pursue any other interests before settling on a final degree?
- Was he or she a good student?
- What did he or she do outside of class?
- What hobbies or extracurricular activities did he or she enjoy?
- Were there any particular relationships that marked this phase of the character's life?
- In what way was your character's youth unique?

Once you've addressed these questions, go back to the skill list and choose another eight skills that represent the things your character did and learned during the developmental period of his or her life. Don't dwell completely on education—think about other interests and activities as well. Some of these skills may be the same as ones you chose for your character's childhood—so long as you don't repeat all of the childhood skills, that's OK. Write the skill names down in the space provided on the worksheet.

Now move on to Characteristics, picking one or two new ones (not repeats of those chosen for your character's childhood). Write them down on your Character Worksheet.

Jessica's parents couldn't send her to flight school, and she was probably a bit too restless for it even if she could have paid her own way. So Jessica signed on to a medium transport making the Earth-Proxima run right out of school. She quickly absorbed as much as she could, learning on the job and taking a few filler courses here and there. The life and education of an independent

If your character is a telepath, remember that telepathy usually manifests itself during puberty, often suddenly and unpleasantly. From that point forward, the character's telepathic ability is likely to color every aspect of his or her life—be sure to account for that as you address the questions above and the skills and Characteristics you choose.

The third phase of your character's history is his or her Adulthood. Think about your character's career and adult life to date (he or she might just be starting off, which is all right). Answer these questions:

- What does your character do for a living?
- Is he or she good at it?
- Is your character recognized by his or her peers?
- Does he or she hold a position of responsibility?
- Does he or she like the job?
- What kind of lifestyle does your character lead? Extravagant? Simple? Beyond his or her means?
- Where does he or she live? Any roommates?
- How often does he or she travel?
- What does he or she do to relax?
- What kind of friends does he or she have?
- What do they do when they're just hanging out?
- Any romantic interests? Spouse? Kids?
- Are his or her parents still alive? Still in touch? What about siblings?
- In what way is your character's adult situation unique?

Once again, after you've finished thinking about these issues, work up a list of four skills and one or two new Characteristics and write them down in the space provided on the sheet.

freight hauler isn't limited to flight skills—Jessica spent her fair share of time on the docks and in the seedy bars favored by flight crews and cargo handlers. She had a couple of brief relationships, but found that she liked flying and learning better than she liked shore leave.

Dana chooses eight skills for Jessica: Piloting; Engineering, Mechanical; Engineering, Electrical; Navigation, Aerospatial; Acrobatics (which includes zero-G maneuvering); Acumen; Savvy; and Combat, Hand-to-Hand. For Characteristics, she's stumped, but something on the list catches her eye. She chooses Ally, and adds a bit to her history to account for it: Jessica had a mentor for the first several years of her education— a senior pilot named Bill Whelan. Bill has moved to a position with a major shipping corporation, but they remain good friends.

The line between Jessica's on-the-job training and her professional years is pretty thin, but she recently received her pilot's license, so she's definitely a pro now. She still works for the same shipping company (Dana and the GM agree on a name for the company: ProxTrans), piloting a small cargo transport solo on the Earth/Proxima run. Her leisure time consists of playing pool in dockside bars and reading up on current events while in flight. She's also nurturing a dream of buying her own ship, so she's been hanging out with a lot of independent haulers, talking with her dad about going into business together, and has even had a meeting or two with bank loan officers. For now, she lives alone aboard her ProxTrans ship, which Dana names Ascendant, and still has simple tastes, so she's had a chance to save up a little money. She still sees her family every so often when she's back in Proxima, but has few close friends.

Dana lists four skills that represent this part of Jessica's life: Shiphandling; Piloting; Gambling; and Diplomacy. For Characteristics, Dana chooses Assets.

There's one more area in the Detailed History section, marked Additional Notes. This section is optional, but you might want to consider the questions below, and jot down any additional notes on your character that might result. You may (again, optionally), list one or two additional skills and one Characteristic that result from these character experiences.

- What's the most dangerous thing that your character has ever done?
- The silliest?
- What planet is the furthest from home that he or she has traveled?
- Has your character ever met a member of another race?
- How often has this happened?

The "most dangerous thing" question caught Dana's eye. The small and independent haulers Jessica runs with aren't always the most savory sort—surely something in her background should reflect Jessica's occasional contact with these less desirable elements. Dana decides that Jessica once accepted a smuggling contract, hoping to make a little extra money and bring herself that much closer to getting her own ship. On one of her regular ProxTrans runs, she also took a small packet that she was

told contained grey-market computer chips. Along the way she was wracked with misgivings, and had already decided when she got to Proxima that she'd never do such a thing again. Then it got worse—the handoff to her Proxima contact was ambushed by a competitor. She narrowly escaped serious injury, and cleared the area before the cops showed up, but she did witness two people getting shot, one of them a bystander. Whatever was in that packet, it wasn't computer chips.

Dana adds Combat, Ranged to Jessica's skill list, figuring she took a firearms course shortly after the incident. She selects the Haunted Characteristic as well.

Now you're ready to work out the details on your Learned Skills and Characteristics.

Learned Skills

To the right of the Detailed History section of the Character Worksheet is an area for Learned Skills. Skills reflect the capabilities your character has developed over his or her lifetime, and are rated on a scale of 1 to 5 (though the highest skill your character will begin with is a 4).

Look at all of the skills you wrote down as you worked out your character's detailed history. Pick the one at which your character most excels, and write the name in the space marked "Primary Skill" on the worksheet. As the Character Worksheet indicates, your character's skill level in this skill is 4. Go to the skill description section towards the end of this chapter and choose two Specialties for that skill that represent the areas within it at which your character is especially good, and write those down in the space provided on the Worksheet.

Next, choose three more skills from those that you jotted down earlier and write

them down under "Secondary Skills" in the Learned Skills column. As listed on the Character Worksheet, your character's level in each of these skills is automatically 3. Again, go to their skill descriptions and choose two specialties for each.

Finally, choose any or all of the other skills you listed in the Detailed History section and write them down under "Tertiary Skills" on the Learned Skills list. You have 12 skill points to spend on these skills (unless your character is a telepath—in which case, see the Psionics section, below). For each skill, assign a level of 1 to 3, with each level costing one point. You must choose a Specialty for each skill, at no cost, and may assign additional Specialties (up to two per skill) at the cost of one point per Specialty.

Once you have finished defining your character's Learned Skills, you may want to fine-tune the history of the character, to more accurately describe how and why he or she learned the particular skills you have chosen. You will also want to share what you've done with your GM to make sure that you both agree on the skills. If you discover at this point that you really want your character to have a particular skill but it is not reflected in the character's history, feel free to alter the history to more closely match what you want. This is an iterative process, so alternate between editing your character history and your skill list until you and the GM are both happy with the result.

As mentioned elsewhere, while your character can begin the story at any chronological point in his or her life, he or she will still be a starting character in game terms, and will thus not be totally awesome at everything. A starting character should not be better than Adept (level 4—see the sidebar) at any skills, and should only be Adept at a maximum of one skill. However, a character can have as many Specialties in one skill as you choose to spend points buying.

Jessica's skill list is a piece of cake. Looking at the lists she's compiled while working on Jessica's history, Dana puts Piloting down as the primary skill, choosing Space Transport and Atmospheric Shuttle as Specialties. For her secondary skills, Dana chooses Navigation, Aerospatial (with Insystem and Hyper-

space as Specialties); Engineering, Electrical (Electronic Design, Electrical Applications); and Acumen (Veracity and Attitude). For tertiary skills, Dana picks Shiphandling at level 1 (for 1 point) with a Specialty in Light Gravitational Ships; Engineering, Mechanical at level 2 (for 2 points) with a Specialty in Mechanical Applications; Acrobatics at level 2 (2 points) with a Specialty in Zero-G Maneuvering; Combat, Ranged at level 2 (2 points) with a Specialty in Pistol; Combat, Hand-to-Hand at level 1 (1 point) with a Specialty in Punch; Gambling at level 1 (1 point) with a Specialty in Pool; Diplomacy at level 2 with Specialties in Inquiry, Obfuscation, and Emotion (4 points—2 for the skill and 2 for the extra Specialties); and Savvy at level 1 (1 point) with a Specialty in Underworld. Totalling that up, Dana sees she's spent 14 points, so she goes back and reluctantly removes Shiphandling (figuring Jessica has much more experience with single-pilot vessels than larger ships) and the Emotion Specialty to Diplomacy. That brings her total down to 12. Several skills picked during character history didn't make the list—that doesn't mean that the history is wrong, just that the experience Jessica has had in those areas didn't add up to any real skill.

Characteristics

Your character is almost complete. The last step is to read up a little on the Characteristics you selected as you thought about your character's history. You'll need to make a few more decisions about how they relate to your character's history, and many of them require you to specify a few details.

Characteristics can be advantages for the character, or disadvantages. Many can be advantageous at one time and disadvantageous at another, depending on the situation. They differ from skills, which define precisely what your character can do and how well, in that Characteristics add special opportunities to get into the role of your character and examine how his or her mind works. The best chances to roleplay are those in which your character is dealing

with personal demons and learning about his or her weaknesses, and many of the Characteristics give you the chance to do just that.

In play, whenever a Characteristic allows you the opportunity to roleplay your character well, try to get into the spirit of what he or she is feeling and doing. The rewards for this are not just a better adventure, but also Fortune Points that you can use to help your character during the game (see Fortune Points on page 114). However, with the opportunity to roleplay things comes a bit of responsibility. There is such a thing as overdoing it, and you should avoid getting stale or repetitive with your Characteristic, as the GM will not reward dull roleplaying. Your character

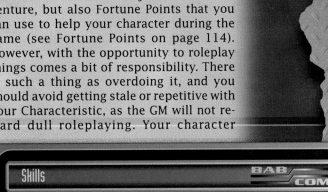

Skills

Skills have five levels. A character who has one level of a skill is Familiar with basic concepts of the skill, although he or she may not have had much practice at the skill. A character with two levels in a skill is Competent and can easily perform routine tasks involving the skill, having had both training and practice in it. At three skill levels, the character is Proficient at the skill, with a good knowledge of the skill and a great deal of practice, and can perform a wide variety of tasks. A character with four levels of a skill is Adept, practiced in a wide variety of tasks, with a great knowledge in the subject matter. A character with five levels of a skill is an Expert, with comprehensive knowledge of the subject matter and the ability to perform most tasks involved in the skill.

Each skill also has Specialties, which indicate narrowed areas of expertise within the broad skill. A Specialty adds two to the level of the skill, but only when the skill is used for a task within the Specialty. A character whose total including a Specialty is six or seven is a Master or Accomplished Master (respectively) in the skill, or at least the area of the skill covered by the Specialty. Masters have a great deal of experience at the skill and a strong fundamental understanding of the concepts involved. Such a person may even have contributed significant research to the field.

When a character first learns a skill, the player must choose a Specialty: a specific aspect of that skill in which the character excels. This might be the aspect of the skill that first interested the character or that which the character most used during training. This is a good way to generate a background story for why the character has the skill. Examples of Specialties are included in the description of each skill, but they are not exhaustive. If you think of an unlisted Specialty that you feel your character should have, consult your GM so that the two of you agree on its scope and purpose.

As your character learns more about the skill, he or she will learn extra Specialties. This happens in one of two ways. The first is automatic Specialties. In addition to the automatic Specialty that the character gained when first learning the skill, a character gains a second automatic Specialty when he or she becomes Proficient (level 3), and a third automatic Specialty at the Expert level (level 5). The second way is to use points to gain Specialties: a skill point can always be used to buy a Specialty within a skill that the character is already at least Familiar with.

should evolve and grow over the course of your story, and some disadvantages can be overcome. It is not unusual to outgrow one disadvantage only to gain another one—a part of growth is to change over time. If you feel that the character is changing during your roleplaying, you and the GM can always come back to this section and refine the character a bit more.

One final warning about Characteristics. Just as with other sections of character creation, you are trying to define a person who has lived a realistic seeming life, not a superhero. While you are encouraged to give your character some Characteristics, make sure that you have a reason and can explain to your GM how or why these Characteristics came about. The character may not even realize that he or she has these Characteristics (particularly those that relate to personality or psyche), but you the player know, and should understand the reasons behind them.

Write the Characteristics that you selected while generating your detailed history down in the space provided on the Character Worksheet, along with a few notes on each to cover the relevant details. If you feel that one or more of the Characteristics are not quite right at this point, you may discard them or replace them with others so long as you end up with at least three and no more than seven Characteristics.

The Characteristics Dana selected for Jessica while making up her history include Curious, Attractive, Ally, Assets, and Haunted. Dana decides to drop the Curious Characteristic, feeling that it's more a reflection of her childhood than her adult personality. Dana can still roleplay Jessica as the curious sort, of course—it's just no longer a driving part of her personality.

Dana starts with the Attractive Characteristic, looking it up in this chapter. It instructs her to specify the nature of her character's attractiveness. Dana notes that Jessica has a slight figure and a pretty, girl-next-door face that draws attention and causes people to forget that she's an experienced, grease-monkey pilot with a bit of a checkered past. For Ally, Dana has already specified Bill Whelan. She further notes that he is now Head of Flight Operations for a major shipping concern. They have a lot of common interests, and he may be good for a favor some time—or he might call on her for one. For Assets, Dana and her GM decide that Dana's savings now total almost 100,000 credits, though all but about 10,000 are tied up in investments, and can't be accessed without a few weeks' notice. Finally, for Haunted, Dana specifies that Jessica feels guilty about the results of her flirtation with smuggling, and can't drive the image of the bystander, lying fatally wounded on the street, from her head. She's definitely leery of involvement in any other unsavory activities, and has an aversion to violence where any innocents might possibly be hurt.

Psionics

Some races have developed members who are able to communicate directly with the minds of others. These individuals, called "telepaths," have appeared in three of the four character races. You may wish to play one. Remember that telepaths are rare in the overall population, though. Only one person in a hundred thousand is a telepath, and only one in a thousand of those is actually strong enough to do more than scan the surface thoughts of others. Your GM must agree with any decision to allow a telepath as a player character, as it will be up to him or her to integrate the character into the story.

Having a Psionics Attribute (that is, being a telepath) is in many ways an advantage, giving a character a way to gain information that many people cannot counteract. However, it is also a burden. Telepaths are not trusted by many people, and they are expected to behave in certain ways and belong to certain organizations. Rogue telepaths, those who do not follow the rules, are always hunted fugitives, on the run from practically every member of their own race, as well as others. As a result, telepathic characters usually live under very strict rules and laws dictating what they can and cannot do. Be very careful when deciding whether or not you wish to play a telepath. Your GM will have more liberty than usual to control your character's actions.

In the game world, telepaths are rated according to their psionic capability. This rating is called the "Psi" rating, and ranges from 1 to 12 in value. For ease of reference this scale applies across all of the races, although internally each race may or may not have such a reference.

While telepaths are usually typical people in every respect other than their abilities, the natural Psionic ability must be trained or practiced in order for the telepath to learn to use it. If you are going to play a telepath, decide what Psi rating your character will have before you assign your character's skills. The highest Psi rating a starting character should have is a P5, which translates to an Attribute value of 4.

Most characters, of course, have a Psionic Attribute level of 0. To give your character a Psionic Attribute level, you must, as just mentioned, first get permission from your GM. If he or she allows it, you may set your Psionic Attribute at any level from 1 to 4. This is aside from the

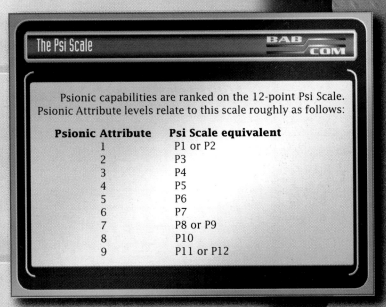

The Psi Scale

Psionic capabilities are ranked on the 12-point Psi Scale. Psionic Attribute levels relate to this scale roughly as follows:

Psionic Attribute	Psi Scale equivalent
1	P1 or P2
2	P3
3	P4
4	P5
5	P6
6	P7
7	P8 or P9
8	P10
9	P11 or P12

process of generating your other Attribute levels—you do not need to balance the other Attributes to account for the Psionic Attribute level. The telepathic capability is not without a price, however. Individuals with Psionic abilities spend much of their lives learning to cope with their talent. To reflect this, the pool of skill points available for buying tertiary Learned Skills is reduced by twice the number of your Attribute level. Thus, a character with a Psionic Attribute score of 2 will have only 8 points to assign

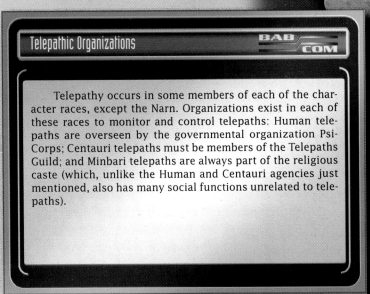

Telepathic Organizations

Telepathy occurs in some members of each of the character races, except the Narn. Organizations exist in each of these races to monitor and control telepaths: Human telepaths are overseen by the governmental organization Psi-Corps; Centauri telepaths must be members of the Telepaths Guild; and Minbari telepaths are always part of the religious caste (which, unlike the Human and Centauri agencies just mentioned, also has many social functions unrelated to telepaths).

to skills rather than 12 (2 doubled is 4, subtracting 4 from 12 leaves 8).

The Character Sheet

You've finished creating your character. Transfer all of the final information (those items in grey boxes) from your Character Worksheet to the appropriate spaces on a clean Character Record. Feel free to transfer any notes that you'd like to keep, as well. You may choose to keep the Character Worksheet around, if you've written notes or other items of interest on it, but it will not be used in the game, and you should not rely on it for info required for play.

You'll notice that there are a few specific spaces on the Character Record for which there are no equivalents on the Character Worksheet. Most (name, profession, and gender, for example) are self-explanatory and are easily derived from your initial concept. Others (like everything in the

Wounds box, for example) stay blank for the time being—information may be added during play. Still others require a little additional filling in.

The first of these is the Fortune Points box. Your character starts the game with 5 Fortune Points. During play, the number of Fortune Points you have will fluctuate frequently, so be prepared to change that number often.

The other missing information relates to possessions and equipment owned by the character. Have a look at the equipment section in this book, and draw up on a sheet of scrap paper a list of the things your character is likely to own (remember that the equipment list presented isn't the outer limit—your character probably owns a great many mundane and personal items that aren't detailed in this book). Limit your list to things that your character owns prior to the start of the game—not items that you think your character will need for upcoming adventures. Remember also that if you're picking rare or high-value items for your character, you should have taken the Assets Characteristics, and your character history should justify it.

Once you've created a rough list, run it past your GM. If your GM approves it, copy the list onto your Character Record. If you've chosen a lot of stuff, or particularly valuable items, your GM may balance that advantage by reducing your starting Fortune Points even if your character has the Assets Characteristic.

Playing Your Character

By this point, you should have a good picture of who your character is. You know what he or she is able to do, what has happened in his or her past, and perhaps a little about his or her goals and aspirations for the future. As you have consulted with your GM, the two of you may have specified a little bit of the recent history of the character that might include some relationship to other players' characters or other hooks into the story that your group will be playing out. The more you have consulted with the GM during the character creation process, the easier it will be for you both to include the character in the story.

This recent history will also include your first opportunity to play the role of your character. As your character is introduced to the people and events that bring you into contact with the other players' characters you will have the chance to play a bit with how your character reacts to these others and to try and think about how he or she would feel about the unfolding circumstances of the story's early stages. This early roleplaying also gives you the chance to feel out the character, and you can play off the GM with several different reactions to events to see which seems to be the best for the character. This chance for practice can come in very handy.

Now you've created the character. You've got the history, and maybe you also have had a chance to play a bit. Hopefully, your friends have done the same. When the group has gotten their characters defined and the GM has the story, you're ready to play.

Section 2: Player Reference

Even a well-crafted character in the hands of a creative player cannot succeed in a vacuum. This section provides players with detailed background information on the cultures from which their characters are drawn, and on the skills and Characteristics upon which they are based.

Humans

Player characters can be Narn, Centauri or Minbari, but the focus of the game is on Humans. Humans are unique among the races in our great diversity and ability to relate to the other races. These are perhaps the reasons why Humanity is one of the more powerful races despite our relatively late arrival among the stars.

History

The Human race is, obviously, the race we are all most familiar with. Humans in 2250 are much like Humans today, complete with the same faults and foibles that we carry around. Humans explored and settled the Sol system before the Centauri discovered us and eventually sold us the secrets to jump gates and interstellar travel. In a few short decades, mankind's sphere of influence spread from the single system where we were born to almost two dozen colonies and outposts spread throughout the sectors near Sol. Earth history is detailed in the introduction to this book.

Government

The Earth Alliance is the formal governing body of the united Human system and its colonies and outposts. The Alliance capi-

tal is Earthdome, a self-contained domed area on the outskirts of Geneva, Switzerland. Housed within this structure are the various parts of Earthgov, which sets policy and legislation regarding Earth and her colonies. Earthgov's structure is a three-branched system. The main ruling arm is the legislature in the form of the Earth Alliance Senate. The Senate is made up of representatives from each country on Earth, usually the elected or appointed leader of that country. Colonies and major outposts may send non-voting representatives to the Senate. The executive arm of Earthgov is the EA president, who serves as the figurehead for the Alliance and the commander-in-chief of the armed forces. The president is nominated from within the Earth Senate and elected by popular vote among the whole Alliance. The final arm, the judicial arm, is the system of courts that address grievances and infractions of EA law.

Military

The military arm of the EA is Earthforce, a military made of several service branches under the command of the EA President, supervised by the Senate Committee on Planetary Security and the Joint Chiefs of Staff. The two main branches of Earthforce are the EA Space Fleet and the EA Ground Forces.

Colonies, Outposts and Stations

BABCOM

The major races have three types of installations aside from their homeworlds: colonies, outposts and stations. Colonies and outposts are installations on the surfaces of other worlds. Colonies are civilian in nature, home to many members of the race, while outposts are military installations, more businesslike in nature and generally restricted to military personnel. Stations are installations in orbit of planets. Sometimes military, sometimes civilian, they are more often transfer points and docking ports of call than permanent homes.

The EA Fleet is made up of a mix of warships, transport ships and scientific vessels, with fighter support wings for ships, outposts, colonies and stations. The EA Ground Forces are a strong army of well-trained forces capable of going where ships cannot, to keep the peace and defend Human lives from harm.

Colonies

Earth has sixteen colonies and eight military outposts. The vast majority of those colonies and outposts, outside the Sol system, were settled within the last century. However, Earth's colonization of other worlds began with its first colony, the Mars colony, in 2090. The first outsystem colony was Proxima III, at Proxima Centauri, one of the three stars that make up the Alpha Centauri system. Along with the Orion VII colony, Proxima and Mars are the major colonies in the Alliance. The newest colony is Tau Ceti IV, established in 2248.

After the EA built its own jumpgate off Io, a transfer station near the gate and a supply outpost on Ganymede were established to control entry to and exit from the Sol system. The Ganymede outpost remains the Alliance's largest outpost, with the outpost at 61 Cygnus A II (informally known as the Signet outpost) and the Altair outpost forming major conduits to other races.

Station Prime, in orbit of Earth, remains the oldest currently inhabited structure off of the planet. Stations orbit planets in twelve different systems, both as colony support vehicles and as diplomatic liaison points for relations with other races. Babylon 5, in orbit of Epsilon Eridani III, is Earth's newest station, and its largest to date, outsizing many outposts.

Diplomatic Relations

The Earth Alliance was never a part of the League of Non-Aligned Worlds, since its rapid expansion precluded Humanity becoming a member of the League. The Alliance maintains very good relations with the League, however, after its tremendous aid during the Dilgar War.

The EA also maintains a slightly better than friendly relationship with the Centauri Republic. The Republic has been very cooperative with the EA over the years, and representatives travel from one world to the other fairly often. Due to the similarities of appearance between the two races, there is also little tension during commercial and social ventures.

The Narn Regime has a less friendly relationship with the Alliance. Suspicion runs high between the two races due to the Narn tendency to attempt force before opening dialogue with others. However, formal relations are amicable, as the Narns were one of the few races to support the EA during the Minbari War.

The relationship between the Alliance and the Minbari Federation is a strained one. Technically, the Minbari surrendered to the EA to end the war, so the races are at peace. But many members of both races were left unsatisfied by the end of the war, and the resulting tension means that official contacts are few, and are carefully handled.

Society

Humanity's most unique feature is its diversity. While many worlds have histories of different tribes, clans or nations, Humanity is the only race to have so many viewpoints and peoples. Its Senate is made up of hundreds of different people of different ethnicities, each with its own cultural traditions. This diversity is unparalleled in the galaxy.

Diversity is evidenced in all things that Humans do. Earth space ships, for example, come in more configurations than those of any other race, with more personal detail than other fleets. Each culture represented in Human space has different beliefs, histories and lifestyles, and all of them live together on many different planets.

Humans are also the most willing to do business with aliens. While all races realize the value of diplomatic and economic relations with other species, Human businesspeople take to the new markets of alien commerce unlike any other. This quality, some say, is one of the key features of Humanity that made the Babylon project possible.

Telepaths

Human telepaths belong to the Psi-Corps, an organization devoted to regulating the use of telepathic powers. It also provides a community for telepaths where they are welcomed and not treated with fear or suspicion. For the protection of all Humans, strict Corps regulations and EA laws govern the use of telepathic powers in the interests of rights to privacy, and all telepaths operating in Human territories are technically bound by the regulations set forth by the Corps.

Human telepaths who elect not to join the Corps are given the opportunity to live normal lives by taking a series of drug treatments that inhibit their telepathic abilities. Regardless of whether or not they use these treatments, all telepaths are offered job placement and educational opportunities. The Corps has training centers and offices in cities and colonies all over the Alliance to make it easier for telepaths to find them, and to make it easier for them to find telepaths.

The Corps provides telepaths for many types of services. The Commercial Telepath Corps is the organization's most often hired arm. They moderate business deals for private clients, often verifying the sincerity of negotiators, for a fee. All national, regional, and colonial governments, and many cities, stations, and other smaller jurisdictions have resident telepaths who are licensed to perform these services.

The other well-known arm of the Corps is Psi-Cops, the internal enforcement arm

of the Corps. Psi-Cops claims jurisdiction over all Human telepaths (and the activity of alien telepaths in Human space), and protect non-telepath Humans from rogue telepaths who do not register with the Corps.

The Corps also has a large public relations force. Despite the protections that the Corps and the EA legal system provide, there is still a measure of distrust of telepaths among non-telepath Humans. The Corps Relations Group is an effort to remind people that "the Corps is your friend."

Narns

A once-peaceful race that learned the lessons of conquest in subjugation to the Centauri, the Narns are, like the Humans, relatively new to the interstellar scene.

History

The Narn Regime is a new government for a civilization a little older than Humanity. The Narns were an agrarian race who lived contentedly on their planet, a world orbiting a red star in a small system out of the way of galactic travel. Learning sea travel early, they settled their northern and southern continents and settled into an agricultural society which they maintained for over a thousand years. While not technologically advanced, the Narns were a content race, and their society was one of the most stable ever recorded.

This society underwent a giant upheaval in 2109 (Earth dating). That was the year that they were first contacted by the Centauri. The mighty Lion of the Galaxy, the Centauri Republic stumbled upon the Narn homeworld during their glorious New Era of expansion. They greeted the Narns in peace, but their plans were not beneficial to the Narns.

The Narns had tales of races who walked the stars from their ancient history, though until then they were thought of as myth. While some of the tales told of wars and strife, the majority were of wise and powerful beings who taught and gave guidance, so the Narns welcomed these new aliens with open arms.

Those arms were soon put in shackles, though, as the Centauri treated the Narns as they did all of their subject worlds. The unique atmosphere of Narn made it not only a place to grow new and exotic food crops, but also a vacation spot, and Narns made excellent servants. At least, at first.

The Narns for their part soon began to realize that these Centauri were not the powerful beings of lore, and that all responsibility and freedom had been taken from them by their technologically superior masters. Over the decades following their subjugation, isolated uprising occurred here or there, and as the years wore on the Narns began to organize. An underground formed that allowed them to fight back against their masters. Narns who had been taken offworld early in the occupation began to use their opportunities for contact with other races to deal for arms and new technology. Narns on homeworld learned to steal munitions and technologies, and to exploit what they stole. In less than a generation, the Narns evolved under the Centauri yoke from a peaceful agricultural world to a world of guerrilla fighters, struggling for freedom and peace.

The occupation of the Narn homeworld came to an end in 2214, approximately one century after it first began. With their supply lines sabotaged, their colonists' lives in severe jeopardy and their "servants" becoming a serious military threat, the Centauri officially "recognized" the Narn wish to be an independent world and withdrew—but not before removing or sabotaging whatever they could.

Narn began to rebuild as soon as the Centauri left, using their new technologies and their vows to never be slaves again to transform their shattered society into an army capable of defending their system. Their newfound might was a gift to them, and to secure their families they began to set up military outposts, then colonies, at nearby stars, to create a buffer zone from which they could defend their world. Races in some of these nearby systems were merely obstacles to this, and the Narns felt no reservations about doing to others what had been done to them, to protect other Narns from the yoke of cruel masters.

In the decades since the liberation of their homeworld, the Narns have grown

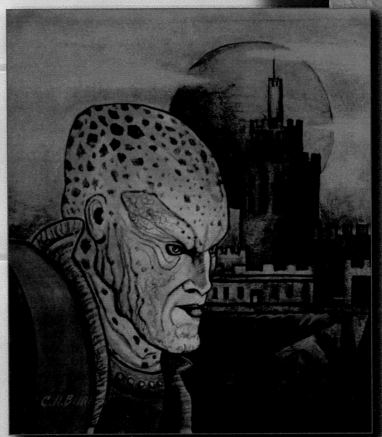

from their single system to a Regime stretching over fifteen systems and holding several races in subjugation. Nine of those are systems that were once controlled by the Centauri. Their thirst for technology has allowed them to become a dominant force in their sector of space, and they have used this dominance to secure military footholds wherever possible.

They have also become much less isolated. After establishing themselves in the galaxy, they began economic relations with as many worlds as possible, believing that trade, the most often used form of interrelation of different tribes on old Narn, was the best way to forge friendships with their neighbors. However, they had little concern for political boundaries at first (only refusing to trade with the Centauri and their "servants"), and quickly gained a mercenary trade reputation. They sold weapons and supplies to three different warring factions within the League of Non-Aligned Worlds, angering all three, before they fully realized the value of diplomatic trade policy.

organization is at present restricted to those who served and led in the overthrow of the Centauri. They must each have years of religious training, as they also serve as the religious leaders of the various worlds where the individual members live, much as the elders of the older tribes guided their extended families before the occupation.

Military

The Narn military is under the direct command of the Kha'ri, with many of the generals and commanders belonging to the Fifth and Sixth Circles. It serves as both a combat force against outside races and a punitive arm within the Regime. Ship captains and fleet commanders are given wider latitude in carrying out the directives of the Kha'ri than those of any other race, making Narn tactics very wide ranging in nature.

Narn ships mix technologies from many different races, and older ships were often equipped with a hodgepodge of systems and components that were barely forced to work together. In the decades since the overthrow of the Centauri, the Narn war machine has become a well tuned instrument, though, and the current Narn fleet is very distinctive, with designs thematically based on classic seagoing vessels from before the occupation.

They were also one of the few races that dealt with the beleaguered Humans, supplying them with badly needed weapons and ships during the Earth-Minbari war.

Despite their troubles, they have risen above what they were and are a race whose star is rising.

Government

The current government of Narn is the Kha'ri, a ruling body both political and religious, hearkening back to the days of familial rule before the occupation began. The Kha'ri consists of eight circles. The First Circle rules the entire Regime, handing down directives to all of the Narn colonies and outposts. Seven Outer Circles provide various executive and advisory functions to the First Circle, each subordinate to the one above it, so that the hierarchical ties reminiscent of the ancient family are reinforced.

The members of the Kha'ri are selected by recommendation from within, and the

Colonies

Narn colonial policy pursues several goals. The first, and perhaps most important to the Narns, is taking a bite out of the Centauri Republic. Vengeance on their old masters is foremost in the Narn mind. The next function of the colonies is as defense posts. The Narns colonized every system near their own, making it difficult for ships to jump into the heart of Narn space without warning. Finally, the colonies provide resources to supply the expanding Regime with raw materials for ships, food for crews and the all important Quantium-40 for jump capabilities.

Due to this eye to defense, the Narn Regime is very compact compared to the other major races. Their main colonies are at Quadrant 37 and Quadrant 14 bordering Centauri space.

Diplomatic Relations

The Narns are a race very new to diplomacy. Despite their long tradition of peaceful planetary rule, the occupation has left a deep wound in their culture, and they are often short tempered and belligerent with other races—a quality that gets them into trouble more often than not. They have emissaries on many worlds, most of whom are members of one of the Outer Circles of the Kha'ri.

They are still known as a race who will sell anything to anyone for the right price. Subtlety is not a tool with which they are familiar, and they do not believe in give-and-take negotiations, as most of the Kha'ri still remembers the occupation. Younger Narns relate a little better to Humans and other races, but they are still taught by those who knew nothing other than slavery.

Society

Modern Narn society is based on the traditional, pre-Centauri structure. In the old days, the Narn were ruled by family tribes and groups of elders, and their society valued the family above all. That remains the case now, though families are often spread out over vast distances, due to displacement by the Centauri, the dispersed nature of modern life, and the demands of an interstellar empire. Also, loyalty to the Kha'ri is high, often rivalling or surpassing family loyalty for some individuals.

Traditional penalties for crimes often followed the eye for an eye philosophy, and were often executed by the members of the family. Retribution took the form of oaths against the perpetrator, from the simple Cha'lar right to property to the Chon'kar, the blood oath of vengeance for wrongful death. Again, this system is still honored, and the Narn rely on almost no governmental justice system.

Before the coming of the Centauri, concerns of importance were discussed at a periodic meeting known as the Kha'ri, a gathering of as many of the familial elders for the tribes as could be gathered. This concept grew into the modern, permanent body of the same name, discussed above.

Telepaths

There are no Narn telepaths. Narn history says that once in the ancient past the talent—or something very much like it—was not too uncommon, but no gene comparable to the one that controls telepathy in other races has been identified. Narn scientists have gone to great lengths in the study of telepathy, and in attempts to develop telepathy through genetic manipulation. So far, efforts spanning from medical experiments to cross-breeding with other races (usually requiring much genetic manipulation), have developed no signs of true psionics in Narns.

Centauri

The Centauri are the oldest of the "younger races" (as all of the other player character races are known by the Minbari). With over a thousand years of space travel, the Republic at its peak spanned over one hundred and fifty systems.

History

The history of the Centauri started with conflict, and it is a part of every day in their life. From physical conflict to social and political conflict, Centauri thrive on challenge. In the early days of their people, two species battled for supremacy on Centauri Prime: the Centauri and a race known as the Xon. In the early years of their civilization, the Centauri were geographically separated from the Xon, and contacts were few. When they occurred, however, they were hostile—the Xon were much larger and more brutal than the Centauri, and invariably treated captured or enslaved Centauri with great cruelty. Eventually, as the generally medieval Centauri society progressed into the early stages of renaissance, the pressures of growing civilizations brought the two races into continual contact—and continual warfare. Despite their physical prowess, however, the Xon were less intellectually and civilly developed (at least according to Centauri histories), and after decades of warfare were eventually defeated and then wiped out.

That was around the year 500, Earth dating, and it set the stage for modern Centauri society. The families whose forces had done the majority of the fighting in the war banded together to form a governing body for the race. Recognizing the nobility of these new houses, the Centauri people became one united nation. The noble houses formed the Centaurum, a ruling and advisory council, and the leader of the highest noble house became the Emperor, the leader of all Centauri.

Some time after the founding of the Centaurum, as Centauri technology was hitting the equivalent of Human twentieth-century levels, an alien ship crashed on Centauri Prime. This ship carried advanced technologies, which the Centauri used to

learn the arts of interstellar travel. They quickly discovered other planets and other races in the nearby systems, none of which was as technologically advanced as they. The Centauri used their technological edge aggressively. Their experiences with the Xon had given them only two models of relations with others on which to base their expansion: slavery and annihilation. Those races that did not fight the Centauri were given the opportunity to serve them, and those that did fight were usually destroyed.

The expansion of the Republic began slowly, and they carefully built their empire, not expanding to the next world until the previous one was under control. This methodical growth served them well, and over the next six centuries, their sphere of influence included over one hundred systems. It boasted a fleet of thousands of ships, and tales of some planets still speak of the ships so numerous that they blocked out the sun.

During this period of expansion, the Centauri also encountered the Minbari and Vorlon races. These older races were far more powerful than the Centauri had ever encountered before, and they were forced to learn another model for relating to other races. Although none of the expeditions into Vorlon space ever returned, those sent into Minbari space were received as guests as long as they did not instigate hostilities. After centuries of politicing at home, the Centauri readily adapted to the arts of interracial diplomacy.

The Republic reached its peak in the 1700's by Earth time. For over two centuries they reigned, known as the mighty "Lion of the Galaxy." On the surface, they were perhaps the most successful galactic empire in known history. But they were torn from within and out by strife. The very foundation of the Republic was conflict and turmoil. Subject worlds became ever more restless over the centuries, as discontent rumbled among the worlds under Centauri rule. And at home on Centauri Prime, the Centaurum was torn by political struggle and backstabbing. The average lifetime of an Emperor was half of what it had been, due to the multitude of mudslinging, innuendo and assassinations that plagued the royal court. The Noble Houses were at each other's throats, and although they didn't know it, they were cutting the heart out of the foundations of the Republic.

While Humans were taking their first fragile steps off of their world far removed from the center of galactic events, the Centauri Republic began to fall to its fate. Discontent moved to hatred, and hatred to resistance on many of the Centauri worlds—far too many fronts for the fleet to defend. Records conflict on which world first moved from resistance to open rebellion, but within the span of two years, the Republic began to fall apart. Those races that had been Centauri subjects began to form their own fleets, from ships that had once been Centauri and ships that had been built under the Centauri rule. The great fleet was reduced, and the Republic began a rapid decline.

The worlds that had broken from the Republic began to explore on their own, first fighting among themselves and then forming the League of Non-Aligned Worlds, made up of both old Republic worlds and others who wished to maintain their independence. Although the Centauri government at first refused to acknowledge the League, their diminishing role in the galactic community eventually forced them to.

The Centauri took their change in circumstance badly. The Noble Houses fought among themselves, blaming one another for the rebellions. While war decimated their forces, the Centaurum argued and debated over which House was to blame for each world.

After only decades the Centauri Republic, which had reigned in glory for centuries, had been reduced to a mere shadow of its former self. But the Republic was not dead by any means. As the older generation of those in power when the rebellions started to die off, a new generation of Centauri took over, with a passion for the glory days of the Republic that outstripped their mutual antagonism.

With a new fervor, the Centauri once again began to explore, heading into new territory rather than attempting to retake their old conquests. When they met a race that already had spacefaring technology, they started diplomatic relations with them. But occasionally, they found rich worlds with simple populations, and then they fell back on the old ways of gaining rule over those worlds.

One of these worlds was the Narn homeworld. To the Centauri, it was a paradise. The natives of the planet were very simple and primitive, in addition to being strong workers. Many plants, animals, and resources of Narn had great appeal to the Centauri, and Narn delicacies, handcrafts, and luxuries became unusually sought after throughout the new empire. Service on Narn was a prime assignment.

But the Narn, unlike most other Centauri subject races, proved a burden rather than a resource. Although they seemed a peaceful people, they turned out to be fierce, hostile and destructive. Measures that calmed other populations only inflamed them. Attempts to remove or relocate instigators were only met with the creation of more instigators. More Centauri resources went into controlling that one planet than had ever been spent before, and only pride and their determination kept them in charge on Narn.

Finally, the Centauri were forced to concede. The Narns had made the planet untenable, so the Centauri withdrew and recognized them as an independent race. Within the councils of the Centaurum, however, much hatred was and still is held for the Narns.

Once it was proven to all that the mighty Republic was a thing of the past, the Centauri lost much of their remaining credibility. They still boasted one of the largest fleets of any known race, and their activities affect most of the surrounding systems, but their time had passed. The Centauri could only watch the decline of the Republic and remember fondly the glory days of old.

Government

The head of the Republic and its leader is the Emperor. From his palace on Centauri Prime, through consultation with his Prime Minister and royal advisors, he sets planetary policy on all issues. He is also advised by members of the Centaurum, a body of senators chosen from their family homes to convey the will of the people to the Emperor.

Since the Emperor, whose family is the highest among the noble houses, is assumed to act for his people by the grace of the gods and goddesses, his word is valued above all others. His advisors have no power of law, and the Centaurum may only override him with a three-quarter vote of its members—a very tricky proposition in the highly-politicized atmosphere of the Centauri government.

The Centaurum, in addition to its other duties, carries out the will of the Emperor in all things. Day to day economic and political matters are handled in the chambers of the Centaurum, with only the highest priority matters going to the Emperor's attention. Members of this august body are elected or appointed, and hold their positions indefinitely. In the event that the Emperor dies with no clear heir, the Centaurum looks within to find another house with a history as noble as the old Emperor, appointing the new Emperor from their ranks.

Military

The Centauri space fleet is the most powerful fleet of the younger races. In both number and capabilities, the Centauri are capable of simultaneously defending all twelve of their remaining worlds. Military actions are ordered by the Emperor and his military advisors, chief among them the Grand Fleet Admiral.

The Centauri Royal Guardsmen make up the bulk of the Republic's ground forces. Originally an escort force for the Emperor in times of war, the Guardsmen's role expanded to include ground operations on rebellious colony worlds. Today, it fills both military and law enforcement roles for the Republic.

Colonies

The remaining Centauri colonies are those systems in which they settled uninhabited worlds. While several are productive agricultural and manufacturing worlds, the chief industry that keeps them self-sufficient is tourism. The Centauri have a longer recorded history than any other race that allows free travel, so their worlds are those with the longest-standing buildings and monuments to the past. Individuals

interested in history eventually visit the Centauri colonies in their search for knowledge.

Their chief commercial colony is Immolan V, one of the first colonies with a proud history. Other colonies include the agricultural colony on Rahgesh 3 and their mineral outpost in Quadrant 27. Colonies near Narn space tend to be military in nature, with little other industry.

Diplomatic Relations

The Centauri maintain cordial relations with the Minbari and Humans, respecting the powers of their empires. While many of the non-aligned worlds also maintain good relations with the Republic, some still hold enmity for the Centauri due to past occupation of worlds. The League of Non-Aligned Worlds keeps relations with them, though, to keep the peace. The Narn Regime shares hatred with the Republic, both still quite bitter about the occupation of the Narn homeworld.

Society

Centauri society is heavily based on family history. The Noble Houses hold the highest levels of respect in society. Members of those houses are the economic, political and industrial leaders of the Republic. To a member of a Noble House, all doors are open, and friends among the Houses are a treasured commodity. Hard work, talent and dedication will move an ambitious Centauri up in the world, but not as quickly as a friend in a Noble House.

Centauri females hold no official positions in society. Males are the leaders of government, industry and commerce. They serve in the military, and all physically demanding jobs are held by men. Women are the protected resource of the Centauri, the nurturers and teachers. They comfort their mates and raise the children—their influence is felt only in subtle ways. This is not to say that they are denied opportunity: women who wish to do things traditionally reserved for males are welcome to try them, but most who do find better opportunity on worlds outside the Republic.

The roles of men and women are not the only differences between the sexes. Men traditionally show their status in society openly, wearing their hair in a wider, taller style the higher they are in society, while women shave their heads of all but a single lock, shunning the trappings of society to emphasize their own roles in society. While many Centauri at some point in their lives have a limited sort of foresight (often they can accurately predict their death from a dream), true gifts of prophecy only appear in women. While the Emperor and his court is respected in one way, among Centauri society those given the most respect on a day to day basis are the seers, those very rare women whose gift of prophecy is strong.

The Centauri also have a strong faith that those above watch out for them. During their conflict with the Xon, many began to trust that those who had gone before would guide them through what was to come. Through faith and prayer, they looked to these spirits to protect them during their fight, and those who proved the most helpful were given more faith, becoming the first of the Centauri gods and goddesses. Today, there are over 50 major gods and goddesses, in addition to the multitudes of household protectors who are gods and goddesses to many families.

The practice of slavery is not uncommon in the Centauri Republic. In the past, both Centauri and subject races were sold into slavery when the occasion warranted it. Although this practice is thought to have played a contributing part in the downfall of the Republic, it is not illegal, nor is it unheard of in the present time. Few of the Houses practice it actively.

Telepaths

The Centauri learned long ago how to trace the gene within their cellular structure that controls Psionics. Now, when a telepathic child is born, he or she is raised by a Noble House and then joins the Telepaths Guild upon the emergence of telepathic abilities. The Guild is a commercial venture of telepaths who are hired out among the Centauri to provide services to the Centauri people.

C.H. BURNETT

There is one very special department within the Guild: the Emperor's Own. This is an organization of powerful female telepaths, raised in groups of four from birth until they are constantly in contact with each other on an unconscious level. They learn to communicate with each other without a line of sight, and each always knows what the others are thinking. When an Emperor takes the throne, he chooses a group from this department to be his personal attendants. Whenever he travels out of the Palace, two of them accompany him, and two remain behind, so that he is always aware of happenings at court and the court is always able to consult with him.

Minbari

The Minbari hold a unique position in the galaxy. They are part of neither the ancient races of the past nor the younger races of the present. After centuries of separation from the affairs of the younger races, and a nearly genocidal war against Humanity, the Minbari are now becoming more involved in interstellar affairs.

History

Minbari recorded history stretches longer by a thousand years than that of any of the younger races. Minbar is a world of beauty and danger. Gigantic mineral deposits formed into crystal over the billions of years of the planet's formation, leaving it a beautiful but largely barren world—a world of rock and glass under hot twin suns, pleasing to the eye but deadly. Early on, the Minbari were a nomadic people. They moved from place to place, growing or gathering what they could on fertile land. They often had to defend such patches from others in need, go for long, harsh periods between times when there was ample food, and migrate across the barrens when fertile areas began to give out.

These nomadic clans developed a structured way of life over several thousand years. During time spent on fertile land, the clan was guided by those who knew the arts of farming and herding, saving and storing supplies as well as feeding their people. In times of conflict or migration, the hunters and gatherers took charge of the people, leading them until another settlement was found, or conflict over fertile terrain was resolved. High respect was always given to the nurturers and healers: those who protected life were the lifeblood of the people. The battle to survive, with its constantly changing priorities, left them without a clear or constant leadership hierarchy, but rather the need for all to act as one, each serving the community to the best of their particular abilities, and the community as a whole acting to protect the individual.

These millennia of struggle gave the Minbari a culture that was deeply contemplative, yet fiercely protective. One that was often dependent on innovation, but still strongly guided by the security of tradition.

Thus, other than their clans, early Minbari had very little organized government. Each Minbari performed tasks according to his or her ability, with none putting personal pride or ambition above the needs of the greater good. Through this service structure, the Minbari advanced. Dedicated service to the whole brought respect, and respect brought influence in the decisions of the whole. The concept of community slowly grew to encompass all Minbari, and the clans began working together, sharing their talents, to build areas where they could live more permanently, which eventually grew to cities. Their nomadic culture evolved into what we now know as the Minbari.

After several thousand years, the Minbari developed the secrets of space travel. Centuries of existence as nomads, dependent on finding new fertile lands to survive, had quite prepared them for the idea of new worlds, and many soon left their world to explore others. After a century, they had established colonies on other worlds and moons in their own system and had begun to reach further. The records are incomplete on exactly how they discovered jump drives, but over the course of a few short decades, they gained jump technology, and had begun to learn about hyperspace travel to other worlds.

Shortly thereafter, they were approached by an ancient race calling themselves the Vorlons, who brought them tidings of peace. Under Vorlon tutelage, the Minbari learned more about the universe and its secrets. This ancient race taught them of other powerful and old races and wars lasting millennia, of how to fight and how to survive. Though uncertain of the purpose, the Minbari learned the arts taught them.

The reason was evident very soon, though, as the darkness of which the Vorlons warned was not long in coming. The Minbari found themselves at war, defending their very lives against a powerful foe. The Vorlons aided as best they could, but they too were beset by the enemy. The Minbari were rapidly loosing ground, not so much because they lacked the technology or tactics for victory, but because they had no experience in warfare on this scale.

At the low point in the war, a Minbari called Valen arose. Under his leadership, the Minbari underwent revolutionary changes. He formalized the three functions of society into groups called castes. The Warrior Caste, drawn from the memories of the hunters and defenders of old, would fight and defend the Minbari from others. The Worker Caste, a reflection of the ancient farmers and herders, would provide the labor and structure to maintain Minbari society from day to day. The healers and nurturers became the Religious Caste, the keepers of the spirit of the Minbari people who teach and watch over the weak.

Valen went on to form a council to coordinate and lead the Minbari. He called three Minbari from each of the three castes together in his Grey Council, a balance of the people to stand as the balance between the ancient races in their war. Together, Valen and the Nine led the Minbari to aid the Vorlons to a victory in the war, bringing a lasting peace.

The Minbari had changed during the war, but the Nine and the One had prepared them well. As the Vorlons withdrew, the Council took a much more active hand in ruling the Minbari, eventually becoming the definitive leaders of their people. Service to the community was still essential to their culture, perhaps moreso now than ever before, but the Council provided the focus, and the vision, to help guide the community. The respect due of old to those who served the most led the people to accept the advice of Valen and his council during the time of rebuilding, and beyond.

As the younger races emerged, the Minbari realized that they were an interstellar power, but they had had enough of war, and had no ambition to conquer others or to rule the galaxy. They kept to themselves, greeting new races when they could, but otherwise staying out of the unfamiliar affairs of others. The Grey Council had sworn to Valen that they would remain the gray between the candle and the star, and since they did not know what the younger races represented, they chose not to disrupt the balance. Watching the rise and fall of the Centauri Republic, they decided that their course had been wisest.

When the humans accidentally killed Dukhat, then leader of the council, the Minbari retaliated as a whole. The community had been attacked, the most respected of them had been killed, and those responsible had to pay. The vengeance was swift, and devastating, as the castes swept through human space like the hot winds that blew through Minbar's crystal deserts.

But on the cusp of destroying the human homeworld, the Grey Council suddenly reversed itself. It ordered not just a pause in the assault, but an actual surrender to the Humans. No explanation was given, or has yet been revealed. The castes, troubled but trusting the council despite their anger, obeyed.

Government

The Minbari are led by the Nine and the One, the Grey Council and its leader. Three members are selected from each caste, with the council choosing a replacement when one of its number can no longer serve. The leader sets policy with the affirmation of the council's majority vote. The council and its leader travel among the people, over all of the Minbari colonies and outposts, ruling by standing between all people.

The Minbari are still in mourning for Dukhat, and the Council leads the people alone.

Military

The military caste performs the day to day operations of defense of the Minbari Federation worlds. While all three castes own and use cruisers and fighters for day to day defense, the military caste is the one that coordinates fleet movements and provides tactical and strategic orders. They are only responsible to the Grey Council and its leader, who determine the overall policy for the Federation.

Colonies

The Minbari Federation covers twenty worlds in eighteen systems. By virtue of their highly advanced technology and powerful ships, they are rarely attacked, and their borders are given a wide latitude.

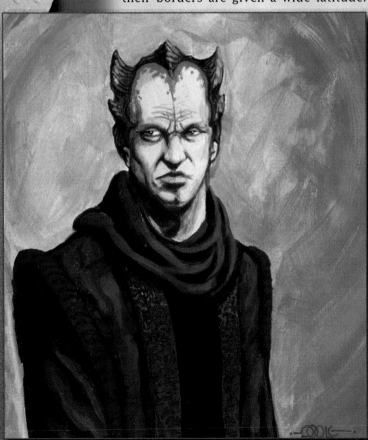

Their chief diplomatic base is on Sh'lek'k'tha. Since few ambassadors are allowed onto Minbar itself, this is where most of the negotiations with the Minbari take place. Their chief industrial base is a colony on Tr'es's'na, from which they produce goods for internal use.

Diplomatic Relations

The Minbari generally stay uninvolved with the younger races, choosing instead to remain neutral. In the aftermath of the Earth-Minbari war, however, they have begun to change their policies. While many in the Federation have no love for the humans, the Federation maintains friendly, albeit strained, diplomatic relations with the Earth Alliance. They have also begun to talk to the Centauri, Narn and Non-Aligned worlds, opening previously closed channels to interact with them.

Society

Minbari life is defined by the caste and clan to which each Minbari belongs. Minbari children are taught and trained in the clans into which they are born. When they reach the age of majority, they choose their caste and clan of adulthood. A Minbari's family is his or her clan, and his or her occupation is the caste.

There are three castes, and each serves the people in its own way. Those in the military caste are raised and trained in the arts of war and defense, providing security to all Minbari citizens. The religious caste members are the guardians of knowledge, holding sacred both all recorded history and the spiritual traditions and legends of the race. Those in the worker caste are the cement that hold the Federation together, performing the day to day tasks that are necessary to survive, each according to his or her talents. Despite their different focuses, each maintains its own internal governance, complete with an executive branch that answers to the Grey Council and a military complement under that caste's command.

In addition to a caste, each Minbari belongs to a clan, a philosophical family of sorts that guides his or her personal beliefs.

The five major clans are the Wind Swords, the Star Riders, the Night Walkers, the Fire Wings and the Moon Shields. The Wind Swords are the most militant among these, often bending the letter of the will of the council to better serve what they believe the intent to be. The Star Riders are the clan who most enjoy the exploration of the stars, and frequently become starship personnel within their caste. The Night Walkers are the custodians of the Minbari homeworld, helping to shape and grow the crystal and biological gardens and crops of Minbar. The Fire Wings are the explorers and inventors of the Minbari race. They were the first to attempt space travel, and the first to master the secrets to hyperspace. They hold a position of respect for their renaissance spirit. The Moon Shields are the guardians of the Minbari people. They care for others' physical and mental wellbeing and tend to the needs of those who cannot provide for themselves.

Telepaths

Like the Centauri, the Minbari have learned to identify those among them who have telepathic abilities. Minbari telepaths are considered to be greatly gifted. The use of this gift is extended as a free service to those in need of it.

Those with the genetic ability are given to the religious caste at an early age, and raised in the ways of Minbari service. Those who serve are valued in the community, and their needs are willingly provided for by the various members of the castes as called upon. All Minbari trained in the ways of this service are bound by their oath to serve.

Skills

The following is a list of skills for all player character races. The list is fairly complete and covers all common (and many uncommon) tasks, but is not necessarily exhaustive. If a character develops a skill not covered on the list, feel free to create the appropriate skill for your game.

Each skill is described in broad terms, followed by a notation on the Attribute or Attributes upon which it is usually based. Beneath each skill description is a list of common Specialties (many other Specialties are possible, of course). Many Specialties are not specified, but simply denoted by the types of Specialty available (for example, the Medical, Diagnostic skill is specialized "by Race"). Note that culture is a subset of race in this regard.

Acrobatics: This skill represents precise movements of different parts of the body at the same time. Tasks requiring this skill are usually based on Agility or Coordination.
Specialties: Climbing, Contortion, Gymnastics, Zero-G Maneuvering.

Acting: This skill represents the ability to convincingly or compellingly portray emotions or assume the roles of different characters or emotions. Tasks requiring this skill are usually based on Presence, Finesse or Charm.
Specialties: Theater, Film, Voice.

Acumen: This perceptive skill is used to assess what someone else is thinking or feeling through observation of behavior and expression, even when the target is concealing such thoughts or feelings (it is not based on telepathic abilities). Tasks requiring this skill are usually based on Finesse.
Specialties: Veracity (detecting the truth of statements), Attitude (judging motivations or general outlook), Emotion (judging emotional state).

Anthropology: This is the study of a race or culture. Tasks requiring this skill are usually based on Intelligence.
Specialties: Archaeology, and by individual culture.

Athletics: This physical skill is based on training, practice and conditioning in sporting activities. Tasks requiring this skill are usually based on one of the Physical Attributes.
Specialties: Jumping, Running, Swimming, Throwing, and by specific sports such as Tennis or Volleyball.

Art: This skill embodies the manipulation of two dimensional media such as paints or inks for aesthetic or informational purposes. Tasks requiring this skill are usually based on Insight or Coordination.

Specialties: Graphic Design, and by specific artistic media such as Painting, Drawing, Photography or Computer-Aided Drafting.

Biology: This skill concentrates on the knowledge and study of plant and animal life. Tasks requiring this skill are usually based on Intelligence.

Specialties: by Kingdoms within a particular biosphere (for example, Earth Plants).

Business: This skill embodies the tricks and techniques used in the world of commerce. Tasks requiring this skill are usually based on Intelligence and Wits.

Specialties: Economics, Management, Marketing, Operations, Ethics.

Combat, Armed: This represents the skills used in hand-to-hand combat with weapons (see Chapter 2 for more information). Note that sometimes, an armed combatant will attempt tasks such as dodging that use the Combat, Unarmed skill. Tasks requiring the Combat, Armed skill are usually based on Agility.

Specialties: Strike (any direct jabbing or thrusting attack), Swing (a swinging attack), Parry (an attempt to use a weapon to deflect or block a blow).

Combat, Martial Arts (specify one school): This represents advanced training in hand-to-hand combat, and allows a character to attempt special maneuvers in combat. Specify the school of martial arts studied—generally, a character only has access to a school developed by his or her race. Specific manuevers are offered as Specialties, and vary with according to school. Martial arts schools include Akido, Karate, and Kenjitsu (Human arts), Then'sha'tur and Katak'eth (Narn arts), Tronno and Coutari (Centauri arts), and Kalan'tha and Pike Fighting (Minbari arts), some of which are used with armed combat actions, and others with unarmed actions. Martial arts tasks are usually based on Coordination, though some are more closely based on Agility or Wits. The use of martial arts, and full descriptions of the use and effects of special maneuvers, are covered in Chapter 2.

Specialties: varies with individual martial arts. See Chapter 2.

Combat, Ranged: This represents the skills used in firing various ranged weapons both in target and in real combat situations. Tasks requiring this skill are usually based on Coordination.

Specialties: Handgun, Longarm, Autofire (applies to the use of any ranged weapon on an automatic setting—use another appropriate Specialty for semi-automatic weapons used in a single-shot mode).

Combat, Unarmed: This represents the skills used in hand-to-hand combat without weapons (see Chapter 2 for more information). Tasks requiring this skill are usually based on Agility.

Specialties: Block (a defensive move that stops the force of a blow by putting something in the way), Dodge (a defensive move that allows a combatant to get out of the way of a blow), Grapple (an attempt to grab and/or hold another immobilized or otherwise controlled, or an attempt to break from such control), Strike (a punch or kick).

Cooking: This skill represents the ability to prepare and serve pleasing foods. Tasks requiring this skill are usually based on Insight.

Specialties: by types of cuisine (such as Earth Tex-Mex).

Dancing: This skill is the ability to express oneself through movement in time with music or in common patterns with others. Tasks requiring this skill are usually based on Agility.

Specialties: by types of dance (such as Earth Ballroom).

Diplomacy: This is the art of manipulating others in social situations to arrive at a desired outcome. Tasks requiring this skill are usually based on Finesse, Presence or Charm.

Specialties: Dulcification (calming someone down or reducing hostility), Ingratiation (working into someone's good graces), Inquiry (getting information out of someone without their realization), Obfuscation (covering or hiding the truth), Persuasion (convincing someone of a different point of view), and Protocol by Culture (knowing the correct diplomatic conventions for that culture).

Driving: This is the ability to guide ground-based vehicles safely and to the performance limits of the vehicles. Tasks requiring this skill are usually based on Coordination or Wits.

Specialties: Cars, Trucks, Motorcycles.

Engineering, Aerospace: This skill covers the design of and concepts behind atmospheric and space-based vehicles and structures. Tasks requiring this skill are usually based on Intelligence.

Specialties: Aerodynamics, Structural Design, Plasma Engine Design, Jump Engine Design.

Engineering, Chemical: This skill represents the knowledge and use of chemicals in production and manufacturing. Tasks requiring this skill are usually based on Intelligence.

Specialties: Alloys, Ceramics, Explosives, Fuels, Plastics, Applications (actual manufacture of and work with materials).

Engineering, Civil: This skill covers large-scale design and knowledge of structures and systems. Tasks requiring this skill are usually based on Intelligence or Insight.

Specialties: Urban Design, Planetary Structures, Orbital Structures, Applications (actual construction and repair of structures).

Engineering, Electrical: This skill covers the knowledge and use of electrical devices and systems. Tasks requiring this skill are usually based on Intelligence.

Specialties: Device Design, Systems Design, Power Systems Design, Computer Systems Design, Device Applications (actual construction and repair of specific electronic devices), System Applications (actual construction and repair of integrated electrical systems).

Engineering, Mechanical: This skill embodies the science and study of moving parts and machinery. Tasks requiring this skill are usually based on Intelligence.

Specialties: Internal Combustion Engines, Robotics, Mechanical Applications (actual construction and repair of mechanical systems).

Gambling: This skill represents facility and experience at the techniques and tricks used in games of chance and skill. Tasks requiring this skill are usually based on Insight, but can be based on Wits or Intelligence depending on the game.

Specialties: by game (such as Poker, Blackjack or Craps).

Geography: This is the study of the physical environment of a particular area. Tasks requiring this skill are usually based on Intelligence.

Specialties: Interstellar, Star System (by specific system such as Proxima System), Planetary (by specific planet such as Minbar), Region (by a specific planet's regions such as North America).

Geology: This is the study of the underlying structure of planets and planetary bodies. Tasks requiring this skill are usually based on Intelligence.

Specialties: by planet type and regional type.

Hiding: This is the knowledge of and ability to use techniques for avoiding notice, either for the self or for other objects.

Tasks requiring this skill are usually based on Finesse, Wits or Agility.

Specialties: Disguise, Concealment (hiding things other than self), Shadowing, Sneaking.

History: This is the study of the past events in a certain area or era of the past.

Specialties: by area, culture and time period (such as Pre-Occupation Southern Continent Narns or Dark Ages Europe on Earth).

Instruction: This is the ability to teach groups of people. It is a knowledge of and aptitude for the techniques of conferring information to others. Tasks requiring this skill are usually based on Insight or Wits.

Specialties: by Race.

Investigation: This is knowledge of and the ability to use tricks and techniques for gathering information. Tasks requiring this skill are usually based on Insight or Intelligence.

Specialties: Research, Forensics, Case Management.

Language (specify one language): This skill represents the knowledge of and ability to use a language and its dialects. A Competent character can generally communicate clearly in the language, while an Adept character is effectively fluent. An Expert speaks with no discernible accent. Tasks requiring this skill are usually based on Intelligence or Wits.

Specialties: Comprehension, Speech, Writing.

Law: This skill embodies knowledge of the laws and their enforcement within a specific community of Humans or aliens. Tasks requiring this skill are usually based on Intelligence.

Specialties: by legal system (such as EA law).

Mathematics: This is the study of numbers and the ability to formulate and prove advanced concepts of number theory. Tasks requiring this skill are usually based on Intelligence.

Specialties: Geometry, Trigonometry, Statistics, Calculus.

Medical, Biotech: This represents knowledge of the safe and effective use of artificial components in biological organisms (for example, limb prosthetics and cybernetics). Note that this skill only covers the implementation, maintenance, and medical interactions of such devices—their initial implantation generally requires additional skills, most notably Medical, Surgery. Tasks requiring this skill are usually based on Intelligence.

Specialties: by Race (for example, Centauri Biotech).

Medical, Diagnostic: This skill covers the techniques and knowledge necessary to use medical instruments and observation to assess the medical condition of a patient. Tasks requiring this skill are usually based on Intelligence.

Specialties: by Race.

Medical, EMT: This skill is the knowledge and ability to treat wounds quickly, both in first aid situations and in situations where the only treatment is to stabilize the wound until more intensive medical treatment can be administered. Tasks requiring this skill are usually based on Wits.

Specialties: by Race.

Medical, Pharmaceutical: This covers the knowledge necessary to create, identify and prescribe drugs and the ability to predict their effect. Tasks requiring this skill are usually based on Intelligence.

Specialties: by Race.

Medical, Psychiatry: This skill represents the techniques and knowledge necessary to correctly diagnose and treat mental illnesses, emotional problems and other personal issues. Tasks requiring this skill are usually based on Intelligence or Insight.

Specialties: by Race.

Medical, Surgery: This covers the techniques, ability and knowledge required to perform surgical operations. Tasks requiring this skill are usually based on Coordination, Wits or Intelligence.

Specialties: by Race.

Metalworking: This represents the techniques and knowledge necessary to work metal into desired designs for aesthetic or utilitarian purposes. Tasks requiring this skill are usually based on Insight or Coordination.

Specialties: Structural Design, Construction/Repair, Ornamentation.

Music: This is the ability to play and write musical pieces, including the knowledge of and ability to play musical instruments and/or to sing. Tasks requiring this skill are usually based on Coordination or Insight.

Specialties: Composition by style (for example Modern Jazz Composition), Performance by instrument (for example Piano or Voice).

Navigation, Aerospatial: This is the knowledge and techniques necessary to successfully chart a course from one point to another in a given aerospace environment and to follow the progress of that course as it proceeds. Tasks requiring this skill are usually based on Intelligence.

Specialties: Atmospheric, Insystem, Hyperspace.

Navigation, Planetary: This skill represents the knowledge and techniques used to successfully chart a course from one point to another in a given planetary environment and to follow the progress of that course as it proceeds. Tasks requiring this skill are usually based on Intelligence.

Specialties: Ground, Water.

Philosophy: This skill embodies the pursuit of truth and wisdom through logical discourse. Tasks requiring this skill are usually based on Insight.

Specialties: by school of thought.

Physics: This is the study of the rules that govern the physical behavior of the universe. Tasks requiring this skill are usually based on Intelligence.

Specialties: Quantum, Mechanical, Optical, Nuclear, Hyperspatial.

Piloting: This represents the knowledge of how to operate single- or dual-pilot aerospace vehicles—those that do not require bridge crews. The atmospheric Specialties are used when atmosphere-capable vessels are piloted within atmospheres—in space, piloting such vessels (like non-atmosphere-capable ships) relies on the appropriate non-atmospheric Specialties. Piloting larger vessels requires use of the skill Shiphandling. Tasks requiring the Piloting skill are usually based on Coordination.

Specialties: Atmospheric Fighter, Atmospheric Shuttle, Atmospheric Transport, Fighter, Shuttle, Transport/Escort.

Religion: This skill represents knowledge of the tenets and doctrines of a given belief system. Tasks requiring this skill are usually based on Insight or Intelligence.

Specialties: Texts by sect (for example Christian Biblical Texts), Ceremonies by sect (such as Jewish Ceremonies).

Savvy: This skill represents knowledge of the rules by which a given society or subculture operates: the ins and outs, do's and don'ts that are followed. Tasks requiring this skill are usually based on Charm or Finesse.

Specialties: Underworld, Politics by Culture, High Society, other specific subcultures (such as Anti-War Earthers).

Sculpture: This is the ability to manipulate three dimensional media such as clay or metal for aesthetic or informational purposes. Tasks requiring this skill are usually based on Insight or Coordination.

Specialties: by medium (such as Metal, Stone, Pottery or Virtual Constructs).

Shiphandling: This skill covers the operation and piloting of large, crewed space vessels (those which require multiple people on the bridge, such as freighters, cruisers or military capital ships). Tasks requiring this skill are usually based on Coordination.

Specialties: Freighter/Liner, Escort, Capital Ship.

Sleight-of-Hand: This is the practice of subtle movements of body and hand that mislead the eye. Tasks requiring this skill are usually based on Coordination.

Specialties: Juggling, Prestidigitation ("magic" tricks), Pick-Pocketing.

Software Design: This represents the skills necessary to manipulate software and computer programs. Tasks requiring this skill are usually based on Intelligence, Wits or Insight.

Specialties: Authoring, Repair, Hacking.

Survival: This skill embodies knowledge of the tricks and techniques necessary to stay alive and functional in a non-standard environment. Tasks requiring this skill are usually based on Wits or Intelligence.

Specialties: Life Support by environment (such as Desert Life Support), Foraging by environment (such as Tropical Rainforest Foraging).

Tactics, Troop: This is the understanding and application of the tactics used by planetary combined-arms forces (including naval forces and air support). Tasks requiring this skill are usually based on Insight or Intelligence.

Specialties: by military doctrine.

Tactics, Space Combat: This skill represents the understanding and application of the tactics of space warfare. Tasks requiring this skill are usually based on Insight or Intelligence.

Specialties: by military doctrine.

Telepathy: This skill is only available to characters with Psionics scores higher than 0. It is the knowledge of the techniques useful in executing telepathic functions. Tasks requiring this skill are usually based on Psionics.

Specialties: Scanning, Blocking, Broadcasting.

Tracking: This covers the knowledge of and ability to use techniques that allow one to follow a specific trail through a given environment. Tasks requiring this skill are usually based on Wits or Intelligence.

Specialties: by environment (such as Forest, Swamp or Urban).

Weapons Systems: This represents skill and practice in operating large weapon systems as well as their guidance systems. Tasks requiring this skill are usually based on Wits or Intelligence.

Specialties: Ship, Planetary, Orbital, Vehicular.

Writing: This skill embodies the ability to effectively, compellingly, and concisely express oneself through a written medium. Tasks requiring this skill are usually based on Insight.

Specialties: Expository, Poetry, Prose.

Characteristics

What follows is a list of Characteristics for *The Babylon Project* player characters. This list is broken down into several parts; Personality Characteristics; Psychological Characteristics; Physical Characteristics; Aspect Characteristics; Relational Characteristics; and Psionic Characteristics. Most can apply to members of any character race, but a few apply only to characters of specific races. In such cases, the description specifies which races may or may not feature the Characteristic.

Personality Characteristics

Personality Characteristics are those elements of a character's personality which are likely to impact in some way on the adventure. Most are somewhat negative in connotation, or are liable to get a character into trouble on occasion. As a result, most offer only cons—their corresponding pros are Fortune Point awards when they become a factor in play.

Contentious: The character can be difficult to get along with. If you choose this Characteristic, specify the degree and nature of the character's contentiousness: he or she might be argumentative or contrary, have a bad temper, be easily upset, or hold grudges. The character may be easily angered or even sent on a rampage. He or she may react very badly at best to taunting or teasing, and may be impatient with manipulation, diplomacy, or bureaucracy. Close friends may or may not be immune to a contentious character's outbursts or moods.

Pros: Fortune Point award for difficulties or particularly good roleplaying that arises from in-character contentious behavior. Also, people who know the character in person or by reputation may find him or her intimidating, or may find it easier to accommodate him or her rather than struggle against a difficult nature.

Cons: Contentious characters often make bad impressions and have difficulty in relationships with friends and co-workers.

"In another place I would have you skinned alive for that!"

Curious: The character has an insatiable desire to figure everything out—from trying to determine why a gadget works the way it does, to trying to uncover the mysteries of the universe (specify a general area of curiosity—some characters love a good deductive challenge, while others are fascinated with, for example, the mysteries of alien cultures). If a question is left only half answered a curious character will try to discover the rest of the answer, and perhaps why it was only half answered as well.

Pros: Fortune Point award for difficulties or particularly good roleplaying that arises from in-character curiosity.

Cons: Snooping can get a character into trouble—and the answers aren't always what was sought.

"Computer, cross reference these things: a name Charlie, and a black rose..."

Dedicated: The character is highly devoted to a particular goal or ideal, which is held above all other priorities (if you choose this Characteristic, specify the goal or ideal). A doctor who is dedicated to the oath taken to preserve life might ignore laws and orders that would violate this oath. A military officer might be extremely patriotic; a telepath might put the Guild above all else; while many people are committed to the ideals of their faith. A dedicated character will see an event through to the end no matter what the cost or the length of time— a very diligent person willing to compromise anything for that to which he or she is dedicated.

Pros: Fortune Point award for difficulties or particularly good roleplaying that arises from following a character's dedication in the face of opposition.

Cons: When it comes down to it, a character's dedication takes precedent of virtually any other motivation.

"We have a safety of the patient precedent on this station—you leave me no choice but to operate without your consent."

Fanatical: The character firmly believes that his or her most passionate viewpoints are the only possible correct ones. Unlike a dedicated character (see the Characteristic above), a fanatical one has difficulty maintaining any sort of relationship with others whose views are even slightly different, and must often keep his or her views a secret in order to interact normally with society. If you choose this Characteristic, specify the viewpoints about which the character is fanatical: extreme religious fervor (of any variety) is not uncommon, nor are racism (in general or against a specific race or culture), or devotion to or hatred of a particular institution.

Pros: Fortune Point award for difficulties or particularly good roleplaying that arises from a character's fanaticism.

Cons: Fanatical characters often have difficulty getting along with others, can easily make enemies of themselves, and may at some difficult point have to reconcile the extremity of their positions with reality.

"It says in the book of G'Quan..."

Heartless: The character has a cruel, or at least a cold, side. If you choose this Characteristic, specify the degree and nature of your character's heartlessness: some characters delight in the pain of others, while others simply lack compassion. Most are more complex—they subscribe to a strict "eye-for-an-eye" philosophy, or take pleasure in the suffering of their enemies while having a more compassionate take on their friends.

Pros: Fortune Point award for difficulties or particularly good roleplaying that arises from the character's attitude.

Cons: Such a character might easily make enemies, and may find him or herself singled out for the receiving end of cruelty.

"I see a million people calling out your name in anguish—your victims."

Impulsive: The character acts first and thinks things through later. If it sounds like a good plan, the character will carry it out without concern for the possible repercussions. An impulsive character is often the first to react in a split-second situation, but such action will not always be the right response and may even be detrimental—an impulsive character will often overestimate his or her chances or fail to see obvious consequences. If you choose this Characteristic, specify the nature of the impulsiveness: some characters are driven by overconfidence in tactical situations, others by a bit too much social bravado, while others are simply impatient, and find ways to "get things going" whenever events slow down.

Pros: Fortune Point award for difficulties or particularly good roleplaying that arises from a character's impulsiveness.

Cons: As just noted, impulsive behavior is rarely well-thought-out, and quick action is sometimes counterproductive.

"It seemed like a good idea at the time."

Proud: The character thinks highly of him or herself. If you choose this Characteristic, specify the nature of the pride: the character might be image-conscious, vain, boastful, or just unable to turn away from a challenge or face the possibility of being seen as a coward.

Pros: Fortune Point award for difficulties or particularly good roleplaying that arises from a character's pride.

Cons: A proud character will focus on superficial issues and may feel obligated to protect his or her image or honor in difficult situations.

"I come from a long line of honorable warriors, whose blood was spilled for you."

Selfish: The character always puts him or herself ahead of everyone else. The character may merely be self-centered (the sort who always eats the last piece of cake without asking if anyone else wanted it first), or may be driven by intense greed or a lust for power or control. Often a character does not recognize his or her behavior, but has simply warped his or her worldview and doesn't give a thought to what someone else might need or think. Sometimes such an attitude is even justified in light of the character's past experiences. If you choose this Characteristic, specify the nature, intensity, and deliberation of the character's selfishness.

Pros: Fortune Point award for difficulties or particularly good roleplaying that arises from the character's selfishness.

Cons: Obviously, a selfish character is likely to gain enmity from people who get tired of the attitude.

*"I believe **I** was first, Ambassador"*

Stubborn: The character is difficult to sway once he or she has reached a conclusion or developed an opinion. If you choose this Characteristic, note how stubborn your character is, and to whom, if anyone, he or she might defer.

Pros: Fortune Point award for difficulties or particularly good roleplaying that arises from the character's selfishness. Also, stubborn characters can sometimes bulldoze their way through people who simply get tired of dealing with their muleheadedness.

Cons: A stubborn character on the wrong side of an issue can be a real liability.

*"You will do it **my** way, commander!"*

Psychological Characteristics

Psychological Characteristics are elements of a character's mental state. They are similar in function to Personality Characteristics, except that most are based on mental or psychological issues which are less fundamental and more easily resolved (or in some cases treated) than personality quirks. As with Personality Characteristics, most are negative, and are offset by Fortune Point awards when the affect play.

Addicted: The character is addicted to a substance—alcohol, tobacco, stims, dust, etc. (specify). Consequences involve not just intoxication and the potential for a dangerous withdrawal, but the issue of obtaining the substance (if illicit) and the more subtle question of whether the character is trustworthy.

Pros: Fortune Point award for difficulties or particularly good roleplaying that arises from the character's intoxication or need to feed the addiction. Also, certain drugs, such as stims and dust, provide temporary advantages.

Cons: The addiction must be fed, and often increases in intensity over time. While it is generally up to the player to decide when the character pursues the addiction, the character is not always in complete control of him or herself (the GM can even take control of the character if necessary) when intoxicated or suffering from the intense need for the substance.

*"I do **not** have a **problem**!"*

Amnesiac: The character's past, or parts of his or her past, cannot be remembered. The character might have suffered a trauma, or been subject to a brainwipe. The character's past may not be a secret—there may be other records that indicate what the character did or who he or she was in the missing period.

Pros: Fortune Point award for difficulties or particularly good roleplaying that arise from the character's uncertainty about his or her past.

Cons: Who knows what really happened in this missing past, or what really caused the amnesia? Even records can be incomplete.

"I have lost part of who I am, captain."

Fragile: The character is extremely sensitive, either to personal confrontation, stress, or violence. This fragility can take the form of outright cowardice, squeemishness at the sight of blood, extreme (or mild) shyness, etc.—if you choose this Characteristic, specify the nature of the frailty.

Pros: Fortune Point award for difficulties or particularly good roleplaying that arises from the character's selfishness.

Cons: Obviously, the character will have a difficult time engaging in activities affected by fragility.

"Please, ambassador. All of this shooting is giving me a headache."

Haunted: The character is dogged by regretful or horrifying memories of a trauma in the past. These memories intrude on the character's life and color his or her ability to make decisions. They may be associated with a specific event (such as the death of a loved one), or with a general period of extreme stress (as in post-traumatic stress syndrome following a character's combat experiences)—if you choose this Characteristic, specify the cause and the depth of its effect. A particularly severe trauma may result in other psychological Characteristics, such as insomnia (below).

Pros: Fortune Point award for particularly good roleplaying or changes in motivation that arise from the character's mental state.

Cons: Many, if not all, decisions the character makes will be affected by a fear of repeating the events in the memories. In most cases, the character will seek to avoid the situation, but sometimes a character will pursue redemption by seeking out similar situations.

"I am not going back in there, sir."

Insomniac: The character has a great deal of trouble getting sleep, or staying asleep for any length of time, and often suffers from fatigue as a result. The character may suffer from nightmares or perhaps just can't drift off.

Pros: Fortune Point award for difficulties or particularly good roleplaying that arises from the character's fatigue. Also, an insomniac character may be able to put some of the extra waking hours to use.

Cons: Severe fatigue acts like an Impairment (covered in the Wounds and Injuries section of chapter 2). The GM may assign an overall Impairment of 1 or more to the character's actions following particularly sleepless nights.

"It's the hour of the wolf. Where's the vodka?"

Paranoid: The character believes that no-one can be trusted and that everyone else is out to exploit, hurt, or kill him or her. Severely paranoid characters (specify the degree of the problem) come up with elaborate conspiracy fantasies aimed at them, and even mildly paranoid characters rarely trust anyone and are always suspicious.

Pros: Fortune Point award for difficulties or particularly good roleplaying that arises from the character's paranoia. Also, sometimes suspicion is warranted.

Cons: Trust is an essential part of any team effort.

"I need protection: an alien guard, very big."

Phobic: The character is completely afraid of a particular situation or object (specify). This character will go to great lengths to make sure that he or she does not have to deal with the subject of the phobia. This fear can be for just about anything: spiders; heights; spaceflight; aliens; etc.

Pros: Fortune Point award for difficulties or particularly good roleplaying that arises from the character's intense fear.

Cons: Irrational fears may limit a character's ability to act in some situations.

"There's a thought eater on the station? I'll be in my quarters."

Physical Characteristics

Physical Characteristics are those that relate to a character's physical state or capabilities. As with other types of Characteristics, pros and cons reflect how the character interacts with others and the world.

Physical Characteristics are often much more obvious than other types, however, and can sometimes impact on the impression that the character makes on others.

Ambidextrous: The character is equally apt with both the right and left hand—very useful if one is injured or otherwise hindered. However, ambidexterity is almost always accompanied by at least mild dyslexia.

Pros: the character may use either hand for any task.

Cons: the character may sometimes confuse right with left at critical moments.

"Left or right? Which way?"

Attractive: The character's physical appearance is pleasing to those who appreciate members of his or her race. If you choose this attribute, specify its nature: the character might have an angelic face, an ideal physique, or a certain bearing, for example, that accounts for his or her appeal.

Pros: In superficial encounters the character will generally receive a better response than others might.

Cons: People are attracted to this character, and not all of their attentions will be welcome. An attractive character will also tend to be noted and remembered by others.

"Don't touch me unless you mean it!"

Handicapped: The character suffers a significant permanent disability: he or she is blind, mute, deaf, partially paralyzed, or missing one or more limbs. If you choose this Characteristic, specify the type and severity of the disability (a blind character may have some sight, just not enough to carry out many common tasks, or might be completely blind on one eye but fine in the other).

Pros: Fortune Point award for difficulties or particularly good roleplaying that arises from the character's disability.

Cons: Varies according to the disability.

"I may be blind, lieutenant, but I'm not stupid"

Aspect Characteristics

Aspects are elements of a character that cannot be defined strictly through Attributes or Skills.

Assets: The character owns one or more specific items of value (anything from a family heirloom such as an antique Rolex wristwatch to a 1,000-ton cargo transport), or has a considerable amount of wealth. If you choose this Characteristic, specify the nature, value, and source of the asset.

Pros: Specific items have specific values—an heirloom might serve as collateral for an emergency loan, while a ship has obvious utility as a transport for the player characters. Wealth speaks for itself.

Cons: The character is responsible for his or her assets. An heirloom implies a duty to look out for it; a ship requires an enormous amount of maintenance and has high operating costs; a family fortune must be

managed. All valuables attract the attention of thieves, swindlers, and the tax collector.

"...so when I found this alien device I saw a way I could make up for my mistakes."

Death Dream: This Characteristic may only be taken by Centauri characters. The character has forseen his or her own death through a dream. While all Centauri may potentially have this dream during their lifetimes, only some actually do, and fewer still remember or note it after waking. Even fewer comprehend the circumstances surrounding the events in the dream. A character with this Characteristic remembers the dream, and the details that will surround his or her death. He or she will probably react badly to circumstances related to those seen in the dream. This dream, like prophecy, is only a shadow of the future, and premature death isn't ruled out—but the future illustrated by the dream is the character's most likely destiny.

Pros: One-time Fortune Point award for the dream itself (if it occurs during play) and any plot hooks that it may give the GM. Fortune Point award for particularly good roleplaying or changes in motivation that arise when the character recognizes (or thinks that he or she recognizes) circumstances or details relating to the dream.

Cons: The character has an increased sense of his or her own mortality, which can result in depression or fear. Events relating to the dream can cause great emotional and even physical distress, including nausea or illness.

"It is a terrible thing to see your own fate."

Gift of Prophecy: This Characteristic is available only to female Centauri characters. Many Centauri women with the gift of prophecy are also telepaths, but they need not be. Note that this Characteristic requires a lot of notice to the GM for effective implementation, and may not be taken unless the GM agrees.

The character has the ability to see events that are yet to come. Such visions are always shadows—not unavoidable facts—but the power and clarity of the vision is directly related how likely the events are to occur, and how strong a prophetess the character is. Each seer has a particular method of invoking visions—one might always look into a teacup, while another relaxes and closes her eyes—but every seer is subject to occasional inadvertent visions brought about when someone touches her. Characters with the gift of prophecy are often haunted by what they come to know.

Pros: Fortune Point awards for visions that further the plot, and for good roleplaying of related actions and reactions.

Cons: Seers are almost always aloof and separate from others, and are looked upon with suspicion by some. Known seers are also constantly plagued by those wanting to ask about themselves.

"I never make jokes about matters of prophecy. This will come to pass, just as I have said."

Missing Basic Skills: The character is missing some of the basic skills of his or her society—skills so fundamental that they are not even accounted among those listed in this chapter. The character may be illiterate, for example, or may be missing even the most basic computer skills.

Pros: Fortune Point award for difficulties or particularly good roleplaying that arises from the character's disability.

Cons: Obviously, the character will be unable to perform many tasks that depend on the missing basic skills.

"I can't read or write."
"You're illiterate?"
"Yes."

Relational Characteristics

Relational Characteristics are those elements of the character's life that affect his or her associations with others. In some cases, the Characteristics define relationships with specific other characters or groups, in others they relate to the character's public persona, if any.

Ally: The character is associated with a person of value to the character. This person may be working towards the same or similar goals, or may be in a position of power or influence. The ally may be a family member, an old school buddy, an ex-lover, or a mate from a previous duty station, and may be a mere acquaintance or a close personal friend. Either way, the ally has reason to assist the character on occasion, either out of friendship, a sense of duty, or a desire to see the character suc-

ceed. If you choose this Characteristic, you must define with some precision the identity of this ally, his or her relationship with your character, and the degree to which the ally can be counted upon. Because the ally will be an NPC played by your GM, and a potentially powerful one at that, your GM will have to understand and agree to your ally.

Pros: An ally can provide important material and informational assistance.

Cons: Not all allies are completely reliable all of the time. Furthermore, any relationship is a two-way street, and the ally may well call upon the character for assistance.

"What do you want?"

Authority: The character is in a position of rank or authority—perhaps he or she is a military officer, a religious leader, or a government official of some rank. Even if the character is not assigned to a specific post, his or her rank commands respect.

Pros: The character has influence and enjoys respect, at least among those to

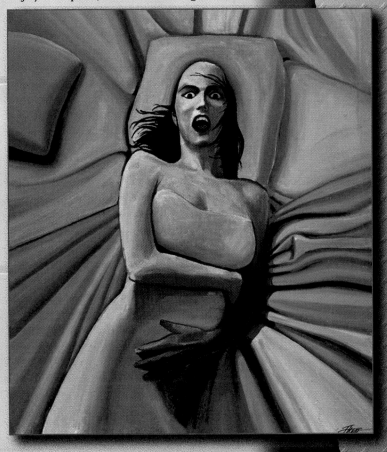

whom his or her authority has meaning (a member of the religious caste will have little direct influence over an EA military unit).

Cons: Authority is limited to its sphere of influence. More importantly, positions of authority entail responsibility—those in the chain of command over the character may make demands upon him or her on short notice, even if the character is on a leave of absence, in an independent position, or otherwise not directly assigned to a position of responsibility. Finally, a character with rank is likely to be held somewhat responsible for the actions of his or her associates.

"We would die for The One."

Dependent: The character has ties to someone or something which he or she must care for: a child; a dog; an ailing parent; even a close friend who relies on the character and isn't the sort that can be brought along into harm's way.

Pros: The dependent can be useful in some circumstances. In some cases, a Fortune Point award may be appropriate for difficulties or particularly good roleplaying that arises from the character's relationship with the dependent.

Cons: The character is obligated to provide for the some or all of the dependent's needs.

*"He is **our** son, and we will do what is best for his soul."*

Enemies: Through some course of action or twist of fate, the character has acquired one or more enemies. These individuals or organizations may wish to kill the character, capture or imprison him or her, stymie the character's objectives, or simply take any opportunity to make life uncomfortable. In fact, the enemy may be little more than a rival, interested only in outdoing the character or making him or her look bad. The enemy may be very powerful, or may never be able to accomplish anything to the character's detriment. If you choose this Characteristic, specify the nature of the enemy, the degree of the enmity, and the source of the conflict.

Pros: Fortune Point award for difficulties or particularly good roleplaying that arises from the involvement of the enemy in the storyline.

Cons: Who knows when the enemy might show up, to throw a wrench into the character's best-laid plans?

"Good to see you again, commander. It's been a while."

Famous: The character is well-known, either to the public at large or to some subset of society. Depending on the nature and cause of the character's fame, his or her face may be well-known, or he or she may be famous simply by name and reputation. The fame may work against the character as well—he or she may be infamous or hated for some real or fabricated public offense. If you choose this Characteristic, specify how famous the character is, and why. Either way, keep in mind that the public's understanding of who the character really is may be quite distorted.

Pros: Fame gives a character a fairly good deal of sway with the common person. If the character's public image is generally negative, a Fortune Point award may be appropriate for difficulties or particularly good roleplaying that arises from his or her infamy.

Cons: It may be difficult to move about unnoticed. Furthermore, everyone has an opinion on public figures, and many people may have developed a specific attitude towards the character long before ever meeting him or her. Finally, remember that not all fame is equal—a famous astrophysicist will not get the same reaction walking into a bar as a movie starlet.

"Stop poking me."
"But you are blessed."
"The plant was blessed, too. Poke the plant."

Justice Oath: The character is the subject or issuer of a Narn judicial oath (see Narns on page 140 for more information on these oaths). This Characteristic generally applies only to Narn characters, though occasionally a non-Narn will find him or herself the subject of an oath. If you choose this Characteristic, specify the nature of the crime on which the oath is based, as well as the specifics of the punishment. Justice oaths are legally binding on the issuer as well as the subject—that is, the issuer is obligated to carry out the oath to its end once it has been sworn. There are three types of oaths, of varying severity:

The most basic is the Cha'lar. As the subject of a Cha'lar, the character owes money or property to the issuer of the oath. If the issuer, the character is owed such a fee. The money or property is generally commensurate with the degree of the crime, although that is obviously quite subjective.

The second form of justice oath is the Chol'tar—the subject of this oath is bound to serve the issuer for a period of time in keeping with the nature and severity of his or her crime.

The highest form is the Chon'kar—an oath of blood. A character who has issued a Chon'kar swears to exact a specific vengeance—death, or perhaps the amputation of a limb—upon the subject as soon as the criminal can be located.

Pros: Characters who have issued these oaths often have a more defined sense of purpose in their lives. Fortune Point awards are given for roleplaying or difficulties related to the oath.

Cons: The oath can often cause the character to ignore other facets of life—and its fulfillment outside of Narn space often runs contrary to the laws of other races. Also, once an has been fulfilled, the sense of purpose can often leave with it, requiring the character to re-assess his or her life.

"I will see you pay with the last breath I take."

Psionic Characteristics

Psionic Characteristics relate to characters with telepathic ability. These Characteristics—even the Latent Telepathy Characteristic—are available only to characters with some Psionic attribute level.

Latent Telepath: This Characteristic is available only to Human characters. The character has unknown and undiscovered telepathic abilities. For whatever reason, these abilities did not manifest during adolescence like those of most telepaths, but are waiting for some event to trigger them.

Pros: The character will probably develop telepathic capability at some point (a fact completely unknown to the character)

Cons: The character cannot use Psionic abilities until this development occurs. The only certainties about it are that it will be a shock, that it will probably occur at a bad time, and that when it does Psi-Corps will develop a serious interest in the character.
"What was that?! Mind-quake."

Rogue Telepath: The character has psychic abilities and is on the run from Psi-Corps or his or her race's equivalent. Life under the watchful eye of a jealous organization is not for everyone, and many telepaths refuse association with their organization. Those that do must become sleepers (see the Characteristic, below), or go on the run.

Pros: Few telepaths are free from organizational "guidance," but a rogue telepath lives free.

Cons: Rogue telepaths are in fact outlaws. Psi-Corps, the Telepath's Guild, or the

Religious Caste will be looking for this character for his or her entire life.

"What choice do I have? The Corps? Drugs? No thanks!"

Sleeper: The character is a Human telepath who has opted out of the capability. Rather than join Psi-Corps, go on the lam, or go to jail (or perhaps simply because he or she didn't like the telepathic capability), the character takes a regular medication to suppress his or her psionic gift. The medication takes the form of monthly government-administered injections. They have a nasty side effect in that they tend to bring about clinical depression.

Pros: Though not active, the character is a telepath. At any given time, he or she could discontinue treatment and gain telepathic ability within a few weeks or so. Of course, the options available at that point are to join Psi-Corps or become an outlaw.

Cons: A sleeper will generally tend to be depressed and tired mentally and physically. Furthermore, the government and Psi-Corps will always have a keen interest in the character's whereabouts and the regularity of his or her treatment, though they will not generally intrude beyond that point.

"Every week, a man in a grey suit would visit, to give her the drugs..."

Chapter 2: Game System

This chapter of the book is mainly for the gamemaster's reference. It contains tools to help the GM create an epic story and adjudicate the actions between the characters in the game once that story is underway. Although this chapter is of the most use to the gamemaster, players who wish to learn how the game works are free to read the rules as well.

This chapter is made up of two sections. The first outlines rules and techniques for building and running an engaging arc story, or campaign. The second section details the mechanics that rule play.

The Role of the Gamemaster

The role of gamemaster is the most challenging task in a roleplaying game. The GM creates and describes the environment in which the characters live. Before the players begin their parts, the GM plans and executes the story within that environment, creating allies and foes for the player characters, and planning events that will motivate and challenge the players to move the story toward its conclusion. This preparation isn't the only task. Once the players arrive on the scene, the GM brings the world to life for them, describing the characters' immediate surroundings and interpreting the actions that the players have their characters perform, from investigation and conversation to physical actions and combat. This requires the GM to think on his or her feet and react to the players' course of action.

The GM's task may be the most demanding, but it is also the most rewarding. As the GM, you see all of the action and learn about all of the characters. You also have the opportunity play many different roles in a single session, from the customs agent that gives one of the player characters a

hard time or the thug who mugs him in downbelow, to the reluctant ambassador whom the characters must convince to go along with a carefully-plotted scheme. The story arc is only a guide, and the players will come up with innovative solutions to the problems presented in the plot, giving both you and the players the chance to learn more about the characters and their hidden strengths and flaws.

Both sections of this chapter are tools to aid you in your role as GM, not regulations that must restrict you. They were created specifically for this setting, and are tailored to capture the realistic feel of the BABYLON 5 television series while helping you create an epic story. The story you tell is yours alone, though—use these rules and guidelines only as long as they help you tell it. If you feel that you can work better without any of them, or if you feel that there are additional rules that you wish to use, add to or remove from them as necessary. In the end, it is your job to give the players a story that they will enjoy and remember. Use the tools that help you to best do so.

Choosing a Campaign Type

Like most television series, many roleplaying campaigns are episodic in nature, consisting of a series of largely unrelated adventures that occur more or less ran-

domly, as the GM thinks them up. The characters change and grow over time, but that change is not integral to any particular adventure during the campaign. This method of storytelling is very popular, as it provides a stable base from which to tell a variety of different stories relating to the characters.

The BABYLON 5 television series, however, tells its story in a different fashion. While some individual episodes are not related to the characters on a personal level, there is an overall arc that is telling an epic tale to the audience. The changes that the characters go through are integral to the story, and there is a definite beginning, middle and end to the arc of events.

The series, and this game, are set in an epic universe, where ordinary people face extraordinary situations. Characters begin the story unprepared for what will face them, and must endure the changes that will give them the power to fight against the odds. This is a different sort of story from the episodic campaign undertaken in many roleplaying games; it is an odyssey upon which the players embark knowing that their characters will be forever changed by the events that they will witness, going down a path from which they can never return.

Episodic campaigns are traditionally open-ended. Generally, players get together regularly, once a week or so, for as long as the game interests them. Sometimes they play for a month or two, and sometimes an episodic campaign goes on for years. An epic campaign is slightly more structured; it will run for a finite length of time. How long is quite variable and difficult to predict at the beginning of the campaign—the guidelines here will generally produce a story taking a few months to well over a year to play out. That's an important factor, one which all of the players should be aware of at the beginning, as it is more difficult to introduce new players (or justify the disappearance of old ones) in an epic campaign than it is in an episodic one.

The choice of story type will ultimately be up to you as the GM to decide. Both episodic and epic campaigns make excellent platforms for roleplaying, though each has a different feel. The tools presented in this book are specifically aimed at GMs who wish to develop epic tales fitting the feel of the BABYLON 5 setting, but many of them are devices and ideas that work well for both types of storytelling.

Section 1: Developing a Story

Before you gather a group of players together to play an epic campaign, you will have to have a story of some sort in mind for them. This section will help by giving you some tools for constructing engaging stories. The BABYLON 5 story draws from epic myths that have entranced people for generations. It retells the struggle of man to become better than he is and nobler than he knows, and touches a chord deep inside many of us. This epic feel is also present in the game, and the stories you and the players tell, while about different people and places, will be very much influenced by the feel of the series. These tips were written with that idea in mind.

Fundamentals of Epic Storytelling

The very first thing you'll need when building a story for *The Babylon Project* is to decide upon a basic idea for your story arc. This does not mean you must have a detailed outline of what you want to do (that will develop as things go on). Instead, you just want a premise outlining where the characters will start and what they will face in the future. The player characters are the protagonists in the story. Although at first they may not realize where events will take them, you'll have an overall arc in mind from the start. Begin by thinking about the basics: the conflict that drives the story; the antagonists that oppose the player characters; and the setting against which the story is cast.

Creating Conflict

Conflict is at the core of any story, large or small. The outline of your campaign must be built around a conflict, which defines the difficulties that the characters face and the course of events that will affect them.

An epic tale can be about many things, but there are a few things that set the epic apart from the mundane. Epic tales involve the struggle of "good" heroes to triumph against the overwhelming odds arrayed against them. These heroes are picked from among the rest of humanity by virtue of some quality that makes them a little bit better than the rest, but are by no means prepared for the task ahead of them. In the game, your players' characters are not special because of any inherent abilities, but because there is a destiny guiding them (see Fortune Points on page 114). They will be subject to failure as much as the next person, and how they overcome their own failings to succeed against the enemy is part of the story. The epic tale is just as much a story of their struggle to overcome their

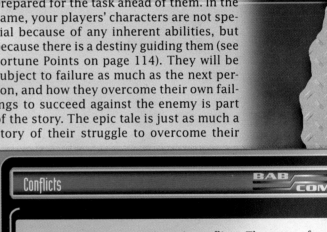

Conflicts   BABCOM

Epic campaigns require epic conflicts. The range of potential conflicts is infinite, but all epic conflicts share one feature: they are big, big enough to dominate the lives of the characters who stand up to them, and big enough to threaten thousands of lives, society as we know it, or the values we hold dear. Some potential conflicts include:

- A new technology or ancient device is discovered, that has the potential to kill millions or totally overthrow the existing order. It is so dangerous that despite some major potential benefit, it must ultimately be destroyed.
- A newly-discovered race faces enslavement at the hands of the aggressive aliens who found them.
- A colony ship lost in hyperspace emerges deep within the space of a hostile or mysterious race (such as the Vorlons), and must contend with that race on the long trek home.
- A powerful telepath has developed a technique for subtle mind control, and is using it for a silent coup.
- Two races stand at the brink of war, deaf to the effects it will have on the stability of interracial relations everywhere.

own weaknesses as it is a fight against the opposition.

In choosing a conflict for an epic story, think on an epic scale. The conflict must be complex—not something that can be fully uncovered, understood, and overcome in a short length of time. It must also be big, serious, and foreboding. Lives—the very future—must hang in the balance. The conflict need not be as sweeping as that portrayed in the television series—it need not threaten all of civilization—but it must be compelling enough to eventually consume the lives of the player characters, and to make heroes of them.

As an example of the story creation process, we'll look at the epic story introduced in chapter 4. This story is being created by Dana's GM, Rob. Rob wants to tie his campaign into the very concept behind the television show: the Babylon 5 station. He bases his conflict on the difficulties encountered in its creation—specifically the destruction of the first three stations. After toying with the idea for a bit, he decides that a powerful conspiracy of Humans opposed to

peaceful interaction with aliens is behind the destruction of the stations. The conflict for the players will be to unmask this conspiracy so that the station can be built. If they don't—if the conspirators succeed—not only will the only hope for lasting peace in the galaxy be quashed, but the emboldened conspirators will move on to even more violent and despicable acts.

Choosing an Antagonist

The epic tale is a battle against the dark foe. Well organized, powerful and deadly, the antagonist in an epic tale is the apparently unbeatable enemy. The antagonist has been around for a long time, either building up power in secret or holding power selfishly, and it is the situation which the antagonist creates that breeds the heroes who must fight. Past actions of the antagonist are often the forces which directly shape the hero. Having created your conflict, the next step is to detail this antagonist opposed to the player characters. To do so, look at the different ways in which the antagonist will affect your heroes.

In its most basic form, the epic story pits good against evil. However, there are many shades of gray between what might be considered "good" and "evil." Heroes in epic stories are not always pure souls who fight for truth and justice, and dark foes are not always ruthless overlords who want to crush the world beneath their feet. When setting up your own story arc, you are not limited to virtuous player characters and two-dimensional dastardly villains. Your characters will have checkered pasts that encourage the players to explore the limits of what they think that they can play. Likewise, give your antagonists history and rationale for what they are doing. Bad guys don't just wake up one morning, look in the mirror and decide, "Gee, I think I'll be evil now." They are passionate characters who can be (as far as they are concerned) patriots, saviors, visionaries or martyrs. So, just as each player decides what motivates his or her character, you must decide what moves the opposition.

An epic story requires an epic foe. In the time period of *The Babylon Project*, there

Antagonists

Antagonists are the opponents against whom the player characters face off over the course of the story. At first they are generally hidden—it often takes several adventures just to figure out who they are. Regardless, a good antagonist is not just a black-hatted villain, but has its own sincere motivations for its activities. Some examples include:

- An aggressive government or race that seeks to expand its power or influence for the glory or security of its people.
- Rebels, terrorists, or factions within and/or opposed to a generally beneficial government.
- A fanatically religious group convinced that theirs is the only true faith.
- A commercial organization or corporation seeking resources, wealth, or advantage.
- A megalomaniac driven towards glory or power by a vision for society that only he can bring about.

are many different antagonists to provide the conflicts and foils behind your story. Most of the aliens have their own agendas, and even many Humans within the Earth Alliance have views that differ from those commonly accepted among the rest of the EA population. Even though the characters will probably not know who the antagonists are at the start of the story, they are an integral part of it, and a well chosen antagonist will provide a really good challenge for the players. Your epic antagonist will usually be at least one step ahead of the player characters through much of the story.

Obviously, your choice of antagonists will be closely linked to your conflict—in fact, your conflict may have already defined who your antagonist must be. When developing that antagonist, mold him or her (or them) into a force that can live up to the player characters, that is powerful, mysterious, and complex. Think of their backstory—what they have been up to prior to the player characters' involvement in the conflict. Decide what their resources are, how far they can stretch their influence, and what other individuals or groups the antagonist controls, can manipulate, or is allied with. Think about the antagonist's methodology—how it goes about accomplishing its goals. Attention to these issues will help build an foe worthy of the player characters and your epic tale.

Rob has already decided that the foe in his story is a conspiracy of radical Humans. He decides that the principal antagonist, at the heart of the conspiracy, is the Homeguard. As befits an epic antagonist, Homeguard (a terrorist organization from the television series) is well outfitted with agents in many different branches of the Earth Alliance. With a well-organized modular structure, they will be hard to root out and defeat. Initially, his player characters would seem to have no chance against such a well-prepared enemy.

The Homeguard is also not a two-dimensional villain. The members of the movement are trying to keep Humanity from being subsumed by alien races and to preserve Human interests. In their minds they are protectors, not vigilantes. They take action not to terrorize oth-ers but to safeguard themselves and their posterity.

Homeguard is led by a group of individuals, many of whom are very influential in government, business, and the military. Rob knows from the television show that Homeguard is related to several lesser nationalist and terrorist organizations, and this gives him a few ideas for his plot—the players may have to investigate their way through several groups before they determine Homeguard's role.

Other Parties

Your choice of antagonist defines the primary opponent that your player characters will face throughout your arc story. However, your characters and their antagonist are not alone in the universe, and the conflict that forms the backbone of an epic story is usually important enough to attract

Third Parties

The conflict behind an epic story is too grand for just the player characters and the antagonists, and will surely draw other interested parties. Some potential third parties that might become involved in an epic story—allied to the player characters, opposed to them, or neutral—include:

- Known alien races.
- Previously unknown alien races.
- Human or alien government organizations, especially those with specific agendas such as Psi-Corps, Earthforce, or an intelligence agency.
- News organizations such as ISN.
- Corporate interests.

---

they might take. As with the antagonist, think about backstory, resources and methods. Give these characters or groups complexity and depth (or leave room to develop it as time goes on), as they may become as influential as the antagonist.

One particular non-player group to think about is the government—if the conflict is one that would involve the authorities, how will they react to the players characters' involvement? Why will fate single out the characters to face down and resolve the conflict, instead of more conventional authorities?

Again, you need not decide completely all of the details surrounding other parties. Leave some room for details suggested by the Characteristics your players choose for their characters, and for characters or groups that arise unforeseen during play.

other interested parties. Some of these will be opposed to the player characters (though not necessarily aligned with the antagonist); others may have goals in common with them. Still others will have completely separate interests, or will change from friend to enemy or vice versa over the course of the plot. You need not define every other faction in the story during the planning stage (especially this early on), but it might help to think bit about it.

Ask yourself who else might be interested in the conflict, and what positions

Rob doesn't have many specific ideas concerning third parties. He's pretty sure that he'll associate the player characters with helpful members of Earthforce (though Homeguard's influence in that organization will mean that it can't always be trusted entirely). He's also got some vague ideas about setting adventures around the destruction of one or all of the early Babylon stations—perhaps he could bring some of the individuals involved in the Babylon Project into the story as recurring characters. Obviously, such personnel would have goals similar to the player characters'. But that doesn't necessarily mean that they'll always be allies, especially if Rob's plan to cast suspicion for the sabotage of the station on the player characters works out...

Choosing a Setting

Having a conflict and an antagonist, the next thing you need to decide upon is the setting. There's a big galaxy beyond the confines of the station featured on the show. Earth has colonies that range in type from well-established metropolitan areas to frontier zones reminiscent of the old west. In addition, stations and other orbital settlements are scattered throughout Human

Settings

Epic campaigns often span great distances and involve many settings. However, some are set largely in one environment. Sample settings include:

- An alien planet or station, on which the player characters are expatriates.
- Babylon 5, Station Prime, or another major space station.
- A mining complex in the asteroid belt, or a colony complex on a world with a unique or hostile environment.
- The rim.
- A massive colony ship.
- Earth.

space, each with its own command style and structure. Several colonies and outposts are mentioned in this book, and others will be detailed in upcoming sourcebooks, so feel free to use one of these or create one of your own. There are also plenty of places outside of Human space for the characters to explore. In the areas near Earth space the Narn and the Centauri both have outposts and colonies, and a number of non-aligned worlds are located near EA space. As the story moves on, you may find that the setting moves from place to place. At this point, however, you only need to have the starting place in mind and a general feel of where things will go in different stages of your campaign.

Rob's story isn't going to be set in one specific location—rather, he foresees the players constantly following events all over Human space. Most adventures will be in space, set on stations or ships, with only a few venturing onto planetary colonies or Earth itself. Towards the middle of the campaign, Rob figures the characters will establish a base of operations on one of the colony planets between Earth and the Babylon Project, though that will be more of a launching

point than the setting for many adventures. As with his thoughts on third parties, Rob will come back to give this issue a little more thought once other aspects of the story come into focus.

Sketching Out a Plot

You've chosen a conflict, an antagonist, and a setting. It's time to sketch out your story.

Any good story has a beginning, a middle and an end. Each of these parts has its own flavor and pace, and each reveals and deals with different aspects of your conflict, antagonist, and player characters. Before launching your epic campaign, you need a rough outline of what's to come—what your player characters will learn and when, and what plot challenges and internal difficulties they'll face and how.

For the purposes of this game each part of the story arc—beginning, middle and end—has been broken into two phases: the beginning of the story consists of the Introduction Phase and the Identification Phase; the middle of the Preparation Phase and the Challenge Phase; and the end of the

Climax and Resolution Phases. Each of these phases has a different tone to it, and each of them requires a different pace of events and different types of adventures.

We'll come back to the individual phases and their adventure requirements in a bit—for now, as you outline your arc story idea, focus only on the differences between the beginning, middle, and end.

The Beginning

As just mentioned, the beginning of an epic campaign consists of two phases: the Introduction Phase and the Identification Phase. The Introduction Phase serves two purposes. The first is to introduce the characters to each other, and the second is to introduce the players to their characters. The first purpose is obvious. Even if some of the characters know each other before the adventure begins, there will still be a period of time where characters who have never met before must meet and learn about each other.

As to the second purpose: it seems odd to say that the players will need to be introduced to their characters, but this is actually a very important part of the game. Until the players actually start playing the game, their characters will be little more than a few words and statistics on a piece of paper. Once they begin the game, the characters will take on more shape, and the players will need time to "grow" into the roles of the characters. This part of the story gives them time to do that. It also gives them time to refine their characters, redefining any characteristics that they feel are inappropriate or do not play well, and answering any last questions that still remain from the character creation process.

The Identification Phase is the part of the story where the players begin to learn what is going on in the story arc. They will not necessarily learn all of the details about their purpose, but they will begin to get some of the pieces of the puzzle. They might learn about who the antagonist is, or how their past relates to the story. Or, they could even challenge and defeat one enemy only to find that they have just begun to discover who the true foe is, layering one story within another. A good way to keep the story compelling is for the characters to suffer defeat at the end of this phase, only then discovering the truth about their enemies. During this phase, you can have a wide variety of adventures, mixing in story elements as you think best for maximum dramatic effect.

To sketch out your plotline, think of the initial impression you want your players to draw from your campaign. You may want to create a sense of urgency right off the bat—if that's the case, you'll want your plot to begin with crisis. Or, you may want your campaign to start off small, transitioning slowly from a mundane feel towards a grander scope. Either way, consider misleading your players at first, obscuring the central conflict throughout the beginning so that the players must first work their way through a series of related conflicts, perhaps coming to believe that the real issue is something completely different. Obviously, by the end of the Identification Phase they must be getting a handle on at least the basics—but that realization, which can come at the turning point between the beginning and middle of your story, can be a real epiphany.

Make a few notes on your thoughts for the opening of your campaign. If you aren't very inspired at this point, don't worry about too much detail. In fact, many GMs prefer to outline the middle or end phases of their campaigns first, then come back to the beginning when they've got a strong sense of where they're going.

Rob decides to open his story with an adventure that ties directly into the destruction of Babylon Station. That'll introduce the conflict—though the players may not necessarily recognize it, as he'll surround the event with two or three unrelated adventures. After that, he'll draw the players back into the investigation of Babylon Station's sabotage, leading them through a series of false leads that first implicate Homeguard's front organizations, associated terrorist groups, and patsies. Finally, in one momentous adventure, the players will at last identify the shadowy Homeguard as the real enemy—but not in time to prevent the destruction of Babylon 2.

This realization, along with the dramatic loss of the second station, will mark the turning point between the beginning and the middle of the story. At this point the players will finally know the identity of the enemy—now they have to figure out how to defeat it.

The Middle

The middle of the story consists of the Preparation and Challenge Phases. The Preparation Phase is usually a bit more directed than the previous phases, and is the part where the characters begin to prepare for their true foe. By this point, they are probably aware that the odds are against them, although they may not yet fully realize exactly what lies ahead. The adventures will relate more directly to the story arc, and will force the characters to get ready for what awaits them. Here they will meet the terrible trials that prepare them for the challenges ahead, where they will either live or die depending on their ability to cope with the adventures they face. It is not unreasonable for a character to die here, or for a character to undergo a life-altering change that cannot be undone. This is where the characters begin to exhibit heroic tendencies and where their destiny becomes apparent. In many ways, this phase is where the characters meet their point of no return.

The Challenge Phase is the part of the story where the characters begin the task for which they have prepared. They have already reached the turning point in the shift from the Preparation Phase; now they begin to take the initiative and act with deliberation. Depending on your story arc, this challenge can be anything from a quiet manhunt to a guns-blazing, galaxy spanning chase. Events are no longer in anyone's control, and are moving inexorably toward a conclusion. This phase is usually very quick and directed, taking only a few adventures to play out. Almost all adventures here will directly relate to the arc, and the end of this phase will lead immediately into the next phase, the climax.

The middle is the meat of the story, where the characters come to grips with and pursue the central conflict. Think about how you expect events to unfold: what situations the characters will be forced into; what other elements beyond the player characters and the antagonists will come to bear; and what general strategy you expect to adopt. Keep your thoughts general at this point—by the time you get into the Challenge Phase, your players' actions and new ideas that occur to you during play will probably alter many of the plans you established beforehand.

Jot down your ideas. If you hadn't come up with much for the beginning of your story (or if your thoughts on the middle changed some of your original thinking), go back and modify your beginning.

The middle of Rob's campaign will focus on the investigation and defeat of Homeguard. This organization is powerful and shadowy, and many don't even believe it exists. Rob decides that for the first few adventures in the middle of his story, the player characters will have to

focus on quiet investigation for the most part, as they seek out the identities of Homeguard's leaders and the vulnerabilities of the organization. This is the time also when Rob foresees the player characters accumulating resources for the battle ahead, and he plans to encourage them to establish the base of operations he was thinking about before.

About halfway through this process, as the characters learn more and more of the terrorists' plans, a new secret will be revealed: Homeguard is planning an act of genocide. They plan on nuking the Markab dome on a colony world shared by three non-aligned races: the Markab, the Drazi, and the Koulani. This will kill hundreds of thousands of innocent Markab, but more than that, it will be timed to coincide with tensions between these races, so that the bombing will inflame a war between them while deflecting blame from Human involvement.

Now that the player characters know about the plan, they can go on the offensive, moving into the Challenge Phase. The next few adventures will center on the players' attempts to unmask Homeguard members and foil their plan. These efforts will culminate in success, with the players (hopefully) preventing the attack on the colony. However, the players will intercept the bomb at the Babylon site, and their inability to defuse it will result in the destruction of Babylon 3.

The End

The Climax Phase is the confrontation that has been building since the beginning. Here, it is force and counterforce, and the fate of the story rests on what happens. This phase will not take longer than one or two game sessions, and will usually not consist of more than one adventure. The characters are meeting their destinies head on and must either triumph or meet the dire consequences of their failure.

As the climax ends, the Resolution Phase begins. Here, the dust settles and the characters must sort out what has happened and make their peace with the changes that they have had to endure. After this phase, the story arc is over. There may be a few bits of unfinished business, but when the characters wrap it up, they have finished the story.

You needn't think too hard about the climax of your story arc this far in advance. If you foresee a particular conclusion or situation against which the climax will play out, go ahead and note it. But be flexible—even more so than the middle, the end of your story will be greatly influenced by the direction your players take and your own new ideas. Once again, if anything occurred to you to change your thinking about the beginning or middle of your story, go back and change them.

The foiling of the terrorist bombing and the destruction of Babylon 3 were just an anti-climax. By now, the players have really put a dent in Homeguard, and the organization is getting desperate. They have a second nuke, and

they're planning to use it. This one won't be aimed at aliens—it's headed for the player characters' base. The climactic adventure will be a race against time as the players struggle to save themselves and their outpost from Homeguard's wrath. If successful, the players will finally unmask Homeguard's top leadership, putting the organization out of business for a while at least.

Putting It All Together

You can run a compelling epic story from just the few notes you've come up with so far, but a little thinking on a few more details can make the difference between a good story and a great one. For starters, read the section on Choosing Adventures, below, which talks about the six phases of an epic story in greater detail. This will give you some additional guidance on the pace of the story, as well as a few ideas on the types of adventures you'll be running at various stages of the campaign.

There are just a few more things to think about. The first is the flow of information to the players. As noted above, the players begin the story knowing little or nothing of the central conflict or their antagonist. Throughout the beginning phases of the story, they come to learn about the antagonist and to face the conflict—but they don't clearly identify either until the story shifts from beginning to middle, and they don't fully come to understand them until later even than that. What will bring your players to these realizations, and how and when will you give them that information?

Think about the seams between the phases—the turning points in the story. Identify a few key pieces of information: the identity of the antagonist or other major players; their plans; key aspects of their capabilities; and other information critical to the player characters' success. Some of these elements will be minor details, others earth-shattering plot twists. Decide which are needed by the players at which stages of the story—and which can't be known prior to a particular point, if the tension and mystery is to be sustained. Develop a few ideas about how the players

might uncover these bits of information (some of which might be the subject of entire adventures), but don't worry too much about it if you're stymied at this point. Like so many other elements, it's good to consider the flow of information as early as possible, but your decisions will likely be altered in play by unfolding events and the actions of your players.

Another element to consider is foreshadowing. In a book or movie, any radically new element that appears late in the story will seem out of place if it hasn't already been hinted at. The same is true in an epic roleplaying game. Foreshadowing will provide the hint needed to bring surprise elements smoothly into the latter stages of the game. That doesn't mean you have to hit the players over the head with every aspect of the plot, or destroy every secret or surprise. In fact, you must be careful not to do that—foreshadowing should be subtle enough to pass unnoticed, or at most be recognized as an isolated piece of the puzzle that doesn't make any sense at

The Story Chart

The Story Chart is a tool for keeping track of where your players have been in your story and what they have learned. It also provides a road map to remind you of what else they may need to know. It is not a rigid setup for the arc—expect to change it to meet the needs of the story as you see new ways to challenge the players and new links that will draw them in. You may also end up dropping events that don't seem critical anymore. In short, the Story Chart is a living document; a guiding device, not a static, set-in-stone blueprint of the story.

The Story Chart for the sample adventure in chapter 4 is on page 171. The story begins at the top of the chart, and progresses down the chart as the player characters encounter the information in each box, or cell, of the chart. Each cell is an adventure that the characters will experience, and can be as simple as few hours of play or as complex as several game sessions. When there are several options for the story, the chart branches out, giving multiple departure points from each adventure depending on the choices the players make.

The cells on the Story Chart represent informational items, not physical locations. While some events in a story, obviously, are tied to specific locations, any given adventure may span many locations, and multiple adventures can be set in the same place.

The Story Chart is based on the standard flowchart that you may have learned in school. It is a directional diagram that uses several pre-defined symbols to allow you to map the story and track its progress. The symbols used in Story Charts for *The Babylon Project* (both here and in future books) are as follows:

This is the most common symbol on the chart. It represents a "non-exclusive" arc-related adventure. Non-exclusive simply means that the events of the adventure do not relate directly to other happenings in the story, so that the adventure can be worked into the story at almost any point. If the players' decisions do not make the adventure appropriate at one point, the GM can work it into the story line later. Often, players can uncover key pieces of information, encounter critical non-player characters, or experience important scenes through any one of several non-exclusive adventures, which together form a tapestry of multiple ways to advance the story. Therefore, all cells that allow the players to find out the same basic information are the same color. Decisions that the you or the players make determine where the story goes next.

This represents an "exclusive" arc adventure that the characters must experience during the story. Exclusive adventures are those that can only happen once, or those that change the nature of the story and cannot be revisited or reversed. These should be used in fewer situations than those that are not exclusive.

This symbol represents an independent or arc-related adventure that is not critical to solving the overall puzzle, but that may help. It may or may not have branches leading to other sections of the story. Those that do not have branches into or out of them can occur at any time during the story, if they occur at all. These can be seeds that develop into other parts of the story arc or standalone adventures designed to give you a break from the epic.

Finally, these connections show which pieces of information are likely to lead to others. The story proceeds along the arrows, in the direction indicated. Again, often there are multiple arrows leading from a single cell—in such cases, the story follows the course determined by the players' actions. These connections do not represent every possible option, and sometimes the players will make choices not represented on the chart. As mentioned above, that's when the GM must make adjustments and bring in new ideas to keep the story flowing as appropriate. No story is ever completely written until it has been played through from start to finish.

the moment even if the players know it will be a key piece later on.

Think about what happens in the middle and end of your arc story—especially about elements, characters, or groups that are introduced (or first brought into the open) in those stages. Jot down a few ideas for how you might hint at the existence of these elements earlier on in the story. Remember, you don't want to give away any surprises or even provide any real clues to the nature of the arc conflict—you just want to set the stage for things to come.

The last element of epic campaign preparation is the Story Chart—a sort of flow chart that outlines each major element of the story and how it relates to the whole. A good Story Chart will help you visualize the story and keep track of what the characters have learned as it progresses. Sketch out a rough story chart according to the instructions in the sidebar, remembering not to be too rigid just yet. Your ideas will likely change during the campaign, and as you integrate the player characters into the background—the next step in preparing your story.

Rob had no idea his story would end so dramatically when he began jotting down his ideas—most of the latter events just occurred to him as he worked his way through the outlining process. Rob has already decided at which points most of the critical information will come to light—the players will identify Homeguard in the last adventure of the Identification Phase, will learn of the plan to nuke the Markab colony dome at the end of the Preparation Phase, and will identify the threat to their own base at the beginning of the Climax Phase.

Rob looks at the latter events for elements that he should foreshadow. The most prominent is probably Homeguard's plan to pit the Markab, Drazi, and Koulani against one another in the war that Homeguard hopes will follow their bombing. In designing his early adventures, Rob will want to bring up the potential tension among those races—in fact, he might want to set an early adventure, unrelated to the arc story, on the very planet that is shared by the three races' colonies. Other ele-

ments he thinks he might want to foreshadow include the use of nuclear weapons, and perhaps, very early on and in very subtle ways, the existence of Homeguard.

The Player Characters

You cannot develop your story much further without taking your player characters into consideration. Who they are, what they are good at, and what their backgrounds contribute are all critical aspects of your story. The character generation system gives you some input into the characters your players create, and your story idea may suggest or even require some particular character types. When working with your players on their character concepts, however, avoid the temptation to micromanage. Let them develop the characters that they want to play, so long as you can work them into your story, and remain open to any ideas or story hooks they come up with.

Integrating Character Concepts

Once you have sketched out the basics of your story, it is time to talk with the players to find out what sorts of characters they want to play. As mentioned above, you don't want to have every little detail of your cam-

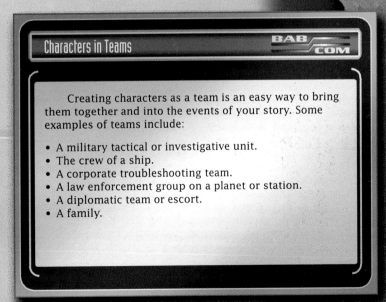

Characters in Teams

BAB COM

Creating characters as a team is an easy way to bring them together and into the events of your story. Some examples of teams include:

- A military tactical or investigative unit.
- The crew of a ship.
- A corporate troubleshooting team.
- A law enforcement group on a planet or station.
- A diplomatic team or escort.
- A family.

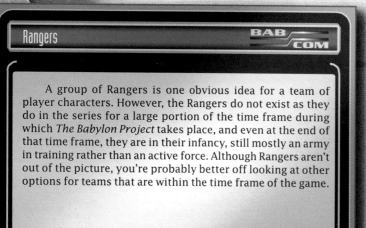

A group of Rangers is one obvious idea for a team of player characters. However, the Rangers do not exist as they do in the series for a large portion of the time frame during which *The Babylon Project* takes place, and even at the end of that time frame, they are in their infancy, still mostly an army in training rather than an active force. Although Rangers aren't out of the picture, you're probably better off looking at other options for teams that are within the time frame of the game.

paign worked out at this point, because the best stories draw the players in by using elements from their characters' backgrounds to flesh them out. Gather your players together and discuss with them who their characters are and exactly why they are together (preferably while they are at the character concept/basic history stage of the character generation process). You can then work those details into your story arc.

How the characters will come together and embark on the beginning of the story is an important issue at this point, one that should affect both character generation and your story design. One of the simplest and most effective ways to put characters together is to make them all part of a team of some sort, with a common goal. No matter what their backgrounds, they will all be mostly working toward the same purpose. They may or may not know each other before the story begins, but they will all have to trust each other to fulfill their common goals.

Teams support long-term stories very well, providing a stable foundation of characters and purpose which can support many adventures in their field (there's always something to threaten Station Security, for example) over the course of the story. If players miss game sessions, it's generally easy to continue play with those who are present. If players want to quit or join the game later, it is also not usually a difficult matter to "reassign" characters as necessary.

The disadvantage of the team approach is that it can occasionally feel contrived or predictable. The characters have a relatively limited range of backgrounds, and the nature of the team sometimes identifies the story to the players long before their characters should be aware of it.

A more difficult way to gather the characters is to develop the group as a part of the story. This requires that the players are all willing to have their characters' histories partially decided by you, as you will need to cultivate the reasons why the characters are brought into the story. They will probably not be together at the start of gameplay, so the events that they play out in the first adventure or two must bring them together. This requires a good deal more planning on your part, as you will have to ensure that you have several different ways to get the group together if the players don't follow the initial plan.

This story-based approach provides a better format for an epic story, as the player characters are drawn together by events that they then have to deal with. It also provides a great deal more diversity to the characters. A Centauri and a Minbari might not serve together on a ship by choice (or be assigned together as members of a team), for example, but if they are both fleeing an exploding passenger liner they might find themselves on the same lifeboat, working for their mutual survival.

Just as with the team approach, the characters on some level share a common goal, although they may not trust each other or even want everyone else to reach the goal with them. This allows for a lot more interplay between the personalities within the party, which can be a very exciting roleplaying opportunity for the players. It also provides a more compelling sense of story, as the reason that they are together is an integral part of that story.

The disadvantage to this approach is that it is not quite as flexible as the team approach in regard to the players. If a player must miss a session or players want to quit or join the story in progress you must figure out a story reason for this to happen, which can be more difficult than with a team. However, with a dedicated group of players and a few "back doors" (ways to explain how a character enters or leaves the story) in place in case of player turnover, this can be the most rewarding story you tell.

These two methods are the extremes. Most campaigns are a mix of these two styles, with part of the party being a partnership or team and others being drawn into events, or with outsiders attached to the team, false team members, or the team being drawn into events with the other characters, events from which they cannot escape. Use the best of each approach in creating your story, and bring the characters into things as you feel it appropriate.

Rob decides to go with the team approach. He decides that EarthGov, realizing that after the euphoria of the victory over the Minbari wears off the prewar anti-alien sentiments will begin to re-emerge, is putting together a special team of investigators and troubleshooters to seek out radical groups. He'll ask the players to create characters that can be part of such a team.

Character Development

Obviously, the method you choose to bring the characters into the story affects the characters' concepts. Now, you will have to sit down with each of the players and determine more specifically how his or her character fits into—and will contribute to—the plot. Some players will have complete characters ready before you meet with them, while others will want you to walk them through the steps of character creation detailed in chapter 1. Determining the history of the character with the player during the first play session will help both types of players get a better handle on the character, and will give you an insight into what the player wants to play and how you might accommodate that.

As you discuss the history of the character with the player, you will also begin to get a better idea of how this character will fit into your overall story. You can suggest changes to the character's background to meet the requirements of your story. An excellent way to do this is to suggest Characteristics that the character will need to overcome during the story or that will in-

volve the character in the events on a gut level.

For example, if you need someone to have a past that involves one of the antagonists, you can suggest to the player who wants to play an retired Earthforce officer that her character left the military when she was injured in a shuttle accident on Mars. This event provides the background for a Characteristic: a phobia concerning atmospheric flight that leaves her preferring to stay on orbital stations. With this Characteristic, you've just created a link between the character and the story. Now you can go back and adjust your story arc. If a faction within Earthforce is tied into your conflict, for example, you could decide that her old superior officer was responsible for the accident—and that he's a part of that faction. The character will discover this during the course of the story, perhaps requiring her to confront her fear to get to the antagonist for a showdown.

Players who have less of an idea what they want to play make this very easy, but

even someone who knows exactly what their character will be is usually open to some suggestion if it will make the story more compelling. This works both ways; if you see something in one of the characters' histories that you feel will strengthen the story, keep it in mind as you are develop the plot. The players will surprise you with how creative they can be, and when something that they have set up turns out to be an integral piece of the puzzle, it gives them a good sense of involvement in the story.

Once you have consulted with each of the players and know how you will work their histories into the story, make adjustments to your story arc as necessary. Some adjustments may come as a direct result of your characters' histories, others may be new ideas that occurred to you as you talked with the players.

Players can throw wrenches into the best-laid plans. One of Rob's players really has his heart set on playing a Narn. Obviously, there aren't many Narns in

Earthforce, so Rob and the player have to work out a plan for bringing the Narn character into the story. After some brainstorming, Rob suggests that they make the character an incidental victim of Homeguard's machinations who is rescued by the team in the first adventure. That'll involve him in events, and if they give the character some crucial skills, his continued involvement with the team from that point on will be justified. The player finishes up his character while Rob makes the necessary adjustments to his initial adventure.

Choosing Adventures

Your story is laid out, your player characters are created and you have a plan for bringing them together. It's time to start planning the actual play of the game.

Although it follows an overall storyline, an epic campaign is made up of individual adventures in the same way that an epic television series such as BABYLON 5 is made up of individual shows and two- or three-part series. An individual adventure sets before the players a conflict smaller than the overall story conflict (although it may be related to or a fragment of the story conflict)—something that can be tackled in an evening or two (or, sometimes, three or four) of play. Some adventure conflicts are best resolved through investigation and deduction, others through tactical action. Creating adventures is fairly easy—you'll get the hang of it after reading the sample adventure in chapter 4.

The type and content of each adventure differs from phase to phase of your story. In terms of relation to your story arc, there are three types of adventures: "independent adventures," which do not directly relate to your arc story at all; "arc adventures," which are directly connected to the conflict of the overall story; and "arc-related adventures," which aren't directly connected to the overall conflict, but which are linked, or which provide important information or insight into the conflict. How you employ these three types of adventures, as well as how you choose their content and pace, varies according to the phase of your story in which they appear.

The Introduction Phase

To begin the story, the characters should hit the ground running. That is to say, they should be immediately drawn into an event that forces them to react as a group. It does not have to relate directly to the overall story arc, as the characters need not be drawn straight into the conflict at this point. The aim is to pull them into their roles and get them familiar with who they are as the story begins.

During this phase, you will want to concentrate on adventures that encourage the characters to act together, not necessarily on adventures that reveal story arc information. Situations where one or more lives are threatened, or where there is danger of future conflict will do this very well.

You might also want to begin to include some references to the story arc. A clue that doesn't fit into the current adventure might be dropped, foreshadowing what is to come. A bit of information about a character's past might be an enigma that the other characters come to learn about. However you handle such elements, remember that such foreshadowing only sets the stage for later events—players should rarely learn anything useful for it, or even notice it right away.

The Introduction Phase represents a time well before fate begins to single out the player characters, and these initial adventures are not usually critical to the outcome of the story arc as a whole. Instead, focus on encouraging the players to roleplay their characters. Make them aware of the uses for Fortune Points and how they are awarded, and reward excellent examples of roleplaying, especially when they are roleplaying the downsides of their characters' Characteristics. Shoot for an average of one Fortune Point per character per game session. That average doesn't mean that you have to give each player a Fortune Point each session, just that if you have, say, five players, you give out around five Fortune Points a night among the entire group. Of course, you don't have to award that many if the players don't earn them. And you can award more—but only under exceptional circumstances.

The Introduction Phase does not last a long time. The players and characters will begin to get used to each other, and will begin to learn how to work with each other fairly quickly. Before they get too comfortable, get the story moving. After two or three independent adventures, move on to the Identification Phase.

The Identification Phase

Once the characters have gotten to know each other and the players are comfortable in their roles, begin to introduce the elements of the story arc that will move

Sample Adventures

In this and other *The Babylon Project* books you will see sample adventures for use either in standalone events or as independent adventures for in your ongoing campaign. These published adventures are presented in the following format:

The Premise: This is the introduction to the story. It gives you, the GM, a basic idea of what's going on and who the players are. Its goal is to give a short teaser to let you know what will happen in the story.

The Background: This is an overview of what's going on behind the scenes of the story. It gives you an idea of who's who in the story and what the characters will face if they are to complete it. The antagonists and other major non-player characters' roles, activities, and approaches are discussed.

The Plot: This is an outline for how events will most likely unfold. It includes the Story Chart and additional details on where the characters must go and what they will likely face to overcome the conflict that drives the adventure.

The Cast: This section introduces the main non-player characters, as well as presenting pre-generated characters (if appropriate) or a list of recommended character types. In the sample in chapter 4, a complete cast of pre-generated characters is included, but other adventures may just give you an outline of who is needed (for example, "a doctor").

Chapters: These are the meat of the adventure. They detail the likely events and encounters that the player characters will go through over the course of the adventure. Sometimes the chapters are followed sequentially, and sometimes their order is determined by the actions of the players and the Story Chart. Each chapter can cover anything from a short incident or plot point to an entire week or more of investigation or travel.

the story forward. This is the first phase in which the players come into contact with the overall conflict, even if it's just in bits and pieces. Set them to adventures that relate to the arc story, so that as they move forward the player characters begin to see where their story is headed. This will probably take an evening by yourself to set the ideas up, but it will greatly enhance the story.

As many adventures in this phase revolve around situations that directly or indirectly set up events later in the story, the player characters should definitely get the feeling that this is leading to something, although they may not learn what that something is until later. By the end of this phase of many of these questions will be answered—although the answers may lead to more questions. The player characters should leave this phase feeling that they understand what will be needed of them in the Challenge and Climax Phases (although there will undoubtedly be a few surprises left).

Controlling the flow of information can make this section very complex, as the characters try to find the clues that allow them to understand what they are up against. Use your Story Chart to control the flow of information to the players.

During this phase, the characters begin to show that they are destined for some-thing a little greater than average. Reward the players more often with Fortune Points (averaging about a point and a half per player per session), though only when they are roleplaying their characters consistently. Remember that during the Introduction phase, the players all had a chance to define the characters by how they played them, so Fortune Point awards should now reward play that is consistent as well as play that exceptionally good.

This phase is much longer than the Introduction Phase. This is the point at which the players have a little time to be side-tracked and can make mistakes and succeed or fail at individual tasks with little consequence to the story. Run four or five arc-related adventures to introduce conflict elements and draw the player characters into the story, and maybe one or two independent adventures just to mix things up a bit.

Once you have reached the end of the Identification Phase, the feel of the story begins to change. At this point, the characters begin to move toward an inevitable confrontation with the foe. To mark this change, the last adventure of this phase should end with a clear turning point, after which the story cannot go back. The characters should recognize this event, and it should have a profound impact on the way that they see

things. It should reveal to the players that what they think they know is just the tip of the iceberg. It will change their perception of the conflict, giving them their first glimpse of the scope of the story.

In Chapter 1 of Rob's story (described in chapter 4 of this book), the characters are assigned together as a team, but as the team comes together, most are meeting each other for the first time. They are immediately drawn into the action by dealing with the consequences of the raider attack, and do not have a chance to get their feet on the ground before their orders come in sending them away. The group's doctor also has a chance to meet So'Shal (the Narn), as a preparation for the next adventure.

Chapter 2 continues the introduction by finishing up the meetings of the characters by bringing So'Shal into the party. All of the characters will have to be on their toes to avoid danger during this act, and some tense interplay between the characters is possible if So'Shal doesn't trust the other player characters. It also leaves a clue to the fact that there is more to come in the arc by presenting an unanswered question: who put So'Shal in the crate, and why?

Preparation Phase

This is the phase of the story arc where the characters commit themselves to the struggle and ready themselves for what is to come. The central conflict has been identified, the story has reached its turning point, and now the characters must reach that point within themselves. Adventures during this phase concentrate on the characters' quest to find out what they need to know to defeat the foe and on preparing themselves to do it.

Adventures that concentrate on the informational quest will follow much the same format as those in the Identification Phase, although they will seem more pressing than before. The Story Chart for this section will help with these adventures, just as before.

The more interesting adventures that appear in this phase from a roleplaying

standpoint, however, are the character preparation stories. As the characters prepare for decisive action, create adventures that break the characters down before building them back up. This is where your work with the players during character creation will really pay off. Not every character will have a tragic flaw or a mysterious past (although that is a goal to strive for), but for those that do you can create stories that make the player closely examine what the character is made of. In the example of the retired Earthforce officer above, for example, you might create an adventure that doesn't just force her to confront her phobia—it relies on it. Her coming to terms with the Characteristic leads to success in the adventure, and prepares the character for what is still to come.

The tone of this phase is much more tense, as the characters learn exact details of what is expected of them. They have been chosen for a destiny, and now they must live up to that destiny. Award Fortune Points for good, consistent roleplaying (averaging two or three points per player per session), and give extra rewards to players when they roleplay their personal preparation adventures. Players whose characters do not have individually-centered adventures that prepare them should receive extra rewards when their characters play an integral role in helping other characters through this preparation.

This phase, while more serious in tone, is also a long phase. The characters will feel tense as they do not know how much time they have, but there will be enough time to let them prepare sufficiently if they buckle down to the task. There should be at least three or four arc adventures in this phase, as well as three or four independent or arc-related adventures that explore individual characters.

Like the Identification Phase, this phase should end at a very clear point in the story. This is the point where, by design or necessity, the characters must begin to undertake what they have been planning, and it is usually triggered by some event that cannot be ignored. From here on, the story is rushing headlong toward its conclusion. This marks the point where the characters' actions shift from reactive to proactive. This turning point generally revolves around the player characters gaining some key piece of information that allows them to begin action.

The events that occur in the example story after the explosion of Babylon 2 comprise the Preparation Phase of the story arc. The player characters have identified the conspiracy, and now their investigations must lead them through Earth First before they can positively identify Homeguard. The investigation against Earth First is almost over, and Homeguard looms ahead.

The example story ends here, giving you a chance to take the story and make it your own. As they prepare to fight the Homeguard, you can reveal what you want about the antagonist, and involve the past histories of your player characters in order to tailor the story to your wishes.

The Challenge Phase

This is the phase during which the characters confront the tasks that they have seen coming and contend with those obstacles that the foe has put in their way—the phase where they go on the offensive, tackling the central conflict with deliberation. Adventures in this phase almost always deal directly with the story arc, and new information that is learned is usually immediately useful. It is a very fast-paced and tense phase, often consisting of only a few adventures. While the previous two phases of the story arc are long and involved, this phase is fast and furious. It marks the beginning of the end of the story, as the major task ahead is the point toward which the story builds.

The characters are heavily involved in the heart of an epic destiny during this phase. They will be performing feats that they thought impossible before. Fortune Points should be rewarded for anything you consider good, be it roleplaying, inventiveness or even good attendance. Shoot for an average of three or four Fortune Points per player per session, and make sure your adventures require their use: they should be passing in and out of the players' hands quickly.

Plotting the story at this point is fairly easy, as the characters are moving toward an obvious goal. Any questions that are left unanswered will either become obstacles now or will have to wait until the Resolution Phase. For example, our ex-military officer may find out here exactly how the antagonist caused her "accident," and she will have to deal with that knowledge quickly and decisively.

Although the action is straightforward, you should still rely on your Story Chart to help keep track of any details that may come up that you haven't planned in advance.

This is a relatively quick phase, as the goal is in sight. It usually consists of no more than two or three arc adventures, which are usually shorter and more action-oriented than adventures in other phases. There are not usually many side adventures in this phase.

The end of the Challenge Phase should be marked yet again by a major plot twist. This time it will be something based not on the characters' actions, but on the actions of the antagonist. The actions of the player characters during this phase have pushed the antagonist up against the wall, and now the antagonist must make a desperate, surprise move that sets up the climax. Prior to this, the player characters may feel that the situation is under control, or almost under control. This sudden turn of events will set up the climax as an even bigger event than what the players expected.

The Climax Phase

The Challenge phase leads directly into this phase; the climax of the story. This is it. The characters have learned a lot, endured even more, and worked hard to get to this point. Rarely taking more than one adventure and only one or two game sessions, this is the point on which the entire story turns.

As in the Challenge phase, the players should be rewarded with Fortune Points frequently and for almost any reason—averaging at least four per player per session. The characters are at the high point of their epic destiny, and will be reaching for every last trick in their arsenal to overcome the odds and their foe.

This phase requires no real plotting, as most of the planning you have already done is paid off here. Events will dictate your plans—no matter your intent, there are no guarantees as to how the story will unfold at this point.

This phase rarely lasts more than one adventure (obviously an arc adventure), although its length may vary depending on exactly what the characters do.

The Resolution Phase

After the action has come to its conclusion, the story will need to wind down. The characters will have to deal with the consequences of the climax, and the players will need to prepare to end the story. This phase serves that purpose. It can be made up of several adventures, however it should not be far from the end of the story.

The resolution of an epic film or novel gives the audience of the story a chance to react to the events of the climax, and this phase of a game gives the players the same thing. Life doesn't end right after the climax of the story, and the characters will need time to get back to some sense of a normal life. The climax of the story will often have permanent consequences, and this is where you must allow the characters to experience those repercussions. While you may know in general terms what you want to happen here, you will definitely have to determine many of the details about what will happen after the climax is over.

The second purpose of the Resolution Phase is to allow the players to prepare to end the story. As mentioned earlier, the epic story has an end, and once that end is reached, the characters have fulfilled their heroic destiny and it's time to go home. By this time, the characters are well-loved personalities that the players are comfortable with and used to. Just as it is a difficult process to start playing a character, it can be a difficult process to stop playing the character once the story is over.

Therefore, adventures in this phase should deal with the results of the climax, and with the resolution of the characters' stories, even though there may still be a few bumps along the way. A good way to do this is to create situations reminiscent of those that they experienced early in the story. This time, however, the characters will have a different perspective on events. This will remind them of how far they have come, and is a good way to provide closure for many characters.

This phase can last anywhere from one adventure of only one game session to three or four adventures that tie up loose ends relating to the antagonist's downfall. Side adventures that reveal how the player characters have changed accent the end of the story.

The final game session should be something that the players will remember, so plan the evening well. In addition to an adventure that ends with a bit of a bang, you might also buy the pizza or surprise the players somehow as a reward for the story. A complex tale could take several months or more to tell in weekly game sessions, so by this point everyone has invested a lot of time and emotion into this story: its end is cause for celebration.

The Sequel

What happens after the story? Now that the characters have fulfilled their destiny, is there another story in their future? The decision of whether or not to have a sequel to your epic story is the last decision you must make in this cycle.

There are a few things to take into account before you decide to take up a sequel. The most important is whether or not it's even possible—often, a story is so grand that any possible sequel will either pale in comparison, diminish the feats of the first story, or reach for heights of drama that are just not sustainable. If you think a sequel is reasonable, you'll also want to consider whether you want to do this all over again. Being the GM for an epic story is a bit like running a marathon, and when it is over, you may need a break. Also, another player in the group may have a new story that he or she wants to tell. Whatever you decide, the epic story you have told will be one that you and your players will remember for some time to come.

Section 2: Game Mechanics

Having created your campaign and generated characters with your players, as GM your biggest role from this point forward will be in determining how events unfold throughout your story. The rules in this chapter are guidelines for adjudicating and interpreting the results of character actions in the game.

Task Resolution

Whenever a player character interacts with other characters or the game environment, you as the GM determine the outcome. In many cases, this outcome will be self-evident; for example, if a player indicates that her character walks across a room and opens an unlocked door, the character will most often be able to do so without a second thought. There are many times, though, when the outcome of the task is not clear, or when a character wants to attempt a task that he or she may not be able to successfully complete. At these times, a way is needed for the GM to arbitrate and determine the outcome of the task: a process called task resolution.

There are four basic factors that influence task resolution, once you establish what the character is attempting. There are also a number of different mitigating factors that you may have to take into account, according to the circumstances of the task. The basic factors are: defining the task; deciding the Difficulty of the task; determining the character's Ability to perform the task; and generating a Random Modifier (also called "rolling" the modifier, since dice are used). These are covered just below. After that follow rules to cover special circumstances and interpretation of the resolution.

Task Definition

The first thing to do when a player decides to have his or her character perform a task is to define that task in game terms. Describe the situation to the player, and have the player describe exactly what the character will do, so that you understand what the attempt entails. Then decide which skill is most appropriate to the task—discuss this with the player if it isn't obvious. Having agreed on the skill, decide if any of the character's Specialties in the chosen skill apply.

Once you've chosen the skill and decided on a Specialty, if any, decide which Attribute the skill should be based on. The skill descriptions listed on pages 51-56 note the Attributes most often used with each skill, but each circumstance is different, and sometimes an Attribute other than the typical is required to perform a task.

Sometimes a character won't have the necessary skill. For basic tasks, that's not a problem—just use the appropriate Attribute, without the benefit of the skill (this lack of skill will reduce the chance of success). For complex or advanced tasks, however, the character must have some degree of skill—no matter how Coordinated a character is, she will not be able to fly a Starfury if she has had no training as a pilot, for example. You must decide whether a character with no skill may attempt a task. Note that in desperate situations, you may allow a character who would not otherwise even be able to attempt a task to do so by spending a Fortune Point—see the section on Fortune Points, towards the end of this chapter.

Finally, if a task might take longer than a few seconds in game time, determine how long the task will take, and how long before the character will know whether or not the task will succeed. For most tasks this is not a factor, but if the character will be at the task for any length of time, tell the player.

Once you have defined the task and established which skill, Specialty, and Attribute applies, move on to determine the Difficulty of the task.

For an example, let's look at Dana's character Jessica. Jessica has been hired to pilot a transport with a small party of personnel (including several other player characters) from Proxima to the new Babylon 5 station. After emerging from the Babylon Station jump gate, the fusion reactor on the transport unexpectedly cut out. Upon investigation, the characters found a critical section of control circuitry burned out, apparently an act of sabotage. While the others went about investigating the cause, Jessica set to work repairing the damage.

The GM tells Dana that the circuitry looks quite bad—the backups were destroyed as well as the primaries. Complete repair will take hours, maybe days, of Jessica's time, and she might not have the necessary spare parts available. After a moment's thought, Dana asks the GM if a temporary bypass could be run, something to give them power long enough to make it to the station. The GM says that doing so increases the risk of a problem later on, but that Jessica could probably run the bypass in an hour or so. Dana will have to make an Engineering: Electrical task check, using the Electrical Applications Specialty if

Keeping Time

BAB COM

There are two clocks to keep track of when you're playing a roleplaying game. The first is the one we're all used to: the clock that measures time in the real world, the one that keeps track of real time. But in a roleplaying game, as in a book or a movie, events don't always pass at the same rate. Often, game time passes at an accelerated rate, especially when the details of events aren't very important. At other times, especially during intense scenes, a few seconds of time in the game will take several minutes of real time to play out. Whenever this distinction is important, the rules specify which type of time is meant.

Jessica has it (which she does). It will be based on Jessica's Intelligence.

Task Difficulty

Not every task is equally difficult, and that variation is represented in game terms by a Difficulty number. Easier tasks have lower Difficulty numbers than harder tasks. To determine the Difficulty of a task, look at the Task Difficulty Levels sidebar and choose an adjective that best describes the task for a typical Human (use the Human standard regardless of the race of the character attempting the task). Take the basic situational and environmental conditions into account—for example, if your adventure is set on a low-gravity planet, a character might have an easier time climbing a fence than in a one-G environment; likewise, a character jumping onto a fast-moving vehicle will have a harder time if doing so in a driving rainstorm than when the vehicle is dry and visibility is clear. Once you've decided on the most fitting adjective, look up the Difficulty Number on the table.

As mentioned above, you should take the situation into account while setting the Difficulty. Furthermore, if you feel that the character has an advantage or a disadvantage that won't be accounted for in his or her Ability (covered just below), raise or lower the Difficulty as necessary, to account for this factor. For example, a character attempting to sneak up on a security guard might have a harder time if wearing clogs. The amount of game time spent on a task may also affect the Difficulty of the task. So, in the example, sneaking up on the guard slowly and carefully may be easier than remaining undetected while moving quickly.

Good roleplaying may also modify the Difficulty, especially for tasks that rely on Cultural Attributes. If the player roleplays the character's action and does a good job, you might improve the character's chances of success a bit by lowering the Difficulty Number one or two points. Never penalize a player for poor performance, however, if he or she is really making an effort at the roleplaying—this game is all about playing the character, and anyone who tries to get into that spirit shouldn't be penalized.

Jessica gets to work on the reactor control circuitry. The bypass isn't particularly difficult, but Jessica is working by flashlight in zero-G. Dana specifies that Jessica will take the necessary time to make sure the job is done right. Taking all of those factors into consideration, the GM decides that the task is Difficult, which gives it a Difficulty Number of 11.

Ability

Next, determine the character's Ability at the task. The factors that make up the Ability are the character's Attribute, Skill and Specialty (if applicable), and any additional modifiers that apply to the character.

The appropriate Attribute, Skill and Specialty were determined during task definition. To get the character's base Ability, add together the Attribute and Skill. If the task matches a Specialty that the character has, add 2 to the Ability (a Competent pilot with a Specialty in Starfury is Adept when piloting a Starfury, for instance).

After you have accounted for the character's statistics, determine any modifiers that apply to this character. The character may have some penalties that modify how well he can perform tasks—for example, someone with a wounded hand may have a more difficult time piloting a ship (impairments from wounds are discussed in the combat section starting on page 108). Likewise, a sight on a PPG may give her an easier time hitting her target (weapon and armor bonuses are given in the description of each item, starting on page 165). Add together the Attribute level, skill level, and Specialty bonus, and then add or subtract any modifiers that you have assigned. The total is the character's Ability for that task.

Jessica is working on the reactor circuitry. Her Intelligence is 5; her skill in Engineering: Electrical is 3; and her Specialty in Electrical Applications adds another 2—all totalling to an Ability of 10. Her GM decides that no additional penalties or bonuses apply.

The Random Modifier

Finally, the element of chance is accounted for through the use of a Random Modifier. The Random Modifier ranges from -5 to +5. To generate the modifier, you need two standard 6-sided dice, of different colors. One die (traditionally a green one) will be the "Positive Die," and the other (traditionally red) the "Negative Die." Roll the dice, and compare the values. The die with

Task Difficulty Levels

BAB/COM

When resolving a task, choose from among the following descriptors, setting the Difficulty at the corresponding number:

Trivial	2
Easy	3
Basic	5
Average	7
Tricky	9
Difficult	11
Very Difficult	15
Next to Impossible	17
Miraculous	25

the lower face value is the Random Modifier. Thus, if you rolled a 2 on the Negative Die and a 6 on the Positive Die, your Random Modifier is -2 (the result of the die with the lower face value). If you rolled a 2 on the Negative Die and a 1 on the Positive Die, your Random Modifier would be +1. If the two dice roll the same number, then neither one is lower, so your Random Modifier is 0.

There are two special results: "boxcars" (a 6 result on each die) and "snake-eyes" (a 1 result on each die). Each of these results is a tie, and thus yields a Random Modifier of 0. However, these results have additional effects beyond the specific resolution of the task, covered under Benefits and Setbacks, on page 95.

Dana rolls the dice. Her Negative Die result is 5, with a Positive Die result of 2. Thus, her Random Modifier is +2.

Interpreting Results

At this point, the process of task resolution begins to vary according to the type of task being attempted. The most basic form of task resolution is the "static task"—any task in which no additional character (player character or NPC) has much impact on the outcome.

To determine success for a static task, add the Random Modifier (remembering that negative results subtract) to the character's Ability, and compare this Result to the Difficulty. If the Result equals or exceeds the Difficulty, the character succeeds in the task. If the Result is lower than the Difficulty, the character fails.

Success and failure are not always black and white, but often come in shades or degrees. The further away a character's Result is from the Difficulty, the better the success (or the worse the failure). A result 0 or 1 point away from the Difficulty is "Marginal," and the degree of success or failure is minimal. A result 2 or 3 away from the Difficulty is "Normal," and no unusual consequences occur. A result 4 or 5 away from the Difficulty is "Significant," and represents a success or failure with consequences that exceed, in a minor way, what might be expected. A result 6 or more away from the

Difficult Tasks

Characters generally perform close to their capabilities. If a task looks more difficult than the character can handle (if the Difficulty Number is 4 or more greater than the character's Ability), you may want to let the player know that the character won't feel comfortable trying the task—the character senses that it is just about beyond his or her capability. The player will probably want to see if there is another approach that works better with that character's skills.

Difficulty represents a "Critical" success or failure, usually with major consequences if warranted.

As noted at the beginning of this section, you will be able to assume that a character can perform a task without a problem in many instances. In cases where the character's Ability exceeds the Difficulty by 4 or more, you may skip the die roll and automatically give the character a Normal success at the task. Skipping the die roll is entirely at your discretion, and simply helps keep the game moving quickly when characters are in their element. Dramatic tasks or tasks that are very significant to the plot should still be resolved using the dice, to add tension and an air of uncertainty to events.

Jessica's Ability in her attempt to bypass the reactor control circuitry is 10. Adding the Random Modifier of +2 just rolled by Dana gets a total Result of 12. That's 1 over the Difficulty of 11 set by the GM—a Marginal Success.

The GM tells Dana that Jessica's bypass has fixed the problem, but that it won't hold up for long, and not at all if the reactor is run at over half its rated power output. Thus, her success in the task resolution fixes the problem, but the GM interprets its marginal nature as a limitation on engine power and fortitude.

Interpretations Beyond the Rules

A static book of rules cannot cover every contingency for every possible situation, and players will come up with great ideas that require interpretation beyond the original scope of these rules. This is why the GM is a integral part of a roleplaying game. In examples throughout the book, the GM will "decide" or "determine" various details about tasks or situations. This represents the on-the-fly decisions that GMs make constantly during play. As a GM, you may feel uncomfortable at first making decisions so quickly, but don't worry. Trust your judgment and common sense, and you'll get a good idea of how to make these snap decisions.

Contested Tasks

A contested task is any task in which two characters (player characters or NPCs) are both directly influencing the outcome. Most often, it's pretty easy to distinguish between contested and static tasks, but if you have any doubt, follow this rule of thumb: if both characters have a roughly equal chance of determining the outcome of the task, treat it as contested. If one character's actions will clearly be the most likely to affect the resolution, treat it as a

Task Resolution Interpretation

The degree of success or failure in a task attempt depends on how much the roll was made or missed by:

roll failed by 6 or more	Critical Failure
roll failed by 4 or 5	Significant Failure
roll failed by 2 or 3	Normal Failure
roll failed by 1	Marginal Failure
roll made by 0 or 1	Marginal Success
roll made by 2 or 3	Normal Success
roll made by 4 or 5	Significant Success
roll made by 6 or more	Critical Success

static task for the most influential character.

Determining the outcome of contested tasks is actually easier on the GM than doing so for static tasks. Instead of comparing a character's Result to a number that you set, you compare it to the Result of the other character (generated by the second player, or by you in the case of a NPC). Each character uses the Attribute and skill appropriate to the task that he or she is performing (they do not necessarily have to be using the same skill, Specialty, or Attribute). The character scoring higher succeeds at the task. If the characters tie, the result is nebulous, and you must determine what has happened if the task test cannot be repeated. Just as with static tasks, the difference between the scores is important, and successes that are Significant or better can have consequences. Levels of success are determined just as in static tasks, and consequences always favor the winner.

After limping her transport into Babylon 5, Jessica and several other characters head for a little R&R at a dockside bar. There's a pool table, and Jessica can't resist. In mere moments, she's into a match with Lefty Lou, the local pool shark (an NPC), and there's money on the table.

The GM tells Dana that she'll have to make a contested roll against Lefty. The skill is Gambling, the Specialty Pool, which Jessica has. The skill list recommends Insight as the Attribute for most Gambling tasks, but the GM specifies Coordination for this pool match. That gives Jessica an Ability of 10 (Coordination 7 + Gambling 1 + 2 for the Pool Specialty). He also determines that Lefty's Ability is 11 (he's not as Coordinated, but he's got a lot more skill). Dana rolls a Random Modifier of -1, giving her a total of 9, while with an RM of +2 Lefty's total is 13. He beats her by 4—a Significant Success for Lefty. The GM tells Dana that though the original bet was only 20 credits, halfway through the game Lefty had talked Jessica into upping the kitty to 30—which he then easily won.

The most common contested task is usually physical combat between characters. This is a very special case of task resolution, and the consequences are usually injuries, even for marginal or normal successes. Combat is covered in detail starting on page 99.

Cultural Tasks

The BABYLON 5 setting has many different cultures and races. Characters dealing with other races are limited by their cultural differences. This limitation is represented by the Xenorelation Attribute. When dealing with characters of another race, a character must use the lower of the Xenorelation Attribute or the otherwise appropriate Attribute. For example, while dealing with an alien a character with a Finesse of 6, a Presence of 4 and a Xenorelation of 5 would use the Xenorelation score when performing a task that would normally call for Finesse, but would use Presence (which is lower than Xenorelation) when attempting to use that Attribute.

This is an important rule; it models the differences between the many alien races and their diverse, and often conflicting, cultural values and mindsets. It also provides an excellent opportunity for roleplaying. If a character is limited in relating to other races, he or she may have to find alternative solutions.

As Jessica leaves the pool table, and angry Narn confronts her. She can barely understand his broken English, but it's clear that he has it in for her or someone in her group. Jessica attempts to calm the alien long enough to understand his grievance and defend herself. The GM calls for a Diplomacy roll, using the Dulcify Specialty. Jessica doesn't have that one—furthermore, she'll have to use her Xenorelation Attribute (in which she has a level 4) instead of the otherwise-appropriate Finesse (level 5). With her Diplomacy skill of 1, that gives her a total Ability of 5. A Random Modifier of 0 gives her a Result of 5—two less than the Average Difficulty the GM had assigned. That's a Normal Failure. The Narn continues his broken accusations, unmoved by Jessica's attempts at pacification.

Physical Tasks

Physical tasks (those involving the Physical Attributes) are resolved in the standard manner, with one added element. A character attempting a physical task can improve the chances for success by "pushing" his or her physical limits; expending a lot of extra effort. To push, reduce the character's Endurance by one point, and add a point to the Physical Attribute being used. Then proceed with the Task Resolution as if the character had the new Attribute level. This bonus to the Physical Attribute lasts only for a short period of time—a task or two in rapid succession, a combat, or a few minutes game time. However, the penalty to the Endurance Attribute remains in effect for the remainder of the game session, or until the character rests for at least an hour of game time. Do not alter the player's Endurance score on the Character Record when pushing—simply note the push in pencil next to the score.

A push is not without its cost—a character who pushes the physical limits too much risks injury. If a character Significantly fails a task (or does worse) while pushing, he or she suffers physical injury. Determine what has happened and how severe the injury is based on the circumstances and the particular task. Sprained muscles and sore backs are common, though you can be more creative. As a rule of thumb, inflict an Impact injury with a Damage of 3 in the case of a Significant failure, increasing the Damage to 6 for a Critical failure (damage and its effects are covered further on in this chapter). For dramatic effect, you might increase the Impairment by a point or two (due to pain) for the first hour or so of game time after the injury occurs.

Pushing is also not an infinite well of power. A character who reduces his or her Endurance to half or less of its original value has gone too far, and after the push is over will need to rest or will risk physical collapse. When a character who is suffering from this effect performs a task, the Random Modifier for that task must equal or exceed the total Endurance penalties from pushes. For example, take a character with an Endurance of 5 who has recently pushed himself three times (thus reducing his Endurance to 2, less than half of its original level). He must generate Random Modifiers of at least +3 on all tasks until he rests—if his Modifier is less than +3, he collapses immediately after performing the task at hand, regardless of success or failure in the task. Treat such collapsed characters as Stunned (see page 108) until they rest sufficiently for recovery.

Teamwork

There are times when two or more characters will want to work together to achieve a common goal. The degree to which this is possible depends on the task, and it is up to you to determine how and whether such teamwork is possible. There are two methods to resolving a team attempted task. The first is by setting an aggregate goal for one task. This is appropriate when the contributions of many characters will clearly make the task easier (such as lifting a large heavy object). The second method is by counting individual contributions over a series of tasks. This is more appropriate when the task is complex (such as investigating the scene of a crime).

For aggregate goal teamwork, set the Difficulty as if one person were performing a task. Have each contributor generate a Result as though attempting a static task, and total the individual Results. Compare this aggregate result to the Difficulty, just as if it were generated by a single character. For example, say a heavy beam has fallen on an innocent bystander. One person might not be able to lift it, but three people working together might. For one person, it would be impossible, so you might set a Difficulty of 26. The three characters might be able to meet or exceed that Difficulty once you add their individual Results.

For teamwork by individual contributions, set a Difficulty for each component

of the task, and have members of the team perform these components until they get enough successes to complete it. Individual contributions to the task can aid or hinder the task, depending on each character's task results. Take, for example, two computer programmers looking through a huge computer database protected by security measures. The GM has decided that to find the disparate information they seek, the programmers must successfully penetrate the security four times, each of which is a Difficult task. The two players generate their first Results, yielding one Normal success and one Significant success. The GM might decide that, as the consequence of the Significant success, the character penetrated the security twice (or once, for twice as long as expected), thus negating the need for one of the remaining rolls. All they need is one more look, and they will have the information.

Long and Complex Tasks

Long tasks (those that take a lot of game time) or complex tasks which involve many different skills or smaller tasks can be handled in a number of ways. There are two things to take into account: the amount of game time put into the task, and the number of steps involved in the task. For very long tasks, the character can put in the requisite time to accomplish the task between game sessions (a solution particularly suited to tasks like long hours of research in a library, for example) or during a session when the player is unable to play for some other reason. If this is not feasible, you can do it during the game by segregating the player or players performing the task from the rest of the group, dividing your time between the two groups as necessary (this is particularly good when different groups of players want to have their characters tackle different tasks all at the same time).

Sometimes you can split a complex task into several simpler steps, or divide a long task into incremental steps. In this case, have the player or players whose characters are performing the task perform the steps in whatever order you determine is appropriate. Depending on the task, you can either tell them the results of each step, or

The rules on teamwork and on long or complex tasks only apply to tasks that don't seem possible for one person alone. There are no hard and fast guidelines on when or where to use them in lieu of standard task resolution. Feel free to use whatever combination of these rules—in whole or in part—that you feel help more accurately simulate the task.

allow them to complete all steps before letting them know the results.

Benefits and Setbacks

In roleplaying games, just as in real life, there are times when, despite all expectations, something unpredictable enters into the picture. Sometimes a minor setback will befall the characters despite all their efforts, and other times, things will just work out in their favor. This is represented in the game by Setbacks and Benefits.

A Setback occurs when a player rolls "snake eyes" (two 1s) when generating a Random Modifier. The Random Modifier result is 0 (as is always the case when the Positive and Negative Dice tie), and the task is resolved as usual. But the Setback indicates that in addition, something minor and unexpected occurs to hamper the characters' progress. A Setback should not be a major consequence that will derail the plot, but rather a small problem that will provide an unforeseen obstacle for the players. For example, suppose a character is attempting to persuade a diplomat to his point of view at an embassy party—a Setback on a Diplomacy roll might indicate that an attractive member of the opposite sex begins flirting with the diplomat, making it very hard to keep the NPC's attention. Or perhaps another guest spills wine on the character, or an obscure acquaintance with a minor grudge against the character appears and is determined to discuss it, loudly. None of these results necessarily affect the immediate success or failure of the task being attempted, but they may easily affect the outcome of the overall situation.

A Benefit occurs when a player rolls "boxcars" (two 6s) on the dice. Again, this indicates a 0 result for the Random Modifier, and task resolution is carried out as normal. However, the Benefit result means that some minor bit of good luck helps the characters out. For example, imagine a character sneaking up on an enemy position. A Benefit might indicate that the NPC in the position is distracted by an animal or a sneezing fit, or that the character stumbles on a weakness in the security. Again, these results probably won't affect the actual task being rolled for, but might make things a little easier for the next few moments.

Benefits and Setbacks are tools for adding a little flair to the story. However, since they can come up in any situation, precise rules cannot cover the exact consequences of every action. You will have to come up with appropriate consequences based on the situation.

In Jessica's attempt to placate the angry Narn, Dana rolled boxcars. That gave her the 0 result on her Random Modifier, and as result she failed the task attempt. But the boxcars also resulted in a Benefit.

The GM knew that all along the Narn was simply trying to distract Jessica and her companions, while a confederate lifted her briefcase which she had left with her companions next to their table. He had determined already, through hidden rolls, that none of the player characters noticed the thief (he didn't tell the players why he was making the rolls, lest he give this plot twist away). The GM decides that, to resolve the Benefit, a bystander spots the thief and calls out a warning.

Jessica is still dealing with the Narn. "Suddenly some guy at the bar points at your table," the GM tells the players, "'Look out!' he yells!"

Telepathy

In general, telepathy is handled through standard task resolution, although since the effects deal with the characters' minds, your interpretation of the results can be tricky. The other players will also have to play carefully, trying to make sure that they know what they can and cannot hide from a telepath attempting to read their characters' minds.

In order to use any telepathic abilities, the telepath needs to focus on the target. This almost always requires a direct line of sight with the target. In some cases, where the telepath intimately knows the target, line of sight may not be necessary, but in practically all cases, it is the least that a telepath needs. The telepath must also concentrate on the target. Distractions make the job more difficult, modifying the Difficulty of the task.

A telepath can perform three types of tasks with his or her abilities: the scanning of another character's mind; the broadcasting of thoughts to another character; or the blocking of another's telepathic abilities. Scanning and broadcasting abilities can be used against both "normals" and other telepaths, while blocking can obviously only be used against a telepath who is attempting to scan or broadcast. Scanning is usually the most frequent task attempted by telepaths.

Scanning

There are four levels of scanning: Accidental Scans; Surface Scans; Probes; and Deep Scans.

Since a telepath can always "hear" the strong thoughts of others, there is always a chance that a telepath will pick up on someone feeling strongly about something, even if the telepath isn't trying to do so. This is called an Accidental Scan.

The most common level of scanning is the Surface Scan, which gives the telepath a picture of what the subject is actively thinking about at the instant of the scan, and no more. Telepaths who are hired out to businesspeople perform surface scans to verify truth in trade negotiations.

The next deepest level of scanning is the Probe, where the telepath burrows into the subject's mind, able to look at many of the concerns prominent in the subject's thoughts. While many things are easy for telepaths to find through probes, some people are able to hide specific secrets from telepaths. Also, the target of a probe can feel the telepath inside his or her mind, and if he or she sees the telepath while the probe is ongoing, can usually recognize the telepath by sight as the source of the probe.

The hardest scan to do is a Deep Scan, during which the telepath forges through the thoughts of the target looking for a specific piece of information. Successful deep scans can discover any information in the mind of the target. Deep scans are painful for the target, as the mind can feel the telepath invading areas usually sacrosanct. The target of a deep scan also may suffer permanent damage if he or she tries to resist the scan.

Telepaths in Society

In many ways, telepaths are more powerful than other characters. This effect is balanced somewhat by the extreme reaction that "normals" have to them. Telepaths are not often trusted, and they are ostracized from the rest of society. This is true across all three of the telepathic character races, though the Minbari would like to think that they are above that. When a telepath goes against cultural traditions or laws, he or she is treated as a rogue and is often hunted down, obstensibly to protect society from a harmful lunatic. If you have a telepathic character who chooses not to follow the laws of his or her race, you can introduce bounty hunters, police officers or Psi-Cops to the story (as appropriate to your campaign) as a counterbalance to any excessive use of power by the character. See the sections in chapter 3 on each of the races' telepaths for ideas on how they enforce telepathy-related crimes.

In order to actively scan another person, the telepath must concentrate long enough to break through the natural mental defenses built into the minds of even "normals," represented by the Resolve score. To perform the scan, a telepath performs a static task with an Ability equal to the Psionics Attribute plus any skill and

Extreme Success or Failure in Telepathy

If a task resolution result indicates that there are some extra consequences to the task (in the case of Significant or Critical successes or failures, for example), some possible consequences include a headache that incurs a 1-point Impairment (see Wounds and Injuries, below) for a couple of hours (a minor negative consequence); recognition by the target even if he or she doesn't see the telepath (a major negative consequence); and unsought but useful information (a positive consequence of varying importance).

Specialty the character may have from extra training. Assuming that the telepath has line of sight and that there are no distractions, the base Difficulty of the task is equal to the Resolve of the target.

This Difficulty can be modified by several things. The level of scan is the first modifier. If the scan is Accidental, subtract 2 from the Difficulty. If it is a Probe, add 2, and if it is a Deep Scan, add 4. If the telepath is physically touching the target rather than just keeping a line of sight, reduce the Difficulty of the scan by 2. If the telepath has been inside the target's mind for more than a surface scan before, that familiarity will reduce the Difficulty of the scan by 2. Distractions always make scanning more difficult; a minor distraction such as a noisy environment might add 1 to the Difficulty, while explosions going off in the room might add 4.

Factors that modify the Difficulty of scans are cumulative. Thus, a probe on a target whom the telepath is touching is still equal to the Resolve of the target (the +2 modifier for the probe is offset by the -2 modifier for touching the target). If this same telepath were attempting this in the noise and bustle of a public place, the difficulty would be perhaps 1 or 2 higher than the Resolve of the target.

There are no telepaths in the bar scene with the Narn, so let's skip ahead in the adventure for an example. The next day, Jessica is in the Babylon Station Zocalo, meeting with a ships systems contractor to see about getting her transport's reactor control circuitry replaced. An unethical telepath, hired by Jessica's still-unknown antagonist, attempts to probe Jessica's mind in an attempt to determine where she and her companions have hidden the briefcase. Her Resolve is 5. The GM adds +2 because the scan is a Probe, and another +1 for the distracting environment, for a total Difficulty of 8. The telepath has an Ability of 5, and a Telepathy skill level of 2. The GM rolls an RM of +3, giving him a Result of 10. A Normal success—he pulls the information he was looking for right out of Jessica's mind!

But he doesn't get away scot free. A probe can be felt by the victim—the GM tells Dana that Jessica is suddenly hit by a flash of dizziness, and disorienting, unfamiliar mental images. He has Dana make a Perception roll—she gets a Significant Success. As Jessica looks about her, bewildered, she sees a woman getting up from a table across the room. "Jessica suddenly recognizes the unfamiliar face," the GM says, "that man was in her mind!"

Telepaths can team up on a target by aggregate teamwork, using the teamwork rules on page 94.

Accidental Scans cannot be deliberately attempted—they require the GM's intervention. If a character (NPC or player character) has a strong reaction to something and a telepath is nearby, have the telepath perform a static task without telling the player the objective. If the target is another player's character, you may want to check with the player to verify what the character

is thinking. Resolve the task as usual after that point.

Broadcasting

Telepaths rarely broadcast their thoughts, but it can be done. In order for a telepath to broadcast, the telepath must (given line of sight and no distractions) succeed in a task with a Difficulty 2 higher than the Resolve of the target. A broadcast generally reaches only a single target, but a telepath can attempt to broadcast to more individuals: each additional target adds 2 to the Difficulty. As with scanning, modifiers for distractions and physical contact apply.

Blocking

Finally, a telepath can block scans of other telepaths. If one telepath wishes to block the scan of another, treat the scan attempt as a contested task with both parties using their Psionic Attribute and telepathy skills. This is the only time that telepathy is contested, as "normals" have no ability to actively defend themselves against telepaths. If the block is success-

ful, the telepath attempting the scanning gets no information. If the block is unsuccessful, the telepath attempting the scan can perform a static task against the target's Resolve just as if the target were not a telepath. Minor consequences on either side include headaches and a temporary reduction in Wits, while major consequences can include the temporary loss of telepathic ability or even unconsciousness or permanent brain damage.

Combat

The term "combat" in *The Babylon Project* refers to physical conflict between two or more characters, player character or NPC (as opposed to large-scale combat such as space battles or tactical wars). Combat works slightly differently than normal task resolution, although the same contested task rules outlined above (including push rules) apply. For game purposes, there are two types of combat: Close Combat, where the combatants are fighting each other hand-to-hand or with handheld weapons; and Ranged Combat, where at least one combatant is using a projectile weapon from a distance. If you are uncertain of which combat rules to use for a character in combat, follow this rule of thumb: any time a combatant can come into physical contact with another within a round, that character is close enough to perform a close combat action, either an attack or a defense. A typical character can move about two meters per round from a standing stop, and a little farther than that if they are already moving.

Initiative

Combat is fought in rounds of approximately two-seconds, with the order of action within each round being decided by the characters' Initiative scores. Compare the Initiatives from the Character Records, adding or subtracting any modifiers that may be granted to characters by weapons being used or armor worn. The character with the highest modified Initiative acts first. That character can maneuver, attack or wait. Then the character with the next highest Initiative acts, and so on until all

characters in combat have had their opportunities to act (a character who chooses to wait may act at any point later in the round, or not act at all). If two characters tie in Initiative, allow the player character to act first if one is a player character and the other an NPC, or decide randomly who acts first if both are player characters or NPCs. If a character maneuvers, it can be to escape close combat, to move in to close combat, or to move for cover. If a character attacks a character with a lower Initiative during close combat, the target character can use his or her action to defend immediately, although that defense counts as that character's action for the round. If a character waits, he or she can choose to act (preempting another action before it is announced) at any point later in the round.

Let's go back to the bar and the Narn. The stranger yells "Look out!" and everyone turns just as the thief reaches for the briefcase. Their cover blown, the Narn goes for a weapon. "Everyone give me your Initiative total," the GM says.

Jessica has an Initiative of 5. She's still holding her pool cue, but she's much better with her fists than a weapon, so Dana ignores any Initiative penalty the cue stick would incur, as she won't be using it. The GM states that the Narn's Initiative is 6, so he'll be going first.

In some cases, due to success in combat actions the previous round, one character may automatically gain (or usurp) Initiative over another even if his or her Initiative number is lower. When the combat involves only those two characters, don't bother to calculate initiative—the usurper automatically goes first. When that's the case, have both characters figure their modified Initiative scores as normal. However, when it comes time for the usurped character to act, the usurper may jump in and act first *if* he or she chooses to attack the usurped character. If the usurper chooses a different action (running away, for example, or attacking a different character), he or she must act according to normal Initiative order, and the usurped character may act uninterrupted according to his or her Initiative number.

Close Combat

Once Initiative has been determined, characters may take their actions in order of Initiative. In close combat, attacks—punches, kicks, stabs, slashes, etc.—are generally the most common sorts of actions. Making a close combat attack involves three steps: first, the attacker declares whom he or she is attacking, and how; second, the defender declares whether or not he or she will defend, and if so, how; and third, the appropriate task roll is made.

In declaring an attack, the player must state whom his or her character is attacking and how the attack is being made. Obviously, the method of attack must be appropriate to the situation, and the character can only use weapons that he or she has available and ready (remember, a combat round is only around two seconds long, so a character generally doesn't have time to ready a weapon and use it in the same round).

Once the target and attack have been specified, the victim may immediately use his or her action for the round to defend against the attack, unless he or she has already acted this round. Again, the victim must specify the nature of the defense—whether the character will dodge the blow, or block or parry it—and again, the defense must be appropriate to the situation and the victim's resources. Parrying requires a weapon appropriate to the task—not too much smaller or lighter than the attacker's weapon. It also requires enough room to fully use the weapon. Dodging obviously requires no weapon, but does require enough room for the character to maneuver, if only a little. Blocking can be done with a weapon or without, and requires very little room.

On his Initiative of 6, the Narn uses his action to pull a knife—he can't attack this round, as his weapon wasn't in hand already. Jessica is next, with an Initiative of 5. Dana states that Jessica will drop the pool cue and punch the Narn in the face. The Narn cannot actively defend himself, as he has already acted this round by drawing his knife.

Life and Death

The main focus of *The Babylon Project* is on the story that you are telling in cooperation with the players, rather than on the exact modeling of every last detail. However, the game does have a very realistic feel, especially in combat, and so combat is one of the areas that can benefit from a little tactical thinking. Characters in combat can easily be seriously injured, and can die if the players are not careful. A PPG is a deadly weapon and a solid hit from one can kill a character of any of the four main races. Players should think very carefully before putting their characters in harm's way.

The next step is the actual task roll. Task rolls for combat attacks are the same as other task resolution rolls, but involve one or two additional steps. For starters, the attacker must choose the point of attack. Look at the Body Map (located below, on the GM Reference Sheet, and on every Character Record). It shows a humanoid figure (which can represent any of the humanoid alien races, as well as Humans) overlaid with a hexagonal grid. In each hex is a point—the one in the center of the body is marked as the Default Aim Point. Unless the

Maps and Miniatures

Combat is one of the times when it is very important to know exactly where the characters are in relation to each other and to their immediate surroundings. If you or any of the players are having problems visualizing the scene, draw a quick sketch to clarify things for everyone. Key scenes in adventures published for this game will have maps included. Another fun way to help the players visualize the scene is to use miniature figures on the tabletop which represent the characters. A wide variety of pewter miniatures are available in most hobby shops that serve this purpose exactly.

attacker specifies otherwise, this is automatically the point of aim for the attack.

The attacker may choose any other point in the hex grid as the aim point for the attack, but doing so incurs a penalty. For every hex away from the Default Aim Point, the attacker suffers a -1 penalty to his or her roll. Also, the GM may change the Default Aim Point, according to the situation. Imagine, for example, an attacker hiding beneath a car, waiting for the victim to walk past. When the victim does, the attacker reaches out to grab her leg. In this case, the GM might specify a point on the victim's lower leg as the Default Aim Point, as the normal Default isn't even visible to the attacker.

Dana looks at the Body Map on Jessica's Character Record. There's an aim point for the face—it's two hexes from the Default Aim Point, so her attack will be at a penalty of 2.

Body Map

Head
Torso
Arm
Default Aim Point
Hand
Vitals
Groin
Thigh
Leg
Foot

Once the aim point is specified, the combatants make their combat rolls using the skills and Attributes used in their attacks and defenses (modified as necessary just like any other task). If the victim is defending him- or herself, the task is contested; if not, the attacker makes a static roll using the defender's Agility as the Difficulty.

Since the Narn isn't actively defending himself, Dana will be making a Static task test against the Narn's Agility. Her Ability is 8 (Agility 5, Combat: Hand-to-Hand skill 1, Specialty in Punch). Dana rolls a Random Modifier of +1, for a total of 9. The GM says that's a Normal Success (he knows that the Narn's Agility is 6).

In order for the attacker to hit the opponent, he or she must succeed in the attack roll—if the defender's roll exceeds the attacker's, or if the attacker fails a static roll against a victim who is not defending, the attack misses the victim. Furthermore, a successful defense may have additional advantages for the defender, covered just below.

As in all task tests, the degree of success in a combat attack affects the outcome. Look at the Hit Diagram (opposite and on the GM Reference Sheet). The center point on the diagram represents the attacker's aim point. As indicated on the diagram, a Significant or Critical success hits that aim point—a Critical success even increases the Damage by 2 (Damage is explained below). A Normal or Marginal success indicates that the attack hit near the aim point. Roll an additional die, called the Direction Die, and consult the Hit Diagram. That indicates the direction in which the attack strayed—a Normal success result indicates that the attack strays one hex in that direction, a Marginal success indicates not only that it strays two hexes, but also that the Damage is reduced by 2.

Now return to the Body Map, and count over the number and direction of hexes indicated by the Hit Diagram. The point in the middle of the resulting hex is the actual point at which the attack hit. If that point is off the body, the attack narrowly missed the victim. If it is on the body, the

Body Map indicates which area of the body was hit.

Jessica's Normal Success in her attack indicates that the punch strayed one hex from its intended aim point. Dana rolls a Direction Die, getting a 6. Looking at the Hit Diagram, she sees that the attack strays to the upper left. One hex to the upper left from her aim point on the Body Map hits the head. The GM describes the scene: "The Narn thought he had the drop on Jessica, but he was surprised at the speed of her reaction. He barely has time to flinch, but that's enough for Jessica's jab to miss his jaw and hit the side of his head."

If the victim chose to defend and was successful in the contested attack roll, several things can happen. If the defender dodges, Marginal success indicates that the defender didn't quite get out of the way. He or she is hit, but takes only half damage. Normal success means that the defender successfully evaded the attack. If the success is Significant or better, the defender automatically usurps initiative over the attacker on the next round. If the defender blocks, Marginal success means that the attack hits the body part (generally an upraised hand or arm) instead of the intended aim point, and that takes all damage from the attack. Normal success means that the damage is halved. Significant success means that the damaged is halved, and the defender usurps initiative over the attacker on the next round. If the defender Parried, Marginal success means that the defender is takes half damage. Normal success means that the is harmlessly deflected, and Significant or better success means that the attack is deflected and the defender automatically usurps initiative over the attacker on the next round.

As mentioned above, dodging and parrying require sufficient space—a character backed into a corner may not have enough space to do either. Parrying also requires an appropriate weapon. Blocking is not generally as effective as either, but doesn't require maneuvering room or a weapon.

A special case of close combat is when the characters begin grappling—particularly common in zero-gravity environments

Hit Diagram

Aim Point

Direction Die Result

Marginal Success
(made by 0 or 1)
count out two hexes, -2 to Damage

Normal Success
(made by 3 or 4)
count out one hex

Significant Success
(made by 4 or 5)
aim point hit

Critical Success
(made by 6 or more)
aim point hit, +2 to Damage

where punches, kicks and other normal combat moves are generally ineffective. The goal when grappling is usually to subdue the opponent by immobilizing him or her.

Characters begin grappling when any one character grabs another. Once involved in grappling, none of the involved characters are free to leave the combat until they escape their foes. Grappling characters do not calculate Initiative, but automatically act at the end of the round. Each round, the grappling characters make contested skill rolls. Marginal success by either character means that neither one has gained the upper hand, and the characters continue to grapple. Normal success means that the succeeding character has gained the upper hand in the combat, and can control the course of action the next round (this usually means that the unsuccessful character suffers a -2 penalty to his or her roll the following round, or, in zero-G, that the successful character can steer the combat). Significant success or better means that the

Martial Arts Schools

There are many schools of martial arts, stemming from the martial traditions of many races. Each is treated as an individual skill, the special maneuvers and capabilities engendered in its students taking the form of Specialties. A few martial arts commonly practiced include:

Akido: This Human art concentrates on defensive techniques and may be used only in unarmed combat. It is taught throughout the Earth Alliance. Its beliefs concentrate on a balanced, centered life with combat only when there is no other option.
Specialties: Parry/Attack, Pull Off Balance, Multiple Defense, Blind Fighting.

Karate: Another Human art, Karate concentrates on stopping an attacker by eliminating the threat. It is used with unarmed combat. Karate is taught by masters throughout the Alliance. It teaches that with power comes responsibility, and highly values the concept of personal honor.
Specialties: Hard Block, Multiple Attack, Block/Hold, Increased Damage Hit.

Kenjitsu: This Human armed-combat martial art is based on the sword, instilling a respect not only of other life, but also of the arts involved in weaponcrafting.
Specialties: Blind Fighting, Increased Damage Hit, Nerve/Vital Strike, Parry/Attack.

Then'sha'tur: This Narn art is used in unarmed combat and uses the strength and toughness of Narns to maximum advantage. It was born during the occupation from a blend of other Narn arts, and teaches that personal freedom is paramount. The ability to defend oneself is the best way to keep personal freedom.
Specialties: Block/Hold, Absorb Blow, Nerve/Vital Strike, Increased Damage Hit.

Katak'eth: This Narn art dates from before the occupation, and values the inner peace of the individual. It concentrates on the sword, and is used with armed combat actions. It teaches the pupil to value life and use combat as a last resort only, when there is no other option. Once a blade has been drawn, it can only be because there was no alternative than to draw blood.
Specialties: Enhanced Defense, Increased Damage Hit, Multiple Attack, Disarm

Kalan'tha: This Minbari art is a school of thought based on structure and form, and is used in unarmed combat. It teaches that a balance in life is achieved by the blending of all aspects of the person into a whole. It also respects the rights of others to achieve their own balance.
Specialties: Rapid Strike, Enhanced Defense, Nerve/Vital Strike, Parry/Attack.

Pike Fighting: This Minbari art uses a pike, and can only be used with armed combat actions. It is a ritual form used in both duels and street fighting, and teaches respect for the structure of life, but acknowledges that force is an effective way to maintain that structure.
Specialties: Multiple Defense, Nerve/Vital Strike, Parry/Attack, Multiple Attack

Tronno: This Centauri unarmed combat form is an ancient art developed during the expansion of the Republic. It instills a respect of tradition into its pupils, that all who came before contributed to what they are, and that their responsibility is to the Republic rather than to the self.
Specialties: Block/Hold, Increased Damage Hit, Jump Kick, Blind Fighting.

Coutari: This Centauri bladed-weapon art is a ritualistic form, taught and executed in honor duels as much as in real life-and-death situations. It may be used only with armed combat. It places high value on form and honor, shunning those who do not act with honor.
Specialties: Flat Hit, Parry/Attack, Increased Damage Hit, Enhanced Defense

Special maneuvers offered by the various martial arts schools are used as follows:

Absorb Blow: When the character makes a stun check in combat, a successful use of this maneuver adds 3 to his or her Random Modifier in determining whether or not the character is stunned.

Blind Fighting: The use of this maneuver precedes a conventional combat action. If the martial arts task check is successful, the combatant suffers no penalty for fighting in darkness this action, and may act as though in a lighted area. This does not mean that the character can see in the dark, only that he or she senses and tracks the movements of the attacker.

Block/Hold: The use of this maneuver follows an block of Normal or better success. If the martial arts task check is successful the character automatically grapples with and gains a hold over the attacker.

Disarm: The use of this maneuver follows an attack of Normal or better success. The

(continues)

Julien was hit in the torso (body zone 2), with a Damage of 13. Reading down the "11-13" column on the Immediate Effects Table to the "torso or thigh" row, Mike breathes a sigh of relief: the space isn't black, so Julien isn't dead, at least not yet.

The Stun Number listed on the table is 2. Mike rolls a Random Modifier, getting a result of +3. That beats a two, so Julien stays conscious. Finally, the table lists an Immediate Impairment of 2. That means that Julien will suffer a penalty of 2 on all task rolls for the remainder of the scene.

When a character is injured or wounded, record the Damage and Immediate Impairment on his or her Character Record, in the section marked "Wounds." Also, record the type of damage sustained: Impact (blunt trauma to internal structures that doesn't necessarily break the skin); Cut (open wounds); Burn (surface damage caused by heat, chemicals, or abrasion); Cavity Shock (cavity wounds created by a high-speed projectiles, abbreviated CC); or Phased Plasma (damage caused by the high-speed impact of superheated projectiles, abbreviated PP).

On Julien's Character Record, under Wounds, Mike writes "2" under Location, "PP" for the Type, "13" for the Damage, and "2" under Impairment on the first line.

Wounds and Injuries: Final Effects

Once combat is over and the action has died down, it's necessary to determine the longer-term, more detailed effects of injuries and wounds, including any life-threatening blood loss, secondary effects like shock or broken bones, and the character's longer-term impairment. All of these effects are covered by the Final Effects Table (below). Final Effects are only for player characters and important NPCs—don't bother with Final Effects for minor NPCs who probably won't ever show up again in the game.

The first step involves the Damage itself—you may need to adjust the number. Read down left side of the Final Effects Table

to find the Damage Modifier for the body zone wounded. Add (or subtract, if the Damage Modifier is negative) it to the Damage, then erase the first Immediate Damage number from the Character Record and replace it with this newly-modified Final Damage. That's the number you'll be using to determine all Final Effects.

If the wound is located on an extremity (arm, hand, foot, or leg) and is pretty severe (with Damage of, say, 13 or greater), you may want to check to see if it exceeds the maximum possible damage for that body zone. Quickly cross-reference the Damage with the body zone on the Final Effects Table, and see if the resulting space has a blue bar along the bottom. If it does, reduce the Damage to the highest level that does not have a blue bar. For example, take a character who has suffered a Final Damage 14 wound to the hand. Reading down the Damage 14 column to the hand location on the Final Effects Table, we come to a blue bar. The highest Damage in that row that doesn't touch the blue bar is 12, so we

reduce the wound's Final Damage to 12. As just mentioned, this maximum damage effect only applies to severe wounds to the limbs—you needn't bother checking it in the case of wounds to the head, body, or thigh, or in the case of mild wounds.

The fight in the bar wraps up after a few rounds, with the Narn and his buddies fleeing the scene. Jessica and her companions check on Julien, who sits bleeding on the floor. The action having slowed a bit, the GM decides that this is a good time to pause to determine the Final Effects of Julien's wound.

Looking next to the torso body zone on the Final Effects Table, Mike finds a Damage Modifier of 0. Julien's wound still has a Damage of 13. Because it's a shoulder wound, he doesn't bother

checking to see if it's past the maximum damage.

Secondary effects start with blood loss, since serious blood loss can threaten to kill a character within minutes. Begin by looking up the Bleed Shift, listed by Damage Type in the lower left of the Final Effects Table. Then, cross-reference the Damage along the top of the table with the location of the wound, listed along the upper left side. Finally, from that point shift over the number of columns indicated by the Bleed Shift (going right if the Shift number is positive, left if it's negative).

The resulting number is the Bleed Number, the number of minutes before the character will bleed to death if medical attention isn't administered. Remember that the clock starts when the injury is sustained—

Final Effects Table

Damage ▶		1	2	3	4	5	6	7	8	9	10	11	12	13	14	15+
▼ **Location**							▼ **Secondary Effects** ▼									
Head (1)	2								240	180	120	80 B	60	35 E	15	12
Torso (2 or3)	0											B 240	130	70	25 E	4
Vitals/Groin (4 or 5)	2									200 B	120	70	45	20 E	8	4
Arm (6 or 7)	-1											200 B	80	16	M		
Thigh (8 or 9)	0											240	160 B	80	40	8
Leg (10 or 11)	0											200 B	100	12	M		
Hand/Foot (12, 13, 14, 15)	-2										240 B	160	25	M		
▼ **Dam. Type**							▼ **Final Impairment** ▼									
Impact	-3	0	0	0	0	0	1	1	1	1	1	2	3	3	5	6
Cut	0	1	1	1	1	1	1	2	2	2	3	3	4	4	5	6
Burn	-5	1	1	1	1	1	1	2	2	2	3	3	4	5	6	6
CS	3	1	1	1	1	2	2	2	3	3	3	4	4	5	6	6
PP	-1	1	1	1	2	2	3	3	3	4	4	4	5	5	6	6
Heal Time ▶		1	1	1	1	1	1	1	2	2	2	3	3	4		6	8
Decline Time ▶														10		4	1

Left side labels: *Damage Modifier* (between Location column and data), *Bleed Shift* (between Dam. Type column and data) if a character has a Bleed Number of 4, and a minute and a half of game time has passed between the injury and when you paused to determine Final Effects, then the character is only two and a half minutes away from death! A blank in the Bleed Number space on the table indicates that the blood loss isn't life threatening (not necessarily that there is no bleeding, though).

Looking on the Final Effects Table, Mike sees that the Bleed Shift for PP damage is -1. He crossreferences a Damage of 13 with the torso body zone, then shifts one column to the left. That yields a Bleed Number of 130. Only twenty or thirty seconds of game time have passed since Julien was shot, so he's still got over two hours before he'll bleed to death.

Once you've determined blood loss, move on to Lasting Impairment. To do so, cross reference the Damage along the top with the Damage Type along the lower left side. The result is the Lasting Impairment. Erase the Immediate Impairment from the victim's Character Record and replace it with the Lasting Impairment (which may be different).

Like the Immediate Impairment, the Lasting Impairment is a negative modifier that applies to the character's actions. However, the Lasting Impairment applies only to physical actions affected by the wounded area of the body (impairment to the head (body zone 1) also affects Mental and Cultural tasks). In the case of the arms, legs, hands feet and head, it is usually fairly obvious if a task requires the use of the impaired region. In the case of body wounds, you will need to determine how much the impairment affects the action. The general rule of thumb to follow in respect to body wounds is to make the character act with half of the impairment (rounded up).

Cross-referencing his Damage of 13 with PP Damage Type, Mike sees that Julien's Lasting Impairment is 5. He writes this down on his Character Record, replacing the Immediate Impairment of 2. From this point forward, until the wound begins to heal, Julien will suffer a penalty to physical actions affected by his injured shoulder. He'll prob-

ably need to keep his arm in a sling. However, unlike the Immediate Impairment, this Lasting Impairment doesn't affect mental or cultural tasks, or physical tasks unrelated to the shoulder wound.

The last element of Final Effects are a handful of secondary effects. Most secondary effects only apply to severe wounds—don't bother even checking on them for wounds with Final Damage of 8 or less. For more severe wounds, cross-reference the Damage by the body zone again (without Bleed Shift this time). You'll notice several colored bars running at the bottom of the row—if any of these bars run along the bottom of the space you've referenced, your character suffers the related secondary effect.

The first bar you might run into is purple (and is marked with a "B" at its leftmost end). If you've intercepted this bar, the character has suffered a broken bone. Broken bones have no particular effect on character's performance, but they do affect the time required for the wound to heal (covered below).

The second colored bar you might run into is red in color, with an "E" at the left end. If you've run into this bar, the wound is eventually fatal. If the character does not receive serious medical attention (first aid isn't sufficient), he or she will get worse over time instead of better, until he or she dies (again, see below).

Finally, you may run into a blue bar with an "M" at the left end. If that's the case, you've exceeded the maximum damage that can be sustained by that body zone. As mentioned above, you should already have reduced the wound's Damage to the highest level not touching the blue bar, and computed all Final Effects from that level.

Cross-referencing Julien's Damage of 13 with the body zone of the wound (torso), we find the purple bar. The wound has broken one or more bones in his shoulder. That won't have any additional effect on his performance, but will affect the amount of time required for the wound to heal.

Multiple Wounds

There are many times when a character who already has a wound will receive another. This could be later in the same combat, or after some time has passed and the character has had a chance to heal a bit. Either way, if the new wound is in a different body zone than the old wound, simply record the new wound on a blank line in the Wounds section of the Character Record. There is no interaction between the Damage levels of the two wounds—that is, two wounds in different areas, each of Damage 6, do not add up to Damage 12. Wherever the Impairments of the two wounds overlap (if both body zones are needed in the same action—for example, if a character wounded in both his right arm and right hand attempted pilot a Starfury), use the most severe Impairment value. Otherwise, each individual Impairment is used only when the affected body zone is used, as normal (note that Immediate Impairments affect every action). If one or both of the wounds has a significant Bleed Number, use the most severe blood loss rate of the two wounds (the fewer number of minutes).

If a character takes a wound in a body zone which has already been wounded, add the Damage of the new wound to the Damage of the wound already there. This total is the Damage for the aggregate wound—calculate all effects based on that new Damage. If the two wounds are of differing Damage Types, treat the wound as being the most severe type (the severity of damage increases as you go down the list on the Final Effects Table, with Impact being the least severe and Phased Plasma being the most severe).

Let's say, for the moment, that Julien was wounded a second time in the bar fight. If he were hit in the same torso body zone again, say for a Damage of 6, the two wounds would combine for a total Damage of 19—enough to kill him. If he were hit in the arm, however, the

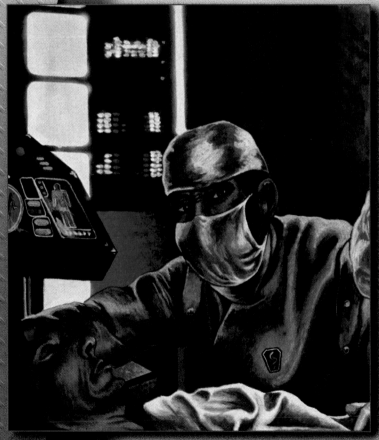

wounds would be treated as individual injuries, and Immediate Effects would be determined again when the second wound was incurred. A check of the Immediate Effects Table indicates no Stun Modifier for an arm wound of Damage 6, and a 0 Impairment. Julien would still suffer the Immediate Impairment of 2 from the torso wound.

Checking the Final Effects Table, the second wound produces no blood loss and a Lasting Impairment of 3. Julien would still be bleeding fast enough to die in 130 minutes (from the first wound). Whenever he attempted a task that required the use of his arm (but wasn't affected by his shoulder wound), he'd suffer an impairment of 3 (from the arm). For a task that affected by both wounds, he'd suffer an impairment of 5 (from the torso wound) if the GM felt that the task was affected by the full impairment, or 3 if the impairment were halved (as is often the case for wounds to the body).

Medical Aid and Recovery

Serious wounds generally take quite some time to recover, even with good medical care, and some wounds can continue to threaten a character's life with even the best medical attention. What does it take to save the life of a wounded character, and set him or her on the road to recovery?

The first step, of course, is first aid. As mentioned above, any character who is bleeding seriously will eventually die if the blood loss isn't staunched. Doing so requires a successful Medical, EMT task roll, generally of Basic Difficulty (though you can set the Difficulty higher or lower based on conditions and the type and severity of the wound). Characters who are not suffering from serious blood loss should also seek first aid if their wounds are significant (Damage of, say, 4 or higher). There are no specific penalties if they don't, though you might choose to increase their impairments by a point or so until they do.

First aid is often carried out at the scene. For serious wounds (any wound of Damage 8 or higher) additional treatment is necessary, at a medical facility if possible. Without this treatment, wounds heal at twice their normal rate (covered below), and eventually fatal wounds get worse over time. If treatment is being provided by player characters, or under primitive conditions, require any combination of Medical, Diagnostic; Medical, Pharmaceutical; and Medical, Surgery task checks that you feel appropriate.

At the bottom of the Final Effects Table are two rows of numbers: the Heal and Decline times. The Heal time indicates the number of days required for a wound to drop one Damage level. Simply reference the Heal time for wound's current Damage level—after the indicated number of days, the wound's Damage drops one level. After the number of days indicated for that new level, it drops again, and so on, until the Damage eventually reaches 0 and the wound is completely healed. As the wound's Damage is reduced, the Final Impairment also drops, as indicated by the Impairment section of the Final Effects Table (for example, when a PP wound drops from Damage 6 to Damage 5, the Impairment drops from 3 to 2—it drops again to 1 when the Damage drops from 4 to 3). Blood loss and other secondary effects, however, are never recalculated.

If a wound is not successfully treated medically, it takes twice as long as usual to heal. Also, if a wound includes a broken bone, the first drop in Damage takes twice the usual time. However, a character kept under supervision and treatment in a state of the art medical facility can heal faster than the indicated time—up to twice as fast, depending on the quality of the care.

If a character is suffering from multiple wounds, monitor the Heal time for the most severe wound only. Every time it drops a Damage level, all other wounds also drop one Damage level.

Eventually fatal wounds get worse instead of better until medically treated. The Decline time is the number of hours (not days!) before the character's condition worsens to the next Damage Level. As with the Heal number, the wound continues to worsen from level to level—if it gets to Damage level 16, the character dies.

Fortune Points and Epic Characters

As you open your campaign, your players will be playing with starting characters, no more special than those around them. They have strengths and weaknesses just as ordinary people do today. What makes them special isn't their abilities, but their fate. Just as BABYLON 5 is about characters who exceed their limits and live up to a nobler potential, the characters in this game have the potential to be more than they know.

This potential is represented in the game by Fortune Points. Fortune Points allow players to influence the performance of their characters, increasing the chances that a character will succeed at a critical task; to temporarily overcome personal limitations; and to attempt tasks beyond their usual means.

This does not mean that the characters are always virtuous, or always succeed at everything they try. Everyone has limitations and quirks that make them unique, and sometimes they succeed at what they try, and sometimes they fail. Fortune Points serve not only as a performance booster, but also to encourage players to develop and build upon the quirks that make their characters unique by rewarding players for good roleplaying.

Granting Fortune Points

Players start the game with five Fortune Points each, but over the course of the campaign they'll gain and spend Fortune Points frequently. Granting Fortune Points is one of the GM's many tasks.

Most Fortune Points are granted as a result of Characteristics affecting play, either in how they impact the game events or limit the character's options, or in how your players roleplay them. The Characteristic descriptions give general guidelines on how to award Fortune Points, and the Story section provides more specific guidelines on the role of Fortune Points in different phases of your campaign. The basic rule of thumb, however, is this: whenever a player makes a decision or takes an action based more on the character's point of view than on his or her own desires, award Fortune Points; and the further into your campaign you are, the more liberal you should be with them.

Always remember that Fortune Points are not a reward for doing things the way you, the GM, want them done, but for doing things that the character would do, given all of the traits that make up that character. On the flip side, Characteristics offer you the chance to put characters into challenging situations, or to complicate already difficult conflicts. Take advantage of that opportunity, then reward the player with Fortune Points when his or her reaction is appropriate to the concept of the Characteristic.

After the bar fight, the GM gave Mike a Fortune Point. Though seriously wounded, Julien could have fought back—after all, he was conscious and only suffering an impairment of 2. But one of Julien's Characteristics is "Dedicated," to the ideal of interracial peace (a veteran of the Earth-Minbari war, Julien is convinced that millions of lives were lost over an avoidable misunderstanding). So instead of shooting back, Julien called out to the Narn, hoping to stop the violence before it got worse. It didn't seem to work—the Narn ran off with the shooter and the thief—but Mike earned a Fortune Point for the in-character attempt.

What Julien didn't realize is that the fight was no misunderstanding. The Narn and his companions were after some legal documents Jessica had in her briefcase, documents relating to her investments. The GM awards Dana a Fortune Point as well, since her Assets Characteristic gave him the hook for this entire subplot to his adventure. He doesn't tell her that, however—in fact, if he was concerned about giving the subplot away, he could hold on to the Fortune Point and award it later, after the subplot plays out.

It's generally a good idea for players to keep a reserve of at least two or three Fortune Points around just in case their characters get into serious trouble, but other than that, players should be willing to use them as often as they want to get a better chance to do things. The pace at which your players use Fortune Points will largely be based on how frequently you give them out, so don't be stingy with them. You will need to decide what is "good" roleplaying, in order to decide how to give them out, but the idea is to make sure that those who put in the effort are rewarded for doing so. For exceptional roleplaying, you can reward a player with more than just one Fortune Point. This will help everyone try to improve their roleplaying. It will also add a lot of enjoyment to the game—players whose characters are accomplishing things have a lot of fun.

Playing Fortune Points

Players can use Fortune Points in several ways. The first way is to improve a character's odds during Task Resolution. The second is to save a character who's life is in the balance, and the third is to allow a character to try a task that he or she wouldn't normally be able to even attempt. Each of these require slightly different uses of Fortune Points.

When a player is resolving a task, he or she can also decide to spend one or more Fortune Points to help during that task. After generating the Random Modifier for the task, the player can spend two Fortune Points to add a "Fortune Die" to the modifier. The player rolls a third die and adds that result to the Modifier. If this result is not satisfactory, the player can spend another two Fortune Points to reroll the Fortune Die, but this second die is not added to the total. Instead, the player must choose the highest of the two results and discard the other. If this second attempt is still not satisfactory, the player may attempt again, and again, etc., but only one result may be kept.

Security and emergency services show up quickly after the battle of the bar concludes. One condition of their employment on this job was that Jessica and her companions keep a low profile, so she tries to fast-talk the investigating officer into letting her and her companions go for the time being. The GM calls for a Diplomacy roll, based on Charm,

---

Recording Fortune Points

The Character Record includes a box for recording Fortune Points. Rather than write down a number, players should keep a running tally of the points in the boxes provided, marking them in when you give them points and erasing them when they're used. Alternatively, you can keep a stock of some sort of counter (coins, chips, beads, or whatever you have handy) to give players and have them give back to you when they gain or lose Fortune Points. Then the players need only mark down their Fortune Points at the end of each game session, so they know how many counters to draw at the start of the next session.

with the Persuasion Specialty. Not having that Specialty, Jessica's Ability is 8. She rolls a -1 for her Random Modifier, for a total of 7—well beneath the 11 required by the Tricky Difficulty set by the GM.

Dana spends two Fortune Points and rolls a Fortune Die. She gets a 3, which, added to her Random Modifier, brings her total up to 10. Still not enough. She spends another two, and rerolls the Fortune Die. Bad luck: the result is a 2. She decides to keep the 3 that she rolled the first time. With the 10 result, her attempt is a Marginal Failure.

Another way to use a Fortune Point to improve a character's odds applies only to Cultural tasks, and only when dealing with aliens. In such cases, a player can spend a Fortune Point to ignore the character's Xenorelation score and use the Attribute that the character would normally use when dealing with a member of his or her own race.

Looking back at Jessica's attempt to calm the Narn, if Dana had chosen to, she could have spent a Fortune Point to bypass her Xenorelation Attribute, and use the normally-applicable Finesse Attribute. That would have given Jessica a total Ability of 6, instead of the 5 that she had in the attempt.

The second use for Fortune Points is in keeping a desperate character alive. There are times when, despite all the player's best efforts, a character ends up in serious jeopardy of losing his or her life. A character on the wrong end of a PPG may simply not have the opportunity to save him or herself if the person on the other end of the gun is quick and is a good shot. When a character, through whatever means, has taken enough damage to die, the player can spend two Fortune Points to reduce the Damage level to 13. This won't prevent the character from suffering a lot of pain, nor will it improve the heal time of the damage—so players shouldn't abandon their character's sense of self-preservation. But it will keep a character around if it's not yet that character's time.

You must use common sense when applying this rule, and you must justify the altered Damage level. Obviously, a character floating naked in space for three weeks, or caught at the epicenter of a nuclear blast, won't survive the resulting damage no matter how many Fortune Points are spent in trying. Even when wounds are less dramatic, there must be an in-game reason for the character's survival. The most common rationale for combat wounds is that the attack missed the most critical areas.

Julien was shot in the torso for Damage of 13. If, as mentioned above, he'd been wounded again in the torso for Damage of 6, the total Damage would have been 19, enough to kill him. Had that happened, Mike would certainly have opted to spend two Fortune Points to reduce the Damage back down to 13. It turns out that the second wound merely grazed Julien's side, and didn't make a significant medical difference in his condition.

Finally, in a very desperate situation, you can allow a character in great need to perform a task that he or she wouldn't normally be able to even attempt. For example, if a character who is not a pilot needs to get a ship out of the way of danger before she and everyone on board are blown into little bits, you could allow her to try the task by use of a Fortune Point. If you decide to allow this use of a Fortune Point, you then set the Difficulty of the task, just as if the character had the skill. The character must succeed just as if she had the skill—though, obviously, since the character has no skill only the Attribute applies when determining the character's Ability. When interpreting the results of a task resolved in this manner, remember that the consequences of extreme success (should it occur) should be somewhat tempered.

Character Evolution: Experience and Learning

People change and grow over time. Just as real people learn and develop, characters in a roleplaying game do, too. To model this in game terms, characters gain Experience Points as the game sessions progress into a longer campaign. Unlike Fortune Points, these are not given out based on the player's performance, but are awarded automatically so long as the character participates in the story. These are points that the player can use to improve the character's statistics as represented on the Character Record. A player can use Experience Points to improve the character in a few different ways: to improve Attributes or Skills; to gain Fortune Points; or to redefine Characteristics.

more rapidly, but remember that building super-skilled characters is not what the game is about.

Dana's group of friends meets every Tuesday night to play The Babylon Project. It took them three weeks to finish their first adventure—at the end of each session, the GM gave each player an Experience Point. At the end of the third evening, he granted each player an additional 2 points, for concluding the adventure.

Granting Experience Points

The rule for gaining Experience Points is simple. For each real time game session that the player attends, give the character one Experience Point. Between individual adventures in the same campaign, give each character one to three points depending on how much happened during the previous adventure. You can vary the number of experience points that characters get if you want the characters to improve

Playing Experience Points

Experience points are used to increase Attribute and skill levels, to purchase Specialties, and to resolve Characteristics. To increase an Attribute from one level to the next, a player must spend seven experience points. To increase a Skill to the next level or gain a new skill (with one Specialty), the player must spend four points. A character may also gain a new Specialty in a skill that he or she already has by spending four experience points. To improve a character's Attributes or Skills, a player must not only spend the appropriate number of Experience Points, but also explain to you how his or her character is learning or practicing the Attribute or skill, and roleplay it if necessary. For example, a character who wishes to improve her Strength will have to do weight training over a period of time. To roleplay that she's doing it, the player makes sure that her character makes time to do weight training every day. This may draw some of her time away from the party temporarily, but she will be able to increase her Strength.

After her first adventure, Dana decides to add the Shiphandling skill to Jessica's list—it was one of the skills she originally wanted, but had to drop during character generation. It'll cost her three points. However, Jessica didn't do any shiphandling during her first adventure, so the GM tells Dana that she'll need some training or experience before he grants Jessica the skill.

There's a flight school on Babylon 5, so Jessica signs up for some courses and simulator time. In a few weeks, she may be able to add Shiphandling to her skill list.

The very nature of the Characteristics means that characters will be losing and gaining them as they evolve. A character might, for instance, overcome his fear of heights while climbing a scaffolding during a critical scene in an adventure. For this reason, Characteristics are very easy to change. Since players are the ones who have to play their characters, allow them to change their Characteristics at will unless you have a very strong reason not to. To get rid of a Characteristic, the player must have some roleplaying reason to lose it (such as the fear of heights example above), and must then spend one Experience Point.

Finally, a player can trade Experience Points in for Fortune Points (although this does not work in reverse; Fortune Points cannot be transferred to Experience Points). In the Beginning of your campaign (the Introduction and Identification Phases), grant players only one Fortune Point per Experience Point turned in this way. In the Middle (Preparation and Challenge Phases), increase that to two, and in the End (the Climax and Resolution Phases), grant three Fortune Points per Experience Point. This exchange must be done between play sessions, however, not in the middle of play.

Chapter 3: The Environment

This chapter is primarily for the use of the gamemaster. It provides details on the settings, races and situations during the time of the building of the Babylon stations—many of which cover things going on behind the scenes, things that most player characters will know nothing about. Players may find the information interesting, but should probably avoid reading it in order to maintain surprise and spontaneity as these secrets are revealed through the game.

The chapter is divided into three sections. The first section details the history and politics of Earth. Next, some extra detail on alien races is given. Finally, there is information on technology and equipment in the 2250s, including spacecraft, weapons, and other gear that the characters may rely upon.

Section 1: Humanity in the 23rd Century

The Introduction to this book, along with chapter 1, provided an overview of

This game takes place in the aftermath of the Earth-Minbari War, during the time of the building of the Babylon Project. This time period begins with the surrender of the Minbari in 2248 and ends with the Narn declaration of war on the Centauri in 2259. If you are familiar with the BABYLON 5 television series, you and your players may know many of the details presented here. Remember, however, that many of the events that occur during the second season of the show and later change the political situation among the known races. Therefore, things may not quite be what your players are expecting.

Humanity's place in the interstellar society of the 23rd century. This section details much of what has changed—and much that has not—between our 20th century society and the future of *The Babylon Project*.

Earth History

Earth's history to date is a mix of struggle and triumph, and the next 250 years between now and the time setting of the game follow the same trend. The Introduction covered the general history of that period, which is also summed up in a sidebar on the next page. These narratives reflect posterity—the elements of history that were acknowledged at the time and recorded in the history books. Often, however, there was more going on behind the scenes than many knew, or than history recorded. You'll find some allusions to such events in this chapter.

This section focuses mainly on recent history—the years just prior to and during the time setting of the game. It begins with the Battle of the Line—the last desperate hope for Humanity in the face of the furious Minbari onslaught.

The Minbari withdrawal after the battle unexpectedly saved Humanity from near-certain destruction. In political circles, this provided unprecedented opportunities for ambitious men and women to give their ideas a receptive forum for realization. One such idea was the Babylon Project, which won unanimous support in the EA Senate. Other trade relations and ambassadorial posts were approved without reservation, and while the Earth Alliance rebuilt itself after the destruction of war, Humans began to much more heavily interact with the other races.

The Minbari had devastated the EA's fleet, but in their haste to destroy Earth they had bypassed many of the Alliance's non-military colonies and settlements. When the Minbari halted their offensive, this single-mindedness proved a saving grace—the EA's interstellar economic base was still largely intact. Though the government and military had been stretched to the limit in the war, several major corporations had the resources to contribute to a rapid rebuilding effort.

In the rebuilding of Earthforce, one of the most important corporations was Mitchell-Hyundyne. Mitchell-Hyundyne sent the SA-23E "Aurora," a fighter which had been prototyped during the last year of the war, into production in late 2248—it was to become the mainstay of the EA fighter fleet over the next ten years. The years after the war also saw the introduction of a new warship, the *Omega*-class destroyer, the first EA warship capable of rotational gravity. It grew quickly, as scores were built to fill in the holes in the critically-weakened Earthforce fleet.

Other corporations helped the Alliance in other ways. Interplanetary Expeditions (IPX), an exploration and trading company, proved invaluable in supplying the necessary Quantium-40 for hyperspace travel and communications. United Spaceways Transport, a small shipping company before the war, took over much of the transport routes that could no longer be handled by EA ships after the war. Quartermaster Corp., a colonial supplier before the war, became the leading supply company for Earthforce during the rebuilding after the war.

Humans and Aliens

Now, in the aftermath of the Minbari War, the political landscape among the vari-

Humanity in Space: a Timeline

2026 Space Station Freedom abandoned.
2047 Station Prime completed.
2064 Armstrong Colony established on the Moon.
2075 Earth Alliance founded as an economic and political conglomerate to colonize Mars.
2081 Psi ability confirmed; Earth governments secretly begin tracking telepaths.
2090 First Mars Colony founded with 100 men and women.
2099 First Mars Colony destroyed.
2105 Permanent Mars Colony founded.
2107 United Nations disbands in favor of Earth Alliance.
2111 Venusian Orbital Station founded.
2113 Centauri occupy Narn.
2122 Earth Alliance formally becomes the governmental structure for Earth.
2130 Skywalker Asteroid Base founded.
2145 Ganymede Outpost founded
2150 San Diego bombed.
2152 EarthGov's Committee on Psychic Phenomena becomes Psi-Corps.
2153 Long range sleeper ships begin leaving Earth system to explore other stars.
2155 Centauri patrol detects humans, Centauri contact Earth.
2156 Centauri jumpgate constructed in Earth orbit.
2161 Centauri sell jump gate technology to humans.
2163 Lockheed-Mitchell Corp. builds Earth's first jump capable exploration ship.
2164 Small orbital station founded in Proxima system.
2165 Proxima III Colony founded.
2169 Procyon II Colony founded; disappeared after two days.
2170 Mitchell-Hyundyne SA-10 Starfury "Aries" makes its debut at Ross 128.
2172 Centauri-Earth border skirmishes begin.
2175 Centauri sign treaty with Earth.
2176 Orion VII Colony founded.
2198 Earth Alliance builds jump gate at Io and deactivates Centauri gate in Earth orbit.
2200 Mars Colony requests independence from Earth.
2209 Centauri leave Narn.
2215 League of Non-Aligned Worlds is formed.
2219 Narn-Earth border skirmishes begin.
2224 Narns sign treaty with Earth.
2230 Dilgar expansion begins.
2231 Earth-Dilgar War formally declared.
2232 Dilgar defeated.
2245 Humans meet Minbari; Dukhat killed, Earth-Minbari War begins.
2248 Earth-Minbari War ends after the Battle of the Line; President Peter Ashton elected.
2249 The Babylon Project begins.
2250 Babylon Station collapses; Babylon 2 destroyed.
2251 Mars food riots
2252 Babylon 3 destroyed.
2253 President Luis Santiago elected.
2254 Babylon 4 goes online and disappears.
2256 Babylon 5 goes online.
2257 First officially known physical meeting between Humans and Vorlons.
2258 Mars revolt; President Santiago dies, Morgan Clark succeeds him.
2259 Narns declare war against Centauri; Centauri Emperor dies on Babylon 5

ous races is changing substantially. As Humanity recovers from the Earth-Minbari War, we are solidifying our systems and refortifying our colonies and outposts. The Narns continue their expansion, particularly into Centauri space. The Centauri, their empire in decline, are defending what is left and trying to establish a foothold in the new political order. The Minbari, following an agenda of their own, have made overtures of peace to the Humans, and have begun to interact more openly with the "younger"

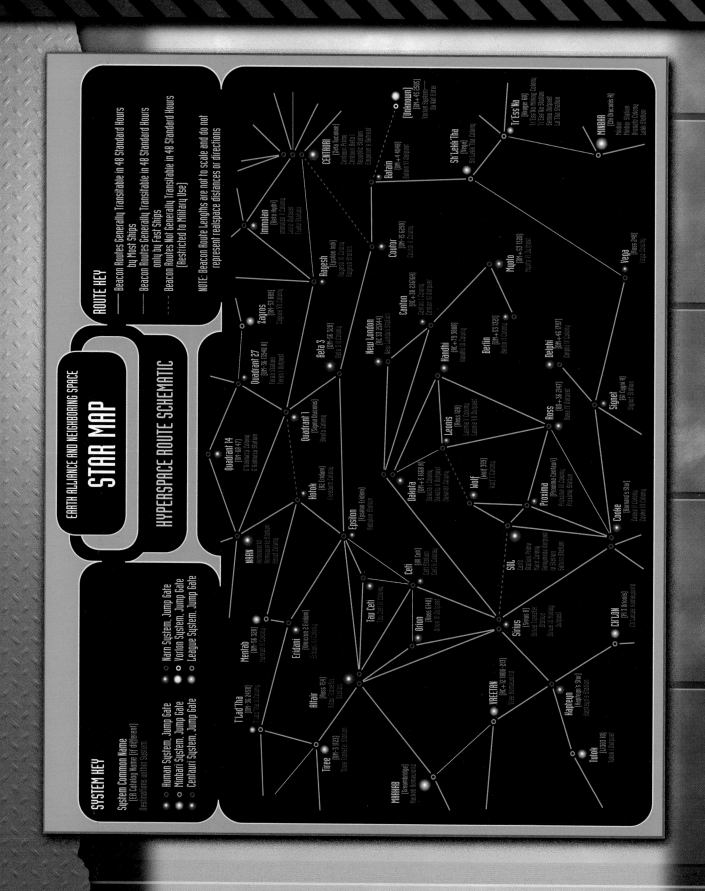

EARTH ALLIANCE AND NEIGHBORING SPACE

STAR MAP

HYPERSPACE ROUTE SCHEMATIC

SYSTEM KEY

System Common Name
[EA Catalog Name (if different)]
Destinations within System

○ Human System, Jump Gate
● Minbari System, Jump Gate
● Centauri System, Jump Gate

● Narn System, Jump Gate
◉ Vorlon System, Jump Gate
● League System, Jump Gate

ROUTE KEY

— Beacon Routes Generally Transitable in 48 Standard Hours by Most Ships

— Beacon Routes Generally Transitable in 48 Standard Hours only by Fast Ships

--- Beacon Routes Not Generally Transitable in 48 Standard Hours (Restricted to Military Use)

NOTE: Beacon Route Lengths are not to scale and do not represent realspace distances or directions races. After the war, however, the Minbari stopped expanding their sphere of influence. Many among the League of Non-Aligned Worlds have begun to ally themselves with one or the other of the larger empires, although the League itself remains a loosely organized independent body. Finally, the Vorlons keep to themselves, as inscrutable as ever. No ambassador sent into Vorlon space has ever returned.

The map opposite depicts Human space and the various empires nearest it. The map is always changing, as new jump routes are discovered, political boundaries shift, and some races skirmish with their neighbors. This version is current as of 2250.

The Babylon Project

The Minbari war caused Humanity to rethink its place in the galactic community. Humankind realized that in order to survive any future challenges like the Minbari War, it would have to know, and be, an integrated part of the interstellar community. Before the war, EA Senator Calvin Natawe, the Nigerian president, had suggested a station in neutral space for commerce and diplomacy. It was little more than an idea when the Minbari War broke out, however. Senator Natawe was a speaker who could galvanize people during times of great conflict, and during the war he became a source of inspiration for many of the Alliance's citizens. From front-line soldiers to those waiting at home, he passed his passion and optimism on to all who saw him. He didn't forget his dream of a place of peace, and spoke of it frequently towards the end of the war. After the war, the notion of peace and diplomacy was very popular, and when he formally proposed it as "The Babylon Project," it won unanimous approval in mid-2249.

As originally envisioned, Babylon Station would be a six-mile long O'Neill colony set in neutral space, housing approximately 500,000 Humans and aliens at any one time. In addition to sectors for Earth Alliance personnel, it would contain sectors for dignitaries from all of the major races, and for representatives from the League of Non-Aligned Worlds. Two counter-rotating sections and multiple customizable habitats would provide varying degrees of gravity suitable for a wide array of aliens. It would be capable of defending itself against attack from all but the heaviest warships, including both defensive weaponry and engines empowering it to move from one place to another. It was the most ambitious project ever taken on by Humans, and the inspiration of one man's dream carried it forward.

The station was also to be home to the Babylon Council, a diplomatic body hosted by the Earth Alliance whose role would be an advisory board to the various alien governments. Initially, the Minbari and Centauri expressed great support for this council, and within a few months, the Narn and League of Non-Aligned Worlds were convinced to join as well. Each of the larger empires—the Humans, Centauri, Narn and Minbari—had one vote on the council, with the League vote breaking any ties. Following their own private agenda, the Vorlons chose not to reply to messages concerning the council.

The Destruction of Babylon Station

BAB/COM

The history of the Babylon Project and the sabotage of Babylon Station by Earth First is at the heart of the example story in Chapter 4. Even if you choose not to run that story as your *The Babylon Project* campaign, you can find more information on the collapse of the station, the involvement of Earth First and other subversive Human organizations, and the history of the Project in Chapter 4.

The dream of peace was not shared by some in the Alliance, though, and some groups played on the fear of the unknown and the former aggression of the Minbari to foster their own agenda. Two such organizations completed plans for sabotaging the station in an attempt to keep out the harmful alien influences. Earth First, a small "family" organization secretly run by EA Senator James Sidhe, sabotaged materials used to build the infrastructure of the station, causing its collapse early in the construction.

The collapse pushed construction costs well over the budget allotted for the station. Since the laws of the Alliance provided very little latitude in budgetary adjustments on that scale, a new budget was drawn up by Senator Natawe mere days after the collapse, and the Senate approved it as Babylon 2. Utilizing many of the undamaged parts of the original station, construction moved forward again mere weeks after the collapse.

The location chosen for the station was a small system of little strategic or economic value in neutral space, Epsilon Eridani. No signs of life were discovered by scanning crews during the survey of the system. The third planet offered an ideal placement for an orbiting station, allowing for temperate zones of heat and light. On January 3, 2250, the station was officially dedicated and construction began.

It was at this point that sabotage by a second organization, the Homeguard, took effect. The Homeguard was a much more organized group than Earth First, with hundreds of members in many different areas of the EA. While Earth First's sabotage was subtle by necessity, Homeguard had the

resources to perform a much more dramatic feat. When the fusion reactor salvaged from the first station went online, it exploded, taking with it many of the completed station components and not a few lives.

This time, the Senate stopped to consider the future of the Babylon Project. An official investigation by a Senate subcommittee ruled both incidents accidental, thanks to some timely intervention by Homeguard and its sympathizers, and the matter was dropped. Behind the scenes, senator Sidhe was implicated and resigned his position in the Senate, but no other action took place. And despite the Homeguard's cover up, rumors and accusations of sabotage began to circulate, although many of them were dismissed as conspiracy theories—at least in public.

The vast majority of EA citizens still believed strongly in Senator Natawe's dream of peace, a sentiment echoed wholeheartedly in the Senate. Those who believed the rumors of sabotage also wished to make the statement that the Alliance would not be bullied in its alien relations policies by small isolationist factions. Accordingly, Babylon 3 was approved and budgeted, and under the watchful eye of the Senate, construction began again. Very little was left over after the explosion on Babylon 2, and the new materials were carefully scrutinized before being sent out to Epsilon 3 for assembly.

By this point, the Homeguard had grown, subsuming several smaller organizations like Earth First, and was well insinuated into some of the highest levels of government and industry. The Homeguard saw itself at war with the EA's foreign policy, and wanted its message to come through loud and clear.

Construction on Babylon 3 crawled in comparison to the earlier versions of the station, with each component being carefully searched and tested before assembly. The infrastructure was eventually completed, with neither structural sabotage nor explosions. Spinup of the rotating sections went smoothly. Soon after the next phases of construction had begun, however, saboteurs struck yet again. A series of small explosives planted at strategic locations damaged the hull and parts of the infrastructure beyond repair. Debris from the

Sabotage Plans

The construction of Babylon 4 was subjected to several minor attempts at sabotage, and there were two notable actions that almost succeeded. The first was an attack by raider fighters (see the sidebar on page 163) in June of 2253, orchestrated by Homeguard using resources from a highly covert bureau within the Psi-Corps. The fighters attacked during a lull in the patrol phase, at a time when the station's main defense screens were scheduled for offline maintenance. Fortunately, the maintenance did not occur on schedule, and the station was just able to meet the attack with the help of fighter squadrons from the EA destroyer *Roanoke*.

The second attempt was in December of that year, as many of the construction workers were changing duty rosters for the holidays. The jumpgate was deactivated by an unknown agent, and a ship of unknown origin (a custom design commissioned by the Homeguard) jumped in danger-close to the station, and on a collision course. The station's maneuver engines were not believed to be online, but construction had been running ahead of schedule. The engines were functional, and the station was able to maneuver long enough for the *Roanoke* to come to bear on the intruder. It self-destructed rather than surrender.

explosions also damaged several nearby ships and the jumpgate generators, causing a temporary delay in transportation to and from the site. 150 people were killed and over 400 injured.

The terrible cost in lives of this attack crippled the resolve of the EA Senate. Debate on the issue went on for months before a budget for Babylon 4 was approved. This time, an accompanying budget was also assigned for military escorts and checks at every point along the way. Senator Natawe, always an advocate of peace, initially balked at military involvement, but eventually agreed that the watchful eye of Earthforce would be an asset in the completion of the station.

Babylon 5

Though only half its original planned size, Babylon 5 is a large space station by any standard. It's built like a giant tube rotating around a stationary core, with the rotation of the tube providing a sense of gravity for those within. The tube is many decks thick, and variation in gravity is achieved by housing closer to or farther from the central core—the further from the center, the stronger the felt gravity. The large open center of the tube is the Garden, where food is grown, water is stored, and plants are allowed to flourish, providing an environment with a natural feel. Color-coded areas are arranged by decks underneath and around the Garden.

The non-rotating sections of the station, including the fusion reactor and the large zero-gravity cargo receiving bays are collectively designated as Yellow Sector.

Blue Sector houses offices, quarters and operations centers for Earthforce and station duty personnel, including the station's Command and Control Center. It also contains the smaller gravitational docking bays and the customs area. All traffic in and out of the station is routed through the docking bay section and customs, allowing the management and control of illegal or improper shipments into the station. Large ships trading at Babylon 5, however, frequently transfer their cargos directly from ship to ship in orbit near the station—a perfectly legal transaction that does not involve station customs.

Green Sector is the home of alien ambassadors and dignitaries, including some very limited facilities for aliens who cannot handle human atmospheric conditions. With the exception of the Vorlon Ambassador, all of the races with votes on the Council house their ambassadorial parties here, and many of the League Worlds' representatives use this area. The Council Chambers are located nearby in Blue Sector.

Red Sector is the center of commerce and recreation. It houses several restaurants, casinos and marketplaces, as well as offering semi-permanent lodging to non-Earthforce humans and other aliens. The top level of Red Sector, along the Garden, houses among other things the fabulous Fresh Aire open restaurant, a recreational sports field, a small freshwater lake (part of the water recycling system, but available for boating and swimming) and a park which features a hedge maze and a Japanese stone garden.

Brown Sector contains temporary lodging facilities and additional commercial areas for travelers passing through. It contains some of the less reputable restaurants and clubs. It also contains the "Alien Sector," the informal name given to the areas of the station set aside for other environments, where many of the different races, including the Vorlon ambassador, live.

Gray Sector is the industrial section of the station, housing construction and maintenance facilities that cannot be located in Blue Sector, including the power regulation stations, the food production facilities and the air and waste recycling centers. Situated on the end of the rotating habitat nearest the fusion reactor, it is a secure area, with access granted only to station operations personnel.

Downbelow is the name given to the undeveloped areas of the station, mostly those situated underneath the colored sectors, where the gravity is slightly higher than Earth normal. Some levels are on the very skin of the station, with windows in the floor that allow a view of the vacuum. Those who come to Babylon 5 with few prospects sometimes wind up in downbelow, unable to find work or to pay for better lodgings or a shuttle ticket home. The combination of undeveloped squalor, the oppressive gravity, and constant crime leave many of the denizens of downbelow, called lurkers, depressed and listless.

Construction on Babylon 4 began in mid-October, 2252. There were additional attempts at sabotage, but none as well-planned as the destruction of Babylon 3. The Earthforce security contingent proved its value, thwarting every sabotage attempt, and after two years of construction the station was at last completed.

But even this effort was doomed to failure. Twenty-four hours after commissioning, the station vanished without a trace. The Earthforce destroyer *Roanoke*, the flagship for the EA security force during construction, had left the system earlier that day, her duties there at an end with the station online and operational. A few hours later, an unexplained explosion was reported near the station. When the *Roanoke* returned four hours later, there was no trace of the station. No debris remained, nor any

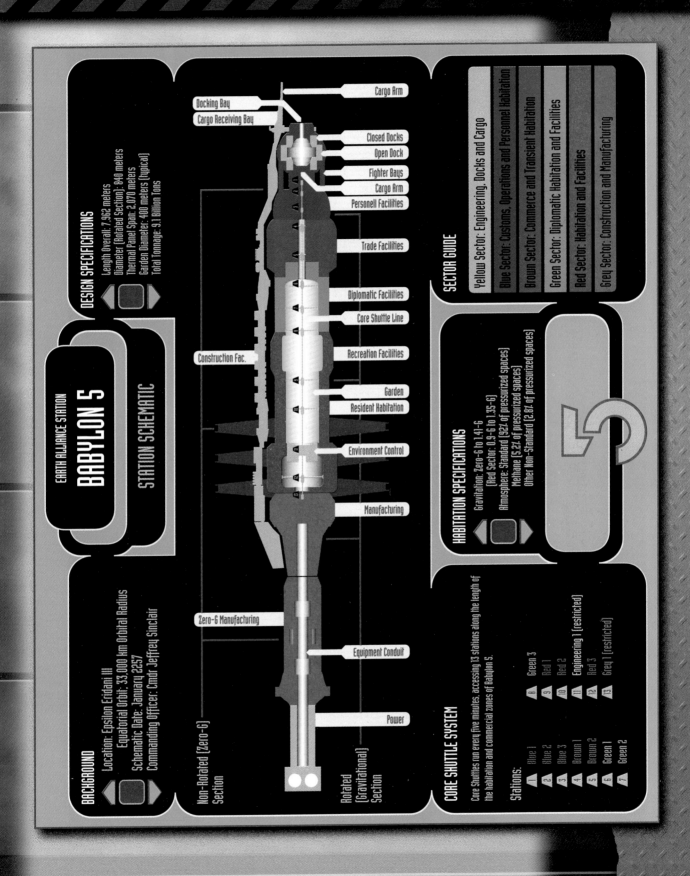

EARTH ALLIANCE STATION
BABYLON 5

STATION SCHEMATIC

BACKGROUND

Location: Epsilon Eridani III
Equatorial Orbit: 33,000 Km Orbital Radius
Schematic Date: January 2257
Commanding Officer: Cmdr Jeffrey Sinclair

DESIGN SPECIFICATIONS

Length Overall: 7,962 meters
Diameter (Rotated Section): 940 meters
Thermal Panel Span: 2,070 meters
Garden Diameter: 400 meters (typical)
Total Tonnage: 9.1 Billion Tons

SECTOR GUIDE

Yellow Sector: Engineering, Docks and Cargo

Blue Sector: Customs, Operations and Personnel Habitation

Brown Sector: Commerce and Transient Habitation

Green Sector: Diplomatic Habitation and Facilities

Red Sector: Habitation and Facilities

Grey Sector: Construction and Manufacturing

HABITATION SPECIFICATIONS

Gravitation: Zero-G to 1.41-G
(Red Sector: 0.9-G to 1.35-G)
Atmosphere: Standard (92% of pressurized spaces)
Methane (5.2% of pressurized spaces)
Other Non-Standard (2.8% of pressurized spaces)

CORE SHUTTLE SYSTEM

Core Shuttles run every five minutes, accessing 13 stations along the length of
the habitation and commercial zones of Babylon 5.

Stations:

1. Blue 1
2. Blue 2
3. Blue 3
4. Brown 1
5. Brown 2
6. Green 1
7. Green 2
8. Green 3
9. Red 1
10. Red 2
11. Engineering 1 [restricted]
12. Red 3
13. Grey 1 [restricted]

Schematic labels

Cargo Arm
Docking Bay
Cargo Receiving Bay
Closed Docks
Open Dock
Fighter Bays
Cargo Arm
Personell Facilities
Trade Facilities
Diplomatic Facilities
Core Shuttle Line
Recreation Facilities
Garden
Resident Habitation
Environment Control
Manufacturing
Construction Fac.
Zero-G Manufacturing
Equipment Conduit
Power

Non-Rotated (Zero-G) Section

Rotated (Gravitational) Section

other signs of conflict. A shuttle leaving the station was the only witness, and crew reported seeing "a white light, then the station was gone." The shuttle's telemetry backed up that general description of events, providing no additional useful insight into the disappearance.

This final inexplicable setback in the Babylon Project sounded a death knell within the Senate, and it looked like the Babylon Station would never be realized. The disappearance was no normal accident, and clearly no mere act of sabotage—it now seemed as though fate itself was against the project. Senator Natawe, however, refused to give up on a dream that he had spent his entire life pursuing. Despite being well into his sixties and close to retirement, he persevered. The Senate no longer wished to expend resources on a project that seemed doomed to failure, so he took his case to the participating alien governments.

The Minbari agreed to help surprisingly quickly, and committed to a substantial portion of the financing of the project provided they had some input on the administration of the station. The Centauri also agreed to help as much as they could, despite "economic problems" on Centauri Prime. Even the Narn pitched in some token support. When Senator Natawe brought this back to the Senate, a budget was grudgingly approved—but only for a vastly cut-back version of the project. The new version would be much smaller than the original station, housing only half the initial population and having far less defensive capability. This final effort only barely passed the Senate, and it was clear to politicos on all sides that this would be the final Babylon Station. If the project didn't succeed here, it never would.

As construction began, the role of Earthforce increased from guard to administration, not only during construction, but on a permanent basis. Senator Natawe, believing this to be a trend that would alienate the other races, fought this change in the Senate. He believed that for the station to truly be a beacon of peace, it could not be run by those who existed to make war. However, many in the Senate felt that it was not wise to leave an area so open to alien incursion under untrained civilian command, and so Natawe was overruled. Due to these differences, as well as fatigue, Senator Natawe resigned shortly after construction was started on Babylon 5, expressing no desire to attend its scheduled dedication ceremony in 2257.

Babylon 5 was finished in late 2256, to much derision in political forums. Many predicted that the station would not last out the year. But it stayed online for several months, surpassing the record of any of the other stations. Given a clean bill of health, as it were, arrangements were made with the alien governments to receive their ambassadors. To the surprise of many, the enigmatic and powerful Vorlons announced that they too would send an ambassador. The Vorlons were of course given a seat on the Babylon Council equal to the four major races, and with their participation the council was formally established.

The Earth Alliance

The Earth Alliance encompasses all Human colonies, outposts and stations, with its seat of government in Earthdome,

---

EA Senatorial Politics

BAB/COM

Most Senators are concerned primarily with matters that relate directly to the countries they represent. All, however, realize the value of commerce and communication with other worlds to keeping peace. Although the President sets foreign policy and appoints ambassadors (with Senate approval), there are two powerful and highly respected committees that have a direct influence on alien relations: the Select Senate Committee on Defense, which works side by side with the president on matters of planetary and system defense for all human worlds; and the Senate Committee on Inter-species Affairs, responsible for trade and commerce regulations.

Several of the more influential senators in the Committee on Defense are Miagi Hydoshi, Paolo Iadoccio and Eileen Dalton. The senior members of the Committee on Inter-species Affairs are Constantin Bespin, Indira Shanthi and Johnathon Moore a self-contained domed district near Geneva, Switzerland. Both EarthGov, the official governing body of the Alliance, and Earthforce, the military and enforcement arm, have their headquarters in Earthdome.

Government

EarthGov is a system of government modeled on the democratic governments of the major countries that comprised its founding members. The central body of the government is the EA Senate. The Senate consists of a representative from each member country, usually the elected or appointed leader of that country. It is the direct ruling body for all EA territorial holdings (colonies and outposts, which are not governed by member states). Most colonies and major outposts send "ghost" representatives to the Senate, who observe and contribute to debate there but cannot vote.

The EarthGov President is chosen from within the Senate. The president relinquishes his or her Senate seat and oversees the executive branch of the government, serving as the commander in chief of the military, the check for the legislative arm, and the head of state. The president also sets foreign policy (relating to alien races),

Earth Alliance Presidents

BAB COM

Over the period of time in which *The Babylon Project* is set, there are three presidents of the Earth Alliance. Sir Peter Ashton of the United Kingdom was elected president in 2248, and served in the aftermath of the Earth-Minbari war. In 2253, Luis Santiago of the Latin-American Federation was elected. He was re-elected in 2258 and served until his death on December 31st of that year. His Vice President, Morgan Clark, served as president thereafter.

acting as the chief ambassador to other worlds. Nominees for president are selected from within the Senate, by two partisan committees. The president is then chosen by popular election of all Earth Alliance citizens in all countries, colonies, outposts and stations. The president's term of office is five years.

The third arm of the EA government is the Judiciary. Within member countries,

disputes and crimes are settled according to that country's own laws. Cases that involve two or more member countries, cases arising in EA territorial holdings, or crimes involving the death of an EA citizen are arbitrated by the Alliance. Local Ombudsmen (magistrates) appointed by the higher courts have jurisdiction over specific districts—smaller colonies or outposts may only have one or two ombuds, with local EA security personnel doubling as the ombuds on the smallest of facilities. Above the ombudsmen are two layers of appeals courts, where decisions by lower courts can be reviewed. Finally, there is Final Appeal, which may be heard by the Senate Appeal Board in serious cases.

Litigation follows the same style as western law today. Suspects are considered innocent until proven guilty, and lawyers may be selected to argue the case for either side. Most civil cases are adjudicated according to EA statues and common law, and are heard only by a ombudsman. Criminal and severe civil cases are given a trial by jury.

The penalties for crimes range from simple fines for misdemeanors to jail time or forced labor on mining colonies for serious felonies. Capital crimes are punishable by the Death of Personality (a process that destroys the criminal's psyche and memories to essentially create a new personality, commonly referred to as "mindwipe"), and the most serious crimes (treason and mutiny) are punishable by death by exposure to vacuum (also called "spacing").

Military

Earthforce is the Alliance's military branch. It serves the EA in both peacekeeping and military capacities, and as the police force in EA territories such as colonies and stations. Earthforce headquarters is nominally in Earthdome, but the bulk of all Earthforce command and control is located at the Ganymede outpost, which also serves as the primary customs stop for all incoming and outgoing ship traffic in Earth's solar system.

There are two main service branches in Earthforce, along with several smaller special branches. The major service branches are the Fleet and the Ground Forces. Both of these are under the command of the president, supervised by the Senate Committee on Planetary Security with the counsel of the Joint Chiefs of Staff. Most EA stations are under the command of Earthforce, as are all outposts.

The EA Fleet is made up of a mix of warships, transport ships and scientific vessels, with fighter support wings for many ships, outposts, colonies and stations. The mainstay of the fleet before the Minbari War was the *Hyperion*-class cruiser. However, as most of the *Hyperion*-class ships were destroyed in the war, the newer *Omega*-class destroyer is becoming the mainstay of the fleet. The SA-23E Aurora starfury is the predominant fighter, a workhorse ship capable of patrol and fighting duties, and the most capable fighter among the younger races.

The EA Ground Forces are a strong army of well-trained troops capable of going where ships cannot, to keep the peace and defend Human lives from harm. They are supported by Fleet transports, usually escorted by warships. Drop ships carried by the transports deliver troops to planetary

Earthforce Leadership

As of 2250, the Chief of Fleet Operations is Admiral Jason Ashvin Singh, who oversees all fleet actions and is a member of the Joint Chiefs of Staff. He is stationed at Earthdome, but he oversees the fleet with a great eye to detail. His aides stationed at Ganymede, whose names occasionally appear on ship orders, include Admiral Gerald Rogers and Admiral Moira Wassen.

The Chief of Ground Operations is General Jennifer Romano, a warrior promoted from within the ranks to the Joint Chiefs. Her strength lies more in battle than in day-to-day management, though, and her Ganymede staff handles the vast majority of the orders and movements of the ground troops. It is usual to see orders from Colonel Michael Atoumbe and Colonel Tyrell Collins rather than from General Romano herself.

defense assignments and provide air support after the troops are deployed, and breaching pods (escorted by starfury wings) are sent in to enter orbital or other space targets.

Colonies

Earth Alliance holdings on Earth itself are limited to Earthdome and a few islands in international waters. All off-world Human holdings, however, are directly subject to the Alliance. The major colonies are those on Mars, Proxima III and Orion VII.

The EA's first civilian colony was the Mars Colony. Closest to Earth, it has also maintained the status as the Alliance's most populous colony, made up of four cities in domed environments. The largest city is Olympus Mons, made up of four domes connected by a network of above-ground transport conduits. The other cities are at Syria Planum, Solis Planum and Xanthe Terra. There are also several other military and research outposts in various places on the planet. The first attempt to colonize Mars was in 2090 on Syria Planum. However, a terrorist attack on the colony (intended to assassinate a dignitary) destroyed the dome, killing many of the colonists. The effort was not lost, however, as the lessons learned allowed a new city at Olympus Mons to be established in 2105. This new city became the capital of the colony, and of the other cities that would be built over the years.

Earth's first outsystem colony was at Proxima III, established in 2164 and located in what was once called the Proxima Centauri system. The system was renamed Proxima shortly after its settlement to avoid confusion with the Centauri Republic. Proxima III is slightly larger than Earth, with an atmosphere similar to Mars. The domed-city approach that was successful on Mars was also implemented here. The Proxima colony is smaller than Mars, consisting of only two large (Olympus Mons-sized) cities located fairly close to one another.

Proxima has become one of the Alliance's leading industrial producers. Many of Earth's interstellar corporations have their main offices on Proxima, particularly those with major orbital manufacturing or construction concerns. The clear orbital trajectories around Proxima drew this business very early on, and the companies that made this move proved profitable over time.

One of the Alliance's more recent colonies is on Orion VII, a settlement located in the star system originally designated as Ross 614 B. The planet, named Orion by the original exploration team, is a small, gray, lifeless world. The Orion system borders on Centauri space, and shortly after the colony's founding in 2178 it became one of the key trade centers between the Alliance and the Centauri Republic. Once relations opened up with the Minbari after the war (and until Babylon 5 supplanted it in 2257), it was also the chief diplomatic post between the Minbari and the Alliance, giving each race the opportunity to learn more about the other in a relatively neutral environment.

The EA's newest colony is on Tau Ceti IV. Established in 2249, following the Minbari War, it is still a frontier world. Consisting of only one city of one dome and a couple of research outposts, it is a rough environment. Those who live there are pioneers and adventurers, people who hope to make their fortunes as founders of a successful colony. The laws of the Earth Alliance apply only as far as the docking bays and other areas under Earthforce's direct supervision. Tau Ceti can be a dangerous place to live, but the rewards can be great for industrious entrepreneurs. Only 5.3 light years from the Babylon Station construction site, it is also near the borders of Centauri and Narn space, making it a trade center between the Alliance and those races.

The alliance has colonized about twenty other worlds, all otherwise lifeless. Most are agricultural or manufacturing sites.

Colonial Politics

When the Mars Colony went online as the first civilian colony (Armstrong, on the Moon, was a purely governmental project), colonists on Mars relied on Earth for everything from transportation and communications to food, water and air. This inspired a great loyalty to the Alliance. As time progressed, however, the colony grew and became more and more self-sufficient. Trade between Martian companies and Earth companies began to make the colony more a peer to, rather than a property of, other EA member countries. In 2150, the EA Senate accepted a non-voting senator from the Mars government as a representative, which allowed the Martian citizens a voice, however limited, in EA matters.

The Mars Colony became much more important in the years that followed, as the discovery of Earth by the Centauri and the acquisition of interstellar travel technologies allowed the Alliance to expand into other solar systems. Those on Mars were the best equipped to handle living on strange worlds, and were the most technically literate in the design and construction of colony domes and cities in alien environments. When the Centauri jumpgate at Earth was deactivated in favor of an Earth-built gate in orbit of Io in 2195, the Mars Colony periodically became a convenient waypoint between Earth and the gate. Its economy boomed. This prompted a tax increase on trade goods in the EA Senate late in 2197, despite the protest of the Martian representative.

As a result of this unequal treatment, the Mars government officially requested its independence from the Earth Alliance on March 3, 2200. The independence request was summarily dismissed by the Senate, and the matter fell by the wayside. But resentment for this treatment from Earth, particularly among those colonists actually born on Mars, did not go away.

Several times over the next twenty years, the Mars Colony requested independence through the Senate or the courts. However, between the occasional small concession from EarthGov and the heavy dependency of the other colonies on Earth, which dampened support among the Mars' only potential allies in the struggle, each attempt ended without success. But by 2225 things were beginning to change. Other colonies, such as Orion and the heavily industrial Proxima, were quickly becoming

Rebellion in the Colonies

In 2253, during the time period of *The Babylon Project*, resentment of Earth's treatment of Mars erupts into violence, as colonists rebel against the food rationing imposed by the EA to keep transports free for construction materials. Threatened by chaos and surrounded by controversy, a divided Senate calls in Earthforce troops to quell the violence. The Senate also installs a provisional government, unseating the territorial government traditionally elected by the colony. This use of force inspires political arguments and division in the Alliance for many years.

This unrest is felt on all of Earth's colony worlds, although the strongest sentiment remains on Mars Colony. Rumors of rebellion and talk of the trouble on Mars (or any colony world) is prevalent in bars and casinos across the Alliance throughout the period of the game. Player groups may find themselves involved with one or more separatist groups during the course of almost any story. Likewise, the EA Senate is always concerned about separatist talk, and keeps an eye out for suspicious activity, occasionally recruiting freelance groups to infiltrate separatist organizations.

The separatist tendencies on Mars reach a head late in 2258, when Mars breaks out in full-scale rebellion. Lightly armed freedom fighters attack a reserve military base outside Olympus Mons before dawn, securing heavy weapons which they then use to assault the capitol building. Troops from Syria Planum and Solis Planum are brought in to quell the fighting, and four days of bloody fighting ensue. Tensions heighten throughout the Alliance, as those with family and friends on Mars worry, unable to contact them and not knowing who is alive and who is dead. In the end the separatists are defeated and peace is temporarily restored, but the cost in lives and morale is high on all sides. The human race has gone to war with itself again; despite the advances in technology and diplomatic relations, we still have not evolved.

self-sufficient, and were becoming receptive to efforts by the Mars government to gain their support in an independence movement.

But the colonies' independence movement would be put on hold over the next few years, as alien concerns forced mankind to put aside internal differences. The Dilgar expansion was drawing humanity into war. With the aid of Earth's forces, the League Non-Aligned Worlds and its allies were able to drive the Dilgar back to their homeworld. A result of this effort was a united Earth Alliance, more powerful than ever—and although many colonial citizens still wished for their independence, official moves were abandoned in favor of the protection that Earthforce offered.

Just as the independence movement was stalled by the Dilgar war, it was again stalled fifteen years later by the Minbari war. The results of the Minbari war were much different, though. The EA fleet was decimated, and EarthGov was left scrambling to protect itself with what little it had left. Taxes were raised all around the Alliance to finance reconstruction and a new fleet. Many of the colonies, their representatives unable to vote in the EA Senate, felt that they were footing an unfair portion of the bill. The issue remains unresolved.

Society

For the most part, day to day life in the Earth Alliance is much like life has always

Society's Cracks

BAB/COM

The underworld is a dangerous place, but it can also be useful for some. Rogue telepaths and others who wish to hide can easily disappear into the underworld, while those looking for illicit or rare goods or services can often find them between society's cracks. Most colonies and stations have undeveloped zones where the poor or the desperate live hidden lives, caught in the gap between the government's inability to dispose of them and unwillingness to pay to ship them elsewhere. On Babylon 5, this area is called "downbelow."

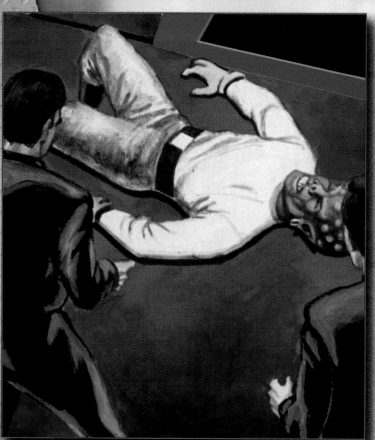

Economics

The standard unit of currency in the Earth Alliance is the Credit (EAcr), with one credit having roughly the buying power of one U.S. dollar today. All of Earth's countries honor the EAcr, and many use it as their sole form of currency. Aboard stations, outposts and colonies it is the only hard currency accepted—aliens generally exchange their own currency for the EAcr upon arrival. However, the most common form of payment is by credit account. There are two types of credit accounts used commonly throughout the Alliance: the named account (equivalent to a bank account with automatic withdrawal, encoded on the identicard); and the credit chit (a card exchanged from hard currency can be used wherever necessary until its value is drawn down to nothing). The credit chit is particularly convenient for travellers. Unfortunately, it can also sometimes be useful to less savory elements of society, and innocent travelers have been known to get entangled in chit scams and snowed over by counterfeiters.

Travel

been. Most EA citizens work normal jobs and earn a living for themselves and their families, trying to make ends meet and raise their children in a healthy environment. If you as a GM are required to make up details about mundane life on Earth or a colony, extrapolate from those details that you know about present-day lifestyles. The biggest differences are in areas of commerce and new technologies.

One important detail about life in the Earth Alliance is the identicard. All EA citizens who enter or leave a member country or territory are given identicards that serve as identification papers, credit cards, passports, and security keys. Aliens staying in EA territory for any length of time are also given cards. When traveling, the identicard is a lifeline. If lost, stolen or destroyed it can be difficult if not impossible to get around. Much like passports of today, they guarantee certain rights to the holder, and are an essential part of travel.

Transportation on Earth itself remains much the same as it is today, albeit faster. Sub-orbital transports make it comparatively trivial to get to any destination with a major airport, and super and hypersonic transports make transcontinental travel as quick and easy as a present-day commute between Los Angeles and San Francisco. Travel between Earth and other planets in the solar system is accomplished by atmospheric shuttles to Station Prime, in Earth's orbit. From there, non-atmospheric shuttles carry passengers and cargo to other destinations within the system, primarily Mars Colony, the Ganymede outpost and the transfer point near Io. From the Io point, ships that have outsystem destinations can access the jumpgate and enter hyperspace. Almost any space ship can use a jumpgate—no special drives or equipment are necessary beyond those required for normal space, with the exception of navigation equipment capable of following hyperspace beacons.

Crime

As noted above, there are always people who are willing to make a living without following the rules. This underworld crosses all societies and all races. It is a world of treachery and danger, with the only loyalty being that of cold, hard cash.

The most common types of crimes on planetary surfaces are the same ones that affect any big city. In space, where governmental control is often spread thin at best, piracy and smuggling are the most dominant crimes. With a small ship and a few bribes in the right pockets, a creative pilot can get in and out of places with no one the wiser.

Smugglers transport many commodities. Weapons are always a popular choice, as are fenced identicards and credit chits. Information, once stolen, can also be a valuable item. Drugs are a problem, the chief trade being Dust, a highly-addictive hallucinogenic manufactured inexpensively in space which is also rumored to have telepathic side effects (though such rumors are unproven).

Telepaths and the Psi-Corps

Humans born with the telepathic gift do not realize it until the ability manifests itself, usually during adolescence. Sometimes the telepath's powers awaken gradually, without obvious signs, other times they appear in a sudden, violent eruption called a mindquake that can be felt by those nearby. Either way, once people start to notice the telepath's ability, he or she comes to feel isolated from friends, family, and associates who do not understand, and often fear, the effects of telepathy.

Telepaths were seen as weird and dangerous for many years after the emergence of psionic powers in Humans. Sensing this discomfort, most felt ostracized. As a re-

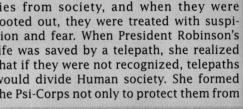

The Psi Corps

The Corps maintains a friendly image, and is glad to answer questions of all who are curious about its operations, as per Earth Alliance regulations. Advertisements in print and on vid feeds note that the Corps is "everywhere, for your convenience." Early in 2256, a scandal breaks out, as some accuse the Corps' vid advertisements of containing subliminal advertising. Nothing is ever proven.

sult, telepaths generally hid their capabilities from society, and when they were rooted out, they were treated with suspicion and fear. When President Robinson's life was saved by a telepath, she realized that if they were not recognized, telepaths would divide Human society. She formed the Psi-Corps not only to protect them from

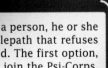

Choices for Telepaths

When telepathic ability manifests in a person, he or she is given two choices under the law. A telepath that refuses either legal option can be fined and jailed. The first option, and that chosen by most telepaths, is to join the Psi-Corps. The ease of finding the Corps centers—and its positive image—make this a very attractive option for most. The other option is to take a series of drugs, informally called "sleepers." Sleepers inhibit telepathic ability, thus allowing the telepath to lead a relatively normal life without the usual mistrust given to unlicensed telepaths. Unfortunately, they also have side effects in many people, making them less mentally acute and somewhat depressed.

A third option, not taken by many, is to go underground. Rogue telepaths are hunted zealously by the Psi-Cops and many other Earth Alliance officials, so this is not an attractive option for most, especially those with families or other close emotional ties.

society and give them a place to feel that they belong, but also to protect society from telepaths.

The Psi-Corps today is viewed by most with respect. Thanks to strict laws governing the use of telepathy and a vigorous public relations campaign, the Corps is looked on as an aid to society and afforded a measure of acceptance not given to early telepaths. The Corps also maintains a lively recruiting program, with offices and testing centers in every major community in the Alliance, for the convenience of those curious about telepathy and so that emerging telepaths can find a place to learn what is happening to them.

The Corps' headquarters is located in London, England on Earth. The administrative offices and office of records are at this site, as well as the main training and evaluation center. There are also major training and evaluation centers in New York, Tokyo and Moscow on Earth, as well as at the Olympus Mons dome on Mars and the main dome on Proxima III.

While the main offices of the Corps are on Earth, the real work of the Corps goes on elsewhere. The Office of the Psi-Cops, those powerful telepaths charged with the enforcement of telepathic regulations, is based in the Solis Planum dome on Mars, and a secret research and experimentation base is located near the Syria Planum dome as well. While most who know that this base

exists believe that it is for the training of Psi-Cops, its real purpose is known only to a very few. Its research deals with the improvement of telepaths and the development of new forms of psionic powers among Humans.

Joining the Corps

New telepaths are taken to the base nearest their home to be tested. Any telepath that registers a probable ability of at least P1 is inducted into the Corps upon the conclusion of testing and transferred to one of the major training centers. Most inductees are entering puberty, at age ten to fourteen, so their schooling is taken over by the Corps. They are given free room, board and tuition while their capabilities are assessed and honed. Those who are older when their abilities awaken are trained by the Corps and given jobs either with the Corps or with a company that offers a partnership labor program.

A young telepath is assigned a mentor— generally an older student—during his or her first year in the Corps training center. During this time, he or she is taught the values of the Corps and given a new home. The transition can be jarring, but telepaths feel more welcome in the Corps than anywhere else once their powers have emerged.

After a telepath has completed training and schooling, he or she is tested for a license. When the telepath entered the Corps, he or she was tested and given an initial "P" rating. At the conclusion of training, an official final test is given. The growth of the telepath's capabilities through adolescence, honed through training and practice, generally results in a higher final rating. Taking into account general knowledge of the laws and regulations affecting the use of telepathy, the telepath is given a Licensed Rating (on the same "P" scale) officially sanctioned by the EA.

Life in the Psi-Corps

The Corps has several branches, and telepaths of many different levels serve in each branch. The four main branches are the Alliance Corps; the Commercial Corps;

Telepathic Review

One of the most dreaded events in a telepath's routine is the telepathic review. Once a month, each member of Psi-Corps must go before a Psi-Cop for a performance review, where his or her past performance is evaluated while under the Cop's scan. Any improper acts can be grounds for reprimand, reassignment, or even banishment from the Corps (and enrollment in the sleeper program). Some telepaths on remote stations or new colonies don't have to be reviewed but once every year or two, but no telepath is ever overlooked if they've done anything that raises the Cops' suspicions. If your player character telepaths are performing illegal acts, it will almost certainly be discovered in their telepathic reviews.

the Training Corps; and the Psi-Cops. When a telepath is training, he or she selects one of the branches for a year's internship. If the internship goes well, the telepath is assigned to a career of duty in that branch upon completion of training.

The Alliance Corps are telepaths assigned to duties within EarthGov. These include diplomatic assignments, negotiations, investigations and the execution of EA penal sentences. Many of the assignments are easier than those in other branches, particularly the diplomatic assignments, but this is balanced by the most arduous duty a telepath can perform: the verification of mindwipe. Duty rotations are short, though, giving the Alliance Corps telepath the opportunity to work with many people over his or her career.

The Commercial Corps is the branch that contracts out to businesspeople for the mediation of corporate negotiations. To serve as more than a functionary in this branch, a telepath must have a rating of at least P5. For the telepath, mediation is simply a matter of scanning the surface thoughts of one or both parties (depending on the arrangements) and verifying the truth of statements made, helping the parties come to a mutually beneficial agreement.

The Training Corps is the branch that administrates the day-to-day business of the Corps and trains and evaluates new telepaths as they are discovered. This is the branch that maintains the offices, public relations campaigns and training centers, and handles the daily operations of the Corps. Telepaths of all ratings serve in this branch, although teachers are required to have a P10 rating in order to train other telepaths in the use of their abilities, and members of the upper administration generally have at least a P11 rating.

The most influential branch of the Corps is the Psi-Cops. They are responsible for ensuring that all Human telepaths follow the laws and regulations that govern the use of their ability. They perform genealogical studies to find likely telepaths and lead them into the Corps, conduct monthly reviews of the performance of other telepaths, monitor those using the sleeper drugs, and hunt down those who refuse all legal options. The Psi-Cops are invested with great power, but also with great responsibility. Whenever a telepath causes harm to another Human or an alien, the Psi-Cops are the ones who take the blame. While telepaths of all ratings may serve in this branch, only those rated P11 or P12 can become actual Psi-Cop officers.

Laws Concerning Telepaths

Telepaths live under strict regulations as to what they can and cannot do with their powers. The right to privacy is one of the highest tenets in the Earth Alliance, and uncontrolled telepathy represents a great threat to that privacy. Therefore, the EA set down a number of laws at the founding of the Psi-Corps to ensure that both telepaths' and non-telepaths' rights are preserved. While it is almost impossible for a telepath to avoid picking up extremely strong emotions, active scanning on the part of the telepath is a violation of privacy.

The cardinal rule on which all laws regarding telepaths are founded is that telepaths cannot violate the privacy of another's thoughts. Thus, scanning is prohibited unless the subject or someone legally empowered to act for the subject (a family member or power of attorney in most cases where someone is unable to given permission for themselves, or occasionally the courts for investigative or medical purposes) has given permission for the scan.

Business negotiations are routinely conducted with a member of the Commercial Corps present when one or more of the parties wishes to ensure the truth of the prospective partners. While it is not legal to force another to agree to a scan, many reputable corporations will not agree to negotiate without a telepath present. Usually both pay a fee, and truth is assured on all sides.

Telepathic scans are severely restricted in courts of law. Since one cannot be made to testify against oneself, involuntary telepathic scans are not admissible as evidence against a defendant—and as just noted, they are generally not even legal. Likewise, as evidence for a defendant, a scan is considered secondhand information and is not usually admissible. The courts may grant exceptions to these rules, but only in unusual circumstances, when a witness is unable to otherwise appear.

In many respects, telepathy is as much a burden as it is a gift. A telepath must always be aware of others and respect society's boundaries. Telepaths must work to maintain that separation at all times.

They must learn to live with the random thoughts and emotions of everyone near them constantly echoing in their minds day and night. It is a burden that some, unfortunately, cannot handle.

Section 2: Alien Races

Human explorers, merchants, and diplomats have come into contact with scores of alien races, and scores more are known to exist. This section not only details the major alien races, but also covers some of the other major players in the known galaxy, including the League of Non-Aligned Worlds and the Vorlons.

Narns

The Narns are a race on the rise. After their overthrow of the Centauri, they vowed to never allow anyone else to enslave them. To achieve this end they went on the offensive, claiming worlds near their own and wresting others from their former masters. Now their cause has vaulted them into the midst of the major interstellar powers, a race whose rise is powered by their own thirst for vengeance.

Government

The government of Narn is the Kha'ri, a ruling body both political and religious in nature. Hand picked, members of the Kha'ri are the heart and spirit of the new Narn, firm in their resolve to never again be slaves.

The Kha'ri consists of eight circles. The First Circle, consisting of eight Narns, rules the entire Regime, handing down directives to Homeworld and all of the Narn colonies and outposts. The Second Circle is the advisory circle, with two advisors for each Counselor in the First Circle. The Third Circle is the diplomatic circle, made up of the senior ambassadors to other worlds and colonies. Twelve Third Circle Counselors split their time between active duty diplomatic posts and Kha'ri sessions on Homeworld, depending on the need for

Narn Leaders — **BAB/COM**

During the time period of the game there is division in the First Circle of the Kha'Ri on how external affairs are to be handled. One faction, led by Counselor T'Bar, espouses the idea that open relations with other races will benefit the Regime. The other, led by Counselor G'Ron, cites the Centauri occupation and holds to the view that other races will do the same if given the chance. G'Ron's faction does not specifically oppose relations with other races—as long as such relations further the end of learning as much about them as possible, to prepare the Narn for battle against them when it inevitably occurs.

Ambassadors. The Fourth Circle is the military circle, a new tradition for the Narns, but more important to them than ever given their past occupation. The Fifth and Sixth circles are the continental and regional governments and military commanders of the planet and colonies. The Seventh and Eighth Circles are the scholars' circles, whose interest is in the histories and traditions of the Narn people.

The first four Circles are permanently in session in the capital city of G'Kamazad, while the Fifth through Eighth Circles only meet periodically, normally performing their duties at their own continental and regional capital cities. While all circles are formally part of the Kha'Ri, the term commonly refers only to the four circles that reside in the capital.

The members of the Kha'ri are selected by sponsorship from within, are voted in by the First Circle, and serve until voted out by the majority vote of their circle or one lower than their own. Sponsorship into a circle is allowed only from a Counselor in the Fifth or lower Circle. At present only those who led in the overthrow of the Centauri serve on the four higher circles, and only those who distinguished themselves during the revolution serve in the First and Second Circles. All Kha'Ri members must

Narn Diplomats

The Narns have no Ambassadors on Centauri Prime, but they do maintain relations with many of the other races during the time period of the game. Ambassador Ta'Kal is the liaison with the Minbari, assigned to Sh'lekk'tha. Ambassador Ta'Lar is the Narn representative on Earth. The Narn representative to the League of Non-Aligned Worlds is Ambassador So'Tal.

In 2256, when Babylon 5 goes online, Ambassador G'Kar takes on the post of liaison there.

have years of religious training as well as training in their specific functions, as they are also religious leaders of the various worlds where the individual members live, much as the elders of the older tribes guided their families in the past.

The Fifth and Sixth Circles of the Kha'Ri fill judicial as well as administrative roles in the government. Although criminal enforcement largely rests with the families of

as fair as they can be, but not perfect. No crime is assumed, but once a crime is evident an accused is assumed guilty until proven innocent by fact. False accusations are punished by the sentence that would be given for the crime, however, so they are fairly rare.

There are several different sentences that the Kha'Ri can pronounce, depending on the severity of the crime and the circumstances surrounding it. The least severe sentence is the Cha'lar right to property, in which the offender must release to the victim property equal to the amount damaged in the crime. The next sentence, and one of the most frequently assigned, is the Chol'tar period of servitude, a sentence in which the offender must devote time in servitude to pay for the crime. The length of this servitude is decided by the tribunal and can either be in service of the victim, or in service of the state, as the tribunal decides. Finally, the most severe sentence is the Chon'kar, a blood oath against the offender. This takes the form of equal injury to the crime. In extreme cases, the Chon'kar can be extended to the family or friends of the criminal, and the obligation to carry out the sentence is taken on by the entire family of the victim. Since there is barely a Narn alive who has not seen a death in the family at Centauri hands, there are many Chon'kars pending on Centauri families.

crime victims, a tribunal of Fifth and Sixth Circle Kha'Ri officials handles sentencing (or determines the validity of sentences in those cases where action has already been taken by the victim's family). Tribunals are

Military

The Narn military is under the direct command of the Fourth Circle, whose Counselors are known as the Warleaders. The military performs both combat and police functions. The Warleaders each have control a domain, with the generals and commanders in the Fifth and Sixth Circles under their direct command. The chain of command is strictly respected. Advice and counsel from the lower circles is given to the Warleaders, but the final orders are theirs alone.

Narn ships mix technologies from many different races, stolen or bought during the occupation. Older ships were often a hodgepodge of parts that could be rigged to work together. Now, the Narn war machine has had time to define itself, and the current Narn fleet hearkens back to the nautical

Narn Officials

Aside from Third Circle ambassadors, members of the inner Kha'Ri (the First through Fourth Circles) rarely if ever leave homeworld, and those who do only leave on official business. They often hire "Ri'Lan," civilian Narns, to execute sentences against Narns who leave homeworld or against aliens who have committed crimes on a Narn citizen. These agents, sometimes called "executors" by outsiders, have authority from the Kha'Ri to carry out sentences as long as it will not cause an interspecies "incident." It is a dangerous job, but for a young, adventurous Narn it's a great chance to travel and meet other races in the cause of justice.

ships that took Narns across the Equatorial Sea. The mainstay of the Narn fleet is the *Th'Nor*-class heavy cruiser, but it is quickly being surpassed by the newer, more powerful *Mak'Aroon*-class heavy dreadnaught. Narn fighters are compact and heavy, capable of both space and atmospheric flight. This results in great ruggedness, but also makes them slower and less maneuverable than the main-line fighters of the other major races.

Colonies

The Narns, unlike most of the established races, have very little in the way of colonial politics. Their colonies and outposts have all been established very recently, in the few decades since the end of the Centauri occupation. Most of their colonies are worlds that they have claimed from the Centauri. These serve mainly military purposes such as surveillance and border establishment, and few of them have any civilian population other than that necessary to uphold the colony. These listening posts are mostly given military designations rather than names related to the stars they orbit. A non-aggression treaty between the Narn and Centauri signed in the mid 2230's divided the border between their space into 40 "quadrants," which defined each territory. The main Narn listening post is in Quadrant 37, with a heavy trading post in Quadrant 14. The Q14 colony became much more of a civilian operation during the 2240's than the Kha'Ri had originally intended—its hyperspace proximity to several of the League worlds allowed it to become one of the Narns' biggest trade relations colonies. Narns are willing to sell the technology and equipment that they have to anyone, for the right price, and Colony Q14 has a reputation as an excellent source for hard-to-find or even restricted merchandise.

Other than military posts, the Narns have taken over three worlds that were formerly Centauri subjects. Two other Centauri subject worlds threw off the Narn once the Centauri were gone, returning to the League of Non-Aligned Worlds. Although the Centauri were harsh, the Narn Regime are strict taskmasters in some ways worse than their former masters. They rule their worlds with

The Narn Military · BAB/COM

Warleader G'Sten, one of the greatest heroes of the liberation from the Centauri, commands the heavy space fleets of Narn. Warleader Na'Dath controls the aerospace pilot and fighter forces of the fleet. The sea fleet is under the command of Warleader G'Ralan. The fierce ground troops are under the hand of Warleader Tu'Kar. The entire Fourth Circle sets policies and makes the tactical decisions that affect the Narn military, but these four are technically the top of the chain of command in each of their arenas. Orders that are signed by anyone else are usually obeyed only after approval of the correct commander.

an iron hand, punishing with death anything that they feel is a crime.

Society

Narn society is based on the traditional familial structure that was prevalent before

Narn Soldiers · BAB/COM

For many Narns, the only way to ensure that they do not fall into slavery again is to contribute their services to the Narn military. An individual's own life is less important than the good of the Narn culture, and giving that life in the service of Narn is a very honorable and noble way to live, and, if necessary, to die. Soldiers come from all walks of life, serve their time, and then return to Homeworld to raise their families. They are typically assigned posts compatible with their individual strengths. Narn ground troops are usually strong and physically able, trained in one or more weapons or in hand-to-hand combat. Narn pilots, like those of other races, are highly coordinated and able to think on their feet, trained to fly in both active combat and passive patrols. Officers are usually a little stronger than average, but are also able to think and react under pressure.

During the time period of the game, the Narns have settled down a bit, content to keep the colonies that they have and build their power base. In 2252, vessels from the Quadrant 37 outpost begin "maneuvers" into what the Centauri claim to be their space, starting a new round of "cold war" type conflicts culminating in a Narn attack on Rahgesh III in early 2257. At the end of 2257, the Q37 outpost vanishes without a trace as the Centauri obliterate it.

These events escalate, culminating in the destruction of the colony in Quadrant 14 in 2259, prompting the Narns to declare war against the Centauri at the very end of the time period outlined in this game.

the occupation. Many early records were destroyed during the Centauri reign, but the religious leaders and teachers kept as many of the tales of the past alive as possible.

The new Kha'ri is more formal than the ruling circles of the past, but it attempts to be as faithful to its ancestors as possible.

Family life on Narn is in many ways like life in other civilizations. Narn males and females mate one-to-one for life, with the female joining the family of the male when she chooses her mate. Narns typically have one to three young at a time. The female carries the child until birth, after which the male cares for the young in his pouch for the first three months of life. Because of this, Narn young are often called "pouchlings."

Teaching and training of children once they have emerged from the pouch falls to the teachers of the Kha'Ri. From the first, Narn children are taught of their culture and of the oppression of the Centauri. The Narns are adamant that they never again will be slaves to another race, and they are passing that on to future generations.

The history of Narn society has been largely preserved by the Seventh and Eighth Circles of the Kha'Ri. The Centauri destroyed many of the academic centers and libraries during the occupation, but due to their own beliefs left many of the places of worship standing. Thus, many of the historical writings of the Narn prophets still survive, and are very complete in some ways.

Those Narns who still believe in a higher power believe that the words of the prophets are the guides to the truth and the will of that higher power. The greatest prophets are G'Lan, whose writings are so ancient that it is forgotten when they were written, G'Ston, who lived 1500 standard years ago, and G'Quan, who lived about 1000 standard years ago. G'Lan is the prophet most often followed, although the followers of G'Quan form a growing movement. The Book of G'Quan describes some very unusual and dark happenings during his life which followers of the other prophets sometimes doubt, and for which there is very little historical corroboration.

Centauri

In the aftermath of their war with the Narn and the near-dissolution of their empire, the Centauri are a race in decline. But even as a shadow of its former glory, the Lion of the Galaxy remains a powerful interstellar force, and a major diplomatic and cultural influence on the other powers of the known universe.

Government

While the great Centauri Republic is not what it once was, it is still a government with a long tradition. The Noble Houses together stand on centuries of tradition and wisdom, and their Centaurum is a body whose politics are unmatched anywhere in known space. Its leader, the Emperor, is the spiritual head of the people and the authoritative leader of the government. The Emperor acts for the good of his people and the glory of the Empire. His word is the law of the land. His advisors, the Centaurum, have no power of law on most matters and may only override him with a three-quar-

ter vote of its members, an unlikely proposition under most circumstances.

The Centaurum, in addition to its other duties, carries out the will of the Emperor in all things. Day to day economic matters are handled by the Emperor's Committee on Finance. General political and diplomatic matters are handled in the chambers of the Centaurum, to avoid troubling the Emperor with sundry details.

Members of the Centaurum (called Senators) are elected or appointed according to the laws of the regions they represent. Centauri are eligible for the Centaurum only in representation of the region in which they were born, not that in which they later come to live. Ties to the noble house of a region are usually the only way to get elected. Females are not technically barred from the Centaurum, but there has never been a female Senator.

Local Courts made up of the members of regional noble houses govern local regions of the Centauri Prime and colony worlds. The Senator for each region is nominally the leader of the Local Court, but his Magistrate usually rules in his place while he maintains his presence in the Royal Court at the Emperor's Palace.

Normally, the Emperor is succeeded by his son or the nearest heir when he passes

Centauri Military Leaders

Military actions are ordered by the Emperor and his military advisors. Chief among them are Grand Fleet Admiral Dromo and Guardsman Elite Tavastani. Like the Emperor's position, these top military roles are ancestral, and both of these advisors are from noble houses that predate the even Emperor's own. Their positions are considered to be unimpeachable and of the highest honor.

The Centauri field the most powerful interstellar fleet of the younger races, in both number and capabilities. Their fighters, though built for both atmospheric and space flight, are surprisingly agile, and their pilots are known to push the capabilities of the craft when closing for the kill—even if it means sustaining enough g-forces to harm them. Their capital ships are an old but reliable design, capable of competing and winning head-to-head against any of the other younger races' ships.

Part of the Centauri advantage is their technology. The Centauri are the youngest race to develop and use gravimetric drives on their capital ships, and although such systems are a costly power drain in combat (and a great liability if the drive systems are hit), they often provide the slight advantage that can make the difference in a fight. Despite the fact that the Centauri have been engaged in almost constant warfare for decades, they have managed to keep their use of gravimetric drives a secret, which they guard jealously against discov-

on. Sometimes, however, there is not a clear heir, either because the Emperor had no offspring, or because he had too many offspring. In the event that he dies with no clear heir, the Centaurum appoints the new Emperor from its ranks—with the guidance of the gods, of course.

ery by the Minbari and the other younger races.

The Centauri Royal Guardsmen make up the Republic's ground forces. Originally, the Guardsmen were the Emperor's personal guards. As the Republic expanded, however, their role grew as well, covering military ground operations on rebellious colony worlds. At the height of the Republic, the Guardsmen also began to take on the role of law enforcement within the Republic itself, becoming not only the militia but the police as well. The uniform of a Guardsman commands great respect among the average Centauri populace.

The CRG is made up of three main branches. The Centauri Guardsmen are the police force that enforce the laws of the Republic. The Military Guardsmen are those who perform the military actions required by the Emperor. The Royal Guardsmen are those who guard the Palace and the person of the Emperor.

Centauri Guardsmen are generally those who were neither smart nor ambitious enough to find another place in life. They are respected as a body, but individual guards are usually ignored as another piece of landscape except when needed. The average Centauri Guardsman is a less-than-average intellect who may or may not be trained to use the weapon that comes with the uniform. The Military and Royal Guardsmen, however, are usually well coordinated and quick, with good training in many forms of combat.

Colonial Politics

The Centauri no longer rule any subject races—the colony worlds that the Republic still controls are those that were uninhabited prior to Centauri colonization. The chief industry of the Centauri Republic is tourism. As the oldest of the younger races, they have a longer recorded history than any of the others, and unlike the Minbari they are willing to allow others to see the wonders of their Republic.

The two oldest Centauri colonies, Centauri Beta I and Immolan V, are centers of tourism open to many of the other races (Narns excluded, of course). There are also several agricultural and manufacturing colonies such as the farming colony at Rahgesh III and the industrial colony on Tolonius VII. The Centauri also maintain a presence against the Narns at outposts along the border between the two spaces. The outpost at Quadrant 27 keeps a watch on Narn space along with the colony in Quadrant 1.

Centauri colonies are governed as provinces of their own, with a local noble house that rules much as a house on Centauri Prime would rule. Some of these houses, such as House Toulani on Beta I, are old, established houses that moved from Centauri Prime to their new provinces for one reason or another, while others, such as House Maro on Tolonius VII, are newly established houses that rose up from one or more of the younger siblings of noble houses during the formation of the colony.

Society

Centauri society is heavily based on the traditions and history of the Republic. The noble houses are the patrons of the people, controlling the economic and governmental interests of the planet, colonies and regional principalities. They hold the highest levels of respect in society. A member of a noble house is an object of respect to

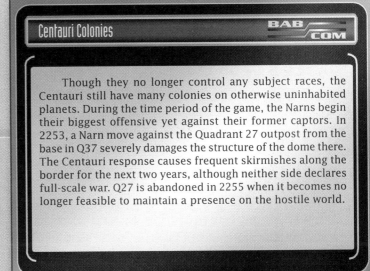

Centauri Colonies

Though they no longer control any subject races, the Centauri still have many colonies on otherwise uninhabited planets. During the time period of the game, the Narns begin their biggest offensive yet against their former captors. In 2253, a Narn move against the Quadrant 27 outpost from the base in Q37 severely damages the structure of the dome there. The Centauri response causes frequent skirmishes along the border for the next two years, although neither side declares full-scale war. Q27 is abandoned in 2255 when it becomes no longer feasible to maintain a presence on the hostile world.

The Emperor during the time period of *The Babylon Project* is Emperor Turhan. Unlike his father and grandfather, Turhan believes that the time has come to make peace with the Narns, and has gone out of his way to grant concessions to them. This has made him very unpopular with some among the Royal Court, and he is always on the lookout for assassination attempts. His allies, however, are stronger than his enemies, and his faction firmly believes that the way to make the most of the future is to open relations with other races, rather than to subjugate them. It is little known outside of the court, but Turhan's first act upon the death of his father was to call off an invasion of Earth that would have proven costly to both sides.

Turhan's only son, Beyon, is tragically killed in a boating accident in 2252. This throws the court into turmoil, as it then leaves no clear heir to the throne. Several houses immediately start planning to have their candidate named Emperor.

In 2253, Turhan evades another assassination attempt, which turns out to have been funded by the Narns. Most of the conspirators, from House Bleda and House Corono, are beheaded as traitors once this is discovered. His Prime Minister, Malachi, escapes the blade in 2254 when a faction supported by House Madrin tries to take the position.

Turhan's health begins failing him in late 2258, and in 2259 he leaves Centauri Prime to visit Babylon 5, where he dies at the end of the time frame of this game.

all who were born in his region. Friends among the houses are a treasured commodity. No amount of work or talent will move an ambitious Centauri up in the world as much as a noble birth. The power of a noble house also carries with it a responsibility to those over which the house claims rule. Nobles are expected to be accountable to the people, and to live as examples of tradition and nobility. Those who do not sometimes lose their position to other, more deserving Centauri. Despite the occasional machinations and heavy politics in the upper regions of Centauri society, this mandate is almost always honored.

The Centauri are unique among the civilized races in that females, although physically similar to males, hold no official positions in society. Males are the leaders of society—they alone serve in the military, and all physically demanding jobs are held by men. Women are kept as a protected resource, nurturers and teachers for the young and old. They work behind the scenes, and their influence is through their training of future generations. Women who are ambitious in politics or industrial circles are not unheard of (though no woman has yet sat in the Centaurum), but they usually find better opportunities beyond the borders of the Republic.

The Centauri also have faith in their gods. Any individual of sufficient fame or public value might someday be deified. Some of these gods watch over the entire Republic, while other, lesser gods watch over smaller portions of Centauri domains. Many families have household gods—those members of the family who have gone before and now watch over their descendants.

The first gods and goddesses, which date back to the ancient wars against the Xon, have ornate temples built in their names adjoining the Emperor's Palace, and are believed to be watching still. There are over fifty major gods and goddesses, with temples in major cities throughout the Republic. The temple to Gon on Immolan V is widely recognized as the most beautiful building ever constructed by a sentient race, and draws millions of pilgrims and tourists each year.

With the rich tradition of thousands of years of history and the importance of family lineage to the Centauri, it is not unusual for marriages among the noble houses to be arranged early in childhood. This practice used to be common among all Centauri, but in recent years it has fallen out of favor in all but the nobility.

The value of romance is not lost on the Centauri people, however. Marriage for love is just as important to the Republic as arranged marriage. After any arranged marriage, many Centauri Nobles choose to marry again. It is not uncommon for a Centauri male to have two or three wives, all of whom serve or love him. This practice, while common all over the Republic, has been losing favor of late. Many Centauri now choose to keep only one wife, which has resulted in a rise in the rate of marriage dissolutions unseen before.

Telepaths

The Centauri use their advanced knowledge of genetics to trace the gene that controls psionics and ensure that the gift does not get out of hand. Now, gifted children are identified before birth, and are raised by a noble house, cared for and trained to handle the responsibility and power that will come when the talent manifests itself. Centauri males and some females with the gift are telepathic, able to read the minds of others like the telepaths of other races. Other females (but never males) instead become prophetic when their ability manifests. These "seers" cannot read thoughts, but have the ability to "read" the future. They see images of what is to come with surprising clarity.

When a telepath's abilities emerge, he or she must join the Telepath's Guild. The Guild is an organization of telepaths that hires out among the Centauri to provide a variety of services. The Guild is a commercial venture, but approved and supervised by the government. Telepaths may not be hired by non-Centauri, or be hired for use against the Emperor or any member of the Centaurum. Those who violate that rule may be fined or banished from the Guild (with their powers suppressed), or even imprisoned. Much like the Psi-Corps, Guild telepaths undergo routine performance evaluations on a regular basis to ensure that they comply with Guild regulations. They are also subject to probes at any time at the request of a member of the Centaurum.

Many Centauri, gifted or not, at some point in their lives have a limited sort of foresight—they foresee the manner of their deaths in a dream. Not all Centauri have this dream, and many of those who do don't remember much of it or recognize its significance. This is often a blessing in disguise, though, because many who come to know the circumstances of their deaths are haunted by it.

While all Centauri have this potential to see a bit of the future, true gifts of prophecy appear exclusively in women. The Em-

Li, Goddess of Passion

The most popular member of the Centauri pantheon is Li, the Goddess of Passion. According to myth, Li lived in the time of the wars with the Xon. She was a vocal advocate of passionate mating and child-rearing, constantly encouraging both large families and promiscuous behavior. Though branded a woman of perversion and even persecuted during her own lifetime, her reputation improved after her death as the Centauri realized the value of her teachings—after centuries of war, the Centauri population grew even as the Xon shrank. This frenetic rate of reproduction, modern Centauri scholars now believe, was one of the deciding factors in the Centauri success over the Xon.

Li was granted her godhood late in the Xon war period. Her message of the importance of mating and passion has been embraced warmly by the Centauri, and though such large families are not so much in vogue today, she remains one of the greatest historical and religious figures of the Centauri.

peror and his court are respected for the power over the people that they hold, but those given the most respect on a day-to-day basis are the seers, those women whose gift of prophecy is strong. They represent the truth unquestioningly, and the information that they can give to the Republic is

The Telepath's Guild

In addition to being bound by the rules of the Guild, telepaths cannot violate the laws of the Republic. However, members of the Centaurum have, at times, been known to bend the rules to get something done. In 2254, a telepath by the name of Vetrello Motro was caught scanning the mind of Senator Foresi after a meeting of the Centaurum. His life was forfeit until he confessed to performing the scan under orders from Senator Mareau. House Mareau was asked to resign from the Centaurum in the aftermath, with House Lorem taking its place.

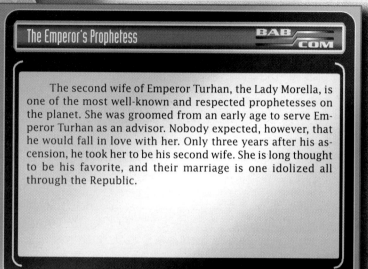

The second wife of Emperor Turhan, the Lady Morella, is one of the most well-known and respected prophetesses on the planet. She was groomed from an early age to serve Emperor Turhan as an advisor. Nobody expected, however, that he would fall in love with her. Only three years after his ascension, he took her to be his second wife. She is long thought to be his favorite, and their marriage is one idolized all through the Republic.

on a long tradition of order and knowledge and guided by the words of Valen and the Nine, their government and social structure have remained stable for almost one thousand years. It has been said that they, like the Centauri, were a race in decline, but the Earth War proved that the Minbari are still a major power in the galaxy. It also showed them the need to adapt their ways to the coming of the newer races. With the death of Dukhat, the Grey Council's leader, Minbari society is beginning a new period of change. Many, however, refuse to acknowledge this.

Government

The Minbari are led according to the structure laid down by Valen. The Grey Council and its leader are the head of the Minbari people. They oversee the entire Federation, and as such do not rule from one location. Instead, to rule all equally they travel the stars aboard the War Cruiser *Valen'tha*. The Minbari people may speak freely to any Council member at any time, but they leave the affairs of the rulers to the Council.

The Council consists of nine members, three from each caste. Decisions are made by consensus. When a member must be replaced due to loss or (very rarely) expulsion, the replacement is chosen by the Council from among the appropriate caste.

The Council rules in the best interests of the Minbari people. In making decisions, it draws upon the wisdom and opinions of other Minbari and, on occasion, the counsel of wise members of other races. One of their greatest sources of wisdom is the prophet Valen, who founded the council. His writings form much of the basis for law and society in Minbari life.

No council this small could rule a multi-planetary populace alone, however. Much of the day-to-day work of the Federation is done by the Worker Caste, whose administrators and technicians devote their lives to the service of the Minbari people. Political ambition is very rare among the Minbari, so posts are granted by merit, not political ties. As such, there is little in the way of intrigue in the Minbari government.

worth more than anything a mere governmental official can do. They do not have any formal organization, choosing to go where they will, and they answer to no-one. A visit from a prophetess is a great gift.

Minbari

Next to the enigmatic and reclusive Vorlons, the Minbari are the oldest race currently active in this part of the galaxy. Based

The members of the Grey Council are a secretive group who shield their identities and activities from outsiders. However, it is imperative that any Minbari citizen who wishes to contact the Council is able to do so. Therefore, petitioners to speak with a Council member can contact the *Valen'tha* and one of the Council will respond.

On all official business, Council Members wear gray robes with deep hoods—a uniform of sorts that shows that the Nine are a united circle. They make their rulings from the Council chamber, where they stand together in a circle to discuss issues at hand and develop their consensus.

Difficult disputes between Minbari are rare, and most of those that do occur are resolved peacefully and quietly between the parties directly involved. Still, there are times when it is impossible to resolve something quietly, and other times when a Minbari becomes "mentally ill" and willfully commits crimes. The Council appoints Justicars to handle these infrequent problems. These Justicars are invested with great responsibility, and are chosen by the Council after a long investigation proves to the Nine that the Justicar is able to perform the duties. They roam the Federation, hearing cases and deciding the fate of those who are guilty of crime. In exchange for their services, they are given room and board wherever they go, so that they need not be distracted by the logistics and hardships of travel.

Minbari who are found guilty of intentional crimes are thought to be mentally ill, not evil. The Minbari people are committed to the reformation of these ill individuals, but they must be respectful of the rest of the populace. The ill are given sentences on the Minbari Penal colony Taralenn II, which is run much like the prisons of any other race, with the exception that it is constantly under military guard. Those who are not violent to themselves or others govern

Minbari Justicars

BAB/COM

Since the death of Dukhat and the unsatisfactory end of the Earth War, more Minbari than ever before have become violent or criminal. The instance of crimes against Minbari and other aliens has increased immensely. There was such a need for new Justicars that in 2249, the Council appointed an Entil'chan "Justicar One" to manage the appointment of the new officials.

the colony, under the supervision of healers and telepaths who try to correct the problems of the residents.

Military

The military caste oversees all operations of defense for the Minbari worlds. All three castes own and use cruisers and fight-

Colonial Politics

Minbari colonies are valued no less highly than their homeworld. The Grey Council travels among them, neither neglecting nor giving preference to any one world. The governments of each world are identical, with Worker Caste functionaries providing the bulk of the day-to-day management and policy set directly by the Grey Council. Only Sh'lekk'tha, the primary diplomatic colony, is governed differently. Given the need there to interact with other races, most of the administrative tasks are performed by members of the Religious Caste, who are better suited to deal with and teach aliens. The Military Caste oversees police and judicial functions there as elsewhere, however, and many thousands of Worker Caste members do attend to mundane aspects of the colony's functions.

Society

A Minbari is defined by his or her caste and clan. From early in life, Minbari are taught and trained by the Religious Caste teachers in their birth clan. Upon reaching the age at which they must take control of their own lives, they choose a caste and clan to which they will belong for the rest of their lives. A Minbari's family is the clan, while the caste is his or her occupation.

The Military Caste is responsible for the safekeeping of the Minbari people. They are the guardians and protectors, fighting against all threats from other races. Military Caste members tend to be physically capable and well-trained.

The Religious Caste is responsible for the spiritual care and intellectual nurturing of the Minbari people. They are the teachers and priests, singers and dreamers of the race and guardians of the words of the prophets. They tend to be well-suited to dealing with others, capable of comforting and nurturing the culture.

The Worker Caste is responsible for maintaining all of the tasks that keep a multi-planet Federation running. They perform the tasks that are necessary to keep everything running, each according to his or her particular talents. They tend to be

---

Minbari Military Leaders

BAB/COM

The awesome Minbari fleet is led by the Shai Alit, Branmer. His captains, given the title "Alit," answer to him with unquestioning loyalty. Branmer was Shai Alit during the Earth War, and personally led the assault that humans called the Battle of the Line.

He never learned the reason for the surrender, but he followed the Council's wishes. On a diplomatic tour in 2257, he dies suddenly and is replaced by Shai Alit Neroon.

---

ers in different capacities, but the military caste is the one that coordinates the fleet and provides orders in times of conflict. They are only responsible to the Grey Council and its leader for policy decisions, acting autonomously once they receive this guidance.

The Minbari use a standard War Cruiser as their primary capital warship. This powerful ship, using advanced magnetic and gravimetric drive technology, and its agile fighters give them superiority over all of the younger races. The Earth War was proof to all of Minbari strength.

The Power of the Council

BAB/COM

The order for surrender at the end of the Earth War came from the Grey Council rather than the military leaders. So strong is the respect for the Council that despite the Council's refusal to give a reason for this order, the war was stopped without objection. While this has caused some dissention in the ranks, the order of the Grey Council is enough to hold the people to its will.

---

intelligent, able to cope with the myriad of details that their jobs demand.

Despite their different focuses, each caste maintains its own internal governance, complete with an executive branch that answers to the Grey Council and a military complement. These internal administrations serve to maintain the independence of each caste while the Council holds them together.

In addition to a caste, each Minbari belongs to a clan. The clan is the philosophical family of sorts that has a given set of personal beliefs. There are five major clans, as well as many minor ones. The five major clans are the Wind Swords, the Star Riders, the Night Walkers, the Fire Wings and the Moon Shields.

The Wind Swords are the most militant among the clans. Most of their members belong to the Military Caste, but some among the other castes claim allegiance to this clan. They have a rich tradition of selflessly serving the castes and the Council with honor, although they feel that intent is more important than form. It is not unusual for one of their number to bend the letter of the Council's policies to better serve what they believe the intent to be.

The Star Riders are the clan who most enjoy the exploration of the stars, and frequently become starship personnel within their caste. They are most at home while travelling, and enjoy the exploration of the stars and trips through hyperspace.

The Night Walkers are the custodians of Minbar, helping to shape and grow the crystal and biological gardens and crops of that world. A love of nature and growth is the hallmark of a clan member, and they are most at peace when surrounded by nature. They also tend to be the ones most likely to stay on foreign planets, learning all about the nature of those worlds.

The Fire Wings are explorers and inventors. They are the tinkerers of the Minbari race, and have mastered many technologies that elude most of the younger races. They were the first to attempt flight and space travel, and the first to learn the secrets to hyperspace—secrets of navigation that prevent Minbari ships from ever being lost in hyperspace. They also invented the gravimetric drives that give ships artificial gravity and make them more maneuverable.

The Moon Shields are the guardians of the Minbari people. They care for others' physical and mental wellbeing and tend to the needs of those who cannot provide for themselves. While many of them tend to join the Religious Caste, there is need for their type in all of the castes, and they are glad to serve.

Minbari posts and ships are not run by single clans (though they are sometimes operated entirely by members of a single Caste). Instead, any given vessel or colony will house members of many clans, though one clan may be dominant, appropriate to the mission. Minbari are always greeted and welcomed as if relatives by other members of their clan.

Telepaths

Like the Centauri, the Minbari have learned to identify those among them who have telepathic abilities. Telepaths are thought to be greatly gifted, and are treated

The Power of Prophecy

Valen's writings hold much wisdom that was recorded to help the Minbari people survive and prosper. Many of those writings are reproduced to be read by all Minbari. However, unknown to all but the Council, Valen also wrote a book of prophecy to help the Minbari when the next dark age would occur. The Council makes its ruling policies based not only on the public information, but also on these prophecies of Valen.

One of Valen's prophecies was that the Minbari would have to unite with "their other half." During the Earth War, Satai Delenn of the Grey Council came to believe that this other half was the human race. She confirmed this theory during the Battle of the Line via the use of a triluminary, one of Valen's artifacts, on a captured human. On this evidence and the word of the prophecies, the Council ordered the surrender that ended the war.

with equally great respect. Much as the Justicars, all of their material needs are provided for so that they may serve others without distraction or need. The use of their gifts is extended as a free service to those in need.

Those with psionic ability are given to the Religious Caste during their childhood,

Minbari and the Vorlons

The fact that the Vorlons helped the Minbari in the last Shadow War is long-forgotten even by most Minbari—a memory preserved only in myths and legends recorded by the Council. The Shadows, an enemy of the Vorlons, were causing conflict throughout the galaxy. In the midst of the War, the Vorlons offered their assistance to the Minbari and were welcomed. A lost legend among the Minbari said that the Vorlons appeared in the form of Valeria, the messenger of the spirit world who appeared to the Minbari early in their pre-history.

and are raised in the ways of Minbari service. They choose their caste and clan in adulthood as all Minbari do, and use their gift as part of the profession and life that they choose.

All telepathic Minbari are trained in the ways of this service and bound by their oath to serve. Those who refuse to serve or who break their oath and use their gift improperly are considered to be mentally ill and are confined for treatment as soon as possible. There is no middle ground. Unlike most other races, Minbari telepaths are not monitored by others, but trusted based on their oath—though disloyalty to that oath can often be sensed by other telepaths.

Vorlons

Little is known of the Vorlon Empire. The Vorlons are one of the oldest races in the galaxy, and are millennia ahead of all of the other races in technology. They keep their own counsel and interact with the other races only when they choose.

The Vorlons protect their secrets fiercely. Every ship that has attempted to reach a Vorlon jumpgate has never been seen again. The Vorlons extend apologies to the governments of such lost ships, but never explanations—Vorlons cite the "dangers" of the hyperspace routes leading to their space, apparently implying that losses are due to accident. What exactly does happen to those who do enter Vorlon space is a mystery to this day, and Vorlons have gained something of a mythical reputation as a result. It is often said that anyone who sees a Vorlon will turn to stone.

Vorlons do, however, interact with the other races. Cordial voice-only communications are maintained with several of the younger races, and the Minbari have a secret relationship with the Vorlons that none of the other races know about. In 2257, Ambassador Kosh arrives on Babylon 5 in an encounter suit, obstensibly to protect him from the human environment (Vorlons are apparently methane-breathers). Despite an assassination attempt on his arrival, Kosh remains on Babylon 5 as the permanent representative to the station. Since he is the first Vorlon known to leave Vorlon space in several years, he is a very popular reason to visit the station. He almost never leaves his quarters and doesn't grant audiences, however, so those who go solely to see him are generally disappointed.

The League of Non-Aligned Worlds

The League of Non-Aligned Worlds is a loosely organized group of alien races that have come together for their mutual benefit. None are great powers or have many colonies—some lack the resources, others the ambition, to colonize many worlds. The League was formed in 2215, shortly after the Narns overthrew the Centauri, and was comprised of worlds that had once been Centauri subjects. They hoped that by banding together they could convince the Centauri to leave them alone, or at least drive them off with a united military front. The League is comprised of over fifty worlds, each having its own cultures and customs, but the Narns, although the catalyst for its formation, preferred their independence over membership in the League.

The Centauri, occupied with the collapse of their own empire, have largely left the League alone. The League remained a primarily informal organization until the late 2220s. As the Dilgar began to invade member worlds, they were required to mount a defensive force. All of the members sent ships to the mutual defense, but even the combined force proved too weak to stop the Dilgar. With little recourse left,

the League called upon the more powerful races to come to their aid. The Earth Alliance's participation formalized the structure of the League as well as cementing the EA as a major power in this area of the galaxy.

In the aftermath of the Dilgar War, the League formed a loose governing council that met periodically to set policy for the member worlds. This council held no force of law, but instead set economic and political policies for interaction among the League worlds. Membership in the League was open to any race with interstellar travel, although the larger races preferred their own governmental structures.

As mentioned above, most members of the League are less powerful races with few colonial holdings. One of the projects the League has started is a co-colonization program: races that don't have the resources to set up colonies alone can found a communal colony world with other races, thus giving each race the opportunity to expand. Generally, such worlds are partitioned, with each race independently setting up its own dome or domes in a separate region.

Drazi

The Drazi are a society founded on the concept of conflict. They believe that those who are physically superior are also mentally superior, and their government rewards this cunning in battle with controlling seats in government. This process manifests itself in the Dro'hannan, a ceremonial battle for the government.

Once every few standard years, all Drazi participate in the Dro'hannan. Wherever they are present, Drazi form into two sides by random lottery. These two sides fight for supremacy via non-lethal combats. Results of individual combats are tallied, and the side that came out ahead overall elects leaders to take the ruling seats in the government until the next Dro'hannan. This process often seems odd to aliens, but it is a system that has worked well for the Drazi for ten generations.

Pak'ma'ra

The Pak'ma'ra are also known across known space as the "carrion eaters." It is not uncommon for them to eat their own dead for nutritional or ceremonial purposes, and this habit has given them a reputation for barbarism among the other races. This is a somewhat unfair view, however, as the Pak'ma'ra are one of the more noble races in the League. They are never known to break their word, and are almost always willing to help others in need. Their fearsome look, however, often combines with their barbaric stereotype to counteract efforts at negotiation and trade.

The Pak'ma'ra have a government based on age. The elders, those who have more experience and wisdom, are granted the positions of authority in the government, ruling and passing their wisdom down to the next generation. Other positions are appointed by the elders, again based on wisdom. As they age, they are revered, and the wisest among them is granted great respect. Once a leader dies, his or her remains are shared among loved ones as tradition dic-

The League and the Babylon Council

BAB/COM

The League of Non-Aligned Worlds helped to a limited extent with the funding of Babylon 5 along with the major races, and were granted a seat on the Babylon Council as a result. However, at the insistence of the Narns and Centauri, both of whom threatened to remove their funding from Babylon 5 over this issue, the League was given only an advisory vote rather than a full seat. The League vote is the tiebreaker on any matter over which the Council's voting members deadlock.

tates, with some portions also being given to those whom the leader governed as a tribute of respect to that leader and in the hope that some of his or her wisdom may be passed on through the flesh.

Markab

The Markab are a private but peaceful race. They have few colonies out of choice, not economic weakness. The privacy of the family is sovereign, and their government recognizes this above all. Since all Markab recognize the need for privacy, all of them know how to respect the privacy of others, making them one of the most peaceful races in the galaxy. Their government is a tribal system. Tribal elders select the Ruling Circle, who create the law of the land. The tribal elders also select their successors.

Gaim

The Gaim are an unusual race, one of the newest to the League. They are bipedal insectoids governed by a hive-like social structure. On each of the continents on their hostile world, a queen rules the land, her duties both legislative and reproductive. Much like other insects, she constantly lays eggs for future generations while she hands out her mandates. The Narn discovered the Gaim soon after their release from the Centauri, and tried unsuccessfully to enslave them. The Gaim joined the League in 2250.

Other Races

There are many other races in the galaxy, some known and some unknown, that do not take part in interstellar politics (EarthGov tallies list close to 100 additional races thought to exist, beyond the sixty or so with which the EA maintains diplomatic ties). Some of these races are extremely xenophobic, some have limited technology, some remain undiscovered, and others just don't care to interact with the rest of the galaxy. Still others are complete mysteries, rumored to exist on the edges of known space or in systems to which hyperspace routes have never been discovered. The trade in rumors of ancient and powerful races runs as thick as commerce anywhere two or more races interact.

Section 3: Technology

Technology in the 2200s has changed quite a bit from our own time. Just a few of these changes are overviewed here.

Space Travel

Though quick and reliable travel between stars is common among all of the major races, no race has yet discovered a way to actually travel faster than light. Travel between stars is instead accomplished via a journey through something called hyperspace—a parallel dimension that is "smaller" than our own "normal space," so that distances of light years in normal space correspond to only hundreds of thousands of kilometers in hyperspace.

To get into hyperspace, a ship must travel through a "jump point." These points are holes between our universe and hyperspace. Theoretically, natural jump points might exist, but no natural points have ever been discovered. Therefore, artificial jump points must be created to allow ships to access hyperspace—and ripping a such a hole in the fabric of space is not an easy prospect.

There are two ways used to open jump points. The first and most obvious

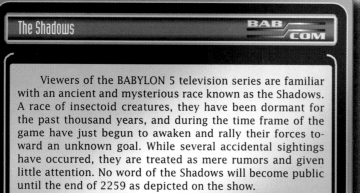

The Shadows

perspace, but there are two very large drawbacks to using them. The first is a matter of economy. Jump engines are massive pieces of expensive equipment that require a great expenditure of power. Only extremely large ships are capable of housing an engine along with the power plant necessary to activate it. The second and most serious drawback is the danger involved in hyperspace travel. Hyperspace is a wild, unpredictable environment. It is very easy for a ship to get lost even if it knows where it is going.

The most common and safest way to travel through hyperspace is to use a jumpgate. Ships of any size can use a gate, and there is an established network of gates that extends to most inhabited star systems. It is still necessary to navigate within hyperspace, but the network of gates again solves this problem. Each gate maintains at least one end of a "beacon." These beacons link gate to gate, and provide a line for ships to follow from place to place.

method is for a ship to carry a jump point generator (called a "jump engine", or "jump drive") along with it, opening a jump point for itself when necessary. The second method is to use a "jumpgate," which is basically a jump engine in a relatively stationary position, which can open jump points for any ship to pass in or out of hyperspace.

Jump engines are by far the most convenient method of getting in and out of hy-

Hyperspace

Hyperspace is a dangerous place. It is a parallel dimension to our own, which relates to our universe in unknown ways.

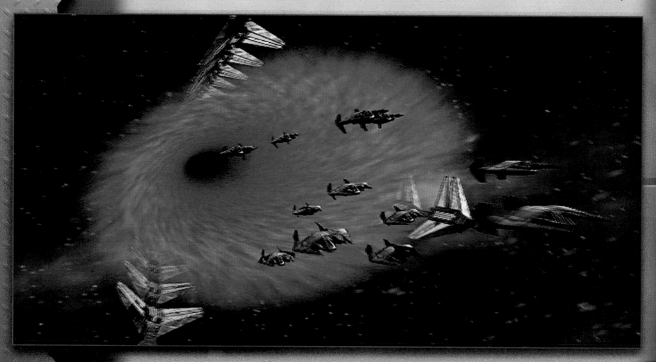

While the distance between stars in our universe is huge and empty, the distance between stars in hyperspace is small and filled with energy waves, gravity inclines and strange currents that ebb and flow seemingly at random.

Hyperspace also does not relate to our universe in a reliably predictable fashion.

While the distance between two points in hyperspace is always shorter than the distance between the corresponding points in normal space, the amount by which it is shorter is unpredictable, and can occasionally change. Points that are equidistant from a given point in normal space are generally not equidistant in hyperspace, also. Hyper-

Ships and Space Travel

As mentioned before, virtually any type of ship—from tiny shuttles to huge military dreadnaughts—can use jumpgates to enter hyperspace and traverse interstellar distances. As a result, there is huge variety in the types of ships that make interstellar journeys, and in the experience of interstellar travel.

Human ships, and most of those of the other younger races, rely upon rocket-type engines for propulsion. These engines use fusion reactors to superheat the propellent which drives the ship. The two types of "fuels"—reaction mass and propellant—are somewhat more efficient than current-day rockets, allowing a high payload-to-fuel ratio.

This technology does not create "artificial gravity" for passengers aboard ship. Many larger ships have rotating sections which provide gravity, but most vessels do not. Acceleration does provide a sense of gravity towards the rear of the ship, and some larger ships are designed to take advantage of this, with their decks aligned with the floors towards the rear. Smaller ships designed to land on planets or in docking bays are built so that the floors are underfoot when the ship is landed—but this means that when under heavy acceleration, the "downward" direction is towards the rear wall, not the floor. Such ships are commonly built with ladders and handholds that allow passengers and crew to move about even under these topsy-turvy circumstances.

Most travel is under weightless, or nearly weightless, conditions. Typically, a ship embarking on a journey travels under heavy acceleration for some period after departure, and then cuts back on its engine output to coast, or travel under only light propulsion, until it reaches its jumpgate. While accelerating, the passengers feel rearward gravity—when coasting perceived gravity is reduced to zero unless the ship has rotating sections.

After passing through the jumpgate, in hyperspace, the ship maneuvers constantly, making minor course changes to counteract the gravity waves and inclines in hyperspace. During this period, the passengers experience general weightlessness (except in ships with rotating sections), with occasional mild impulses in random directions. Emergency maneuvers may be powerful and come without warning, shaking the passengers within the ship like dice in a cup. For this reason, passengers and crew spend most of the time strapped in, and walls and especially corners are padded to reduce the chance of injury.

Finally, when a ship emerges from hyperspace and heads towards its destination, it deccelerates gradually. This provides a sense of very light gravity towards the front of the ship, though the decceleration is often mild enough to feel almost like weightlessness. Again, ships that rotate provide a sense of normal gravity for their passengers, with only a slight forward tug due to deccelerations.

Though it is not widely known, the older races use a different technology, termed "gravimetric" propulsion. These ships are propelled by gravitational fields that their drives generate—an energy- and technology-intensive system, but one with many advantages. One of the biggest is the advent of artificial gravity, which relies on the same technologies. Gravimetric ships provide gravity for their passengers without a need for rotating sections, and regardless of ship size. Not only are the decks always properly underfoot, but outside impulses, such as those due to acceleration or course correction in hyperspace, are partially or completely negated. The Minbari use gravimetric technologies, as do the Vorlons, and though they have never discussed it Earthforce Intelligence (and similar agencies among other races) suspect its use. Among the younger races, only the Centauri have successfully developed the technology. They employ it only in some of their largest military vessels, and have kept their use of it a secret for some time.

BAB/COM

When the Centauri discovered Earth, they leased a jumpgate to the EA, charging a small fee for each ship entering hyperspace. When the Alliance built its own gate it began to subsidize the costs from taxes, so EA citizens leaving Earth no longer have to pay a fee to enter hyperspace. However, use of all other Alliance gates requires a small fee from EA ships, generally based on cargo or passenger capacity. Alien ships traveling through EA jumpgates pay larger fees (although the treaty with the Minbari signed after the War allows their military vessels free passage).

The expense of traveling through alien jumpgates is usually greater than that of EA gates. The exact expense depends on the relations between the Alliance and the race in question. However, when the Minbari, Centauri and Narns agree to the Babylon Project in 2255, they also sign commercial trade agreements that allow free use of the jumpgate at Epsilon Eridani and most gates that connect, by a single jump, to the Babylon Station system.

space is a confusing realm that has confounded all who have attempted to define, map, or understand it.

Unlike traveling through normal space, a ship in hyperspace is constantly buffeted by outside forces—stray gravity inclines and magnetic surges. Thus, a ship in hyperspace must always be correcting its course and maneuvering to follow its beacon. In normal space, when a ship gets up to speed and on course, it can cut its engines and coast to its destination without losing speed. In hyperspace, any ship that cut off its maneuver engines would quickly be rocked off course and lose its beacon. A ship's range in hyperspace, therefore, is limited by its fuel capacity much more than in normal space.

Jump Points

Creating a jump point opens a tunnel between normal space and hyperspace that allows any ship that enters this hole to pass from one to the other. Jump points appear as glowing vortices leading toward an unseen destination. The walls of these tunnels are particle barriers moving at nearly the speed of light. This has two important consequences. The first is that any ship touching the wall of a jump point can be seriously damaged or destroyed. The second is that the walls of a jump gate shift in color depending on whether the observer is entering, traversing or leaving a jump point. The actual color of a jump point's wall is green, however, those entering a jump point see it as yellow, and those leaving see it as blue.

A ship traversing a jump point is not accelerated by the point or its jump engines—although it generally looks that way to a stationary observer nearby. Instead, a ship enters the point under its own power, then proceeds through the tunnel. The length of a tunnel is variable and unpredictable, much like hyperspace itself. It is impossible to measure the length of the tunnel—however, it never takes less than about five seconds nor more than thirty seconds for a ship to traverse the jump point.

Jump Engines and Jumpgates

As mentioned above, jump points are opened by jump engines. While some larger ships carry their own engines, the most common method of opening a point is by using a jumpgate—basically a jump engine assembly situated in a known location in normal space. Both jump engines on ships and jumpgates are expensive, massive devices.

The construction of jump engines is expensive because it requires solid, heavy materials, months of careful precision construction, and one rare ore. This ore, known as Quantium-40, is found mostly in uninhabited, hostile solar systems, particularly in the dead systems of older generation stars, and is rarely found in large quantities. A system considered "rich" in Q-40 might produce enough for the construction of ten or fifteen jump engines over a decade or so of mining operations, while many systems, particularly those with habitable planets, generally produce only enough for one or two engines through decades of prospecting and exploitation. Needless to say, the exploration and mining of systems for Q-40 is an attractive business, luring scouts, miners and dreamers from all races. Those who can find or extract the valuable ore from a system are well rewarded for their efforts.

Jump engines are massive due to the intense power requirements involved in their operation. Opening a hole in the fabric of space-time is not easily done, and even with the necessary technology requires a large discharge of power. Most jump-capable ships require at least a few minutes to recharge their jump engines once they have opened a point before they can open a second point.

Jumpgates provide all ships, regardless of size, with a way to get into and out of hyperspace. Jumpgates are universally state-owned—that is, they are operated by the governments in whose space they are located. Most races allow passage through their own gates into hyperspace by other races through various trade agreements, treaties and tariffs. Passage out of hyperspace via jumpgates is never restricted, given the dangers of becoming lost—though in times of war, jumpgates are sometimes shut down to prevent their use by invaders. Since the power generators in jumpgates are only used for hyperspace functions, it usually takes less than a minute to recharge a gate's jump engines.

Typically, a jump gate or jump-capable ship can hold a jump point open for a

Distances in Hyperspace

BAB/COM

Due to its changing geometry and unpredictable gravitational influences, and to the varying loads and engine power of ships, it can be difficult to reliably quantify hyperspace travel in terms of either distance or time. Since journeys through hyperspace generally run from beacon to beacon, and each leg of a journey requires entering and then exiting hyperspace before moving onto the next leg, journeys are often referred to by the number of "jumps" it takes to get from one place to another, as opposed to the distance to be travelled. A jump might require just a few hours in hyperspace, or up to two days—an average jump represents about one day.

minute or two. While the point is open, one or more ships may pass through it—as many as can fly through the "tunnel" of the jump point while it is open. Thus, it's possible for a jump-capable ship to travel with a contingent of conventional ships, for which it can hold open a jump point when the flotilla enters or exits hyperspace.

Every race has scientific data on millions of stars from centuries of astronomical study. That info, however, is of little interest to the galactic community—of real interest are the stars that can actually be reached. Thus, stars are given relevant names—some new, some traditional—when hyperspace routes to them are opened. In most cases, the captain of the ship that discovers the system names the star.

Planets are usually numbered within a system, from the innermost planet to the outermost. Thus, the eight planets around Tau Ceti are numbered from I to VIII (roman numerals are most common, though standard numbers are sometimes used). The main exception to this rule are homeworlds, which of course were named by their inhabitants long before they even dreamed of space travel.

Among Humans, colonies are generaly named after their planets or systems ("Mars Colony," for example, or "Proxima III"), with individual city complexes named after geographical regions (such as the Mons Olympus dome on Mars). Stations are often given geographical names (like the Ganymede Outpost) or unique names (like Babylon Station).

Navigating and Exploring Hyperspace

Since ships cannot navigate by conventional means in hyperspace, jumpgates perform a navigational as well as transport function. Each jumpgate provides two communications signals in hyperspace. The first is a "local beacon," which broadcasts a signal that any ship passing nearby can follow to the gate. The second is one end of a "beacon pair," which leads to another jumpgate.

Local beacons can only be received a short distance from the gate, and provide a safety net to ships entering hyperspace to ensure that the ship does not get lost before it finds the beacon signal from the destination end of the beacon pair. Once a ship has drifted more than a few thousand kilometers from a gate, the local signal is lost.

Beacon pairs provide navigational signals over long distances in hyperspace. A beacon pair is a matched set of transceivers that communicate via a tightly focused tachyon beam in hyperspace. A ship entering hyperspace simply finds the beacon signal from the gate at its destination and follows

it like a lifeline until it reaches the other end. In order to ensure that they remain in contact and do not lose each other, each end of the beacon pair transmits to its mate continuously. Unfortunately, though each gate can have multiple beacon pair endpoints, interference from multiple transmitters, and the power requirements involved, generally restrict a gate to no more than four or five. Thus, a ship entering the gate cannot opt to travel to any arbitrary destination in the galaxy, but is limited to the four or five beacon routes available from that gate. In heavily traveled systems, this can lead to multiple jumpgates, set a few tens or hundreds of thousands of kilometers apart in normal space. Each gate is beacon-linked to a different set of destinations—ships passing through the system must exit one gate, travel through normal space to one of the other gates, and continue their hyperspace journeys from there.

Travel through hyperspace is dangerous, and standard practices are followed to mitigate that danger. Ships file flight plans before hyperspace journeys, in which they specify which beacons they will follow. At the end of each jump, ships are required to exit hyperspace and send a tachyon signal confirming their arrival to the EA Space Travel Commission (in human space—the alien governments all have similar organizations) before reentering hyperspace.

Civilian traffic cannot plan on jumps that keep them in hyperspace longer than forty-eight hours. Most beacon pair routes are short enough that even slow-moving ships can traverse them in less than forty-eight hours, but this restriction does keep some civilian ships from using some routes. Military ships, of course, are given more leeway—but generally keep their forays into hyperspace to under forty-eight hours anyway, for general safety reasons. In Human space, any ship that does not reach its destination gate within two hours of its flight plan triggers a search and rescue operation. In most such cases, the rescue ship generally finds the missing ship caught in a gravity well somewhere along the beacon, or travelling slowly to compensate for low fuel. In those rare cases where a ship has lost the beacon, it generally cannot be recovered. No Human ship lost in hyperspace has ever been found again.

The exploration of hyperspace is particularly dangerous, as it involves traveling beyond the established network of beacons to add new jumpgates. An exploration ship travels through hyperspace with the materials to build a new beacon and jumpgate. It moves to a location in hyperspace that is thought to correspond to a stellar mass in normal space, and opens a point nearby to reenter normal space. There it constructs the gate and activates the beacon, adding the new point to the jumpgate network. It can then install a second beacon and continue its explorations, or return to its previous port of call.

Quantium-40 is the limiting factor in the growth of the jumpgate network. As more Quantium-40 becomes available, more jumpgates can be built to explore the edge of known space (known as "the Rim"). The EA is the most ambitious empire in looking for new systems. The Alliance's massive *Explorer*-class ships spend years out on the Rim looking for new planets and systems. While some of the stars discovered have no habitable planets and no precious minerals, enough systems are determined to be profitable that the explorer program continues.

Computers and Communication

Computers are prevalent in all aspects of society for most of the races. They are universally used as tools for communication, data analysis and design, and record-keeping. All spacefaring races have mastered some degree of automation as well.

Communications

Interstellar communications are accomplished via use of tachyon links and fast, intelligent computer software. Video telephony and vid-mail messages are the dominant form of personal communication. It is possible (though often very expensive) for anyone in EA space to communicate with another person almost anywhere in known space instantaneously. More common and less expensive, however, are delayed transmissions of video messages via spare bandwidth in the tachyon link. Such messages are pre-recorded by the sender, and transmitted to the recipient when they can be fitted into the transmission dataflow, generally resulting in a delay of two to twenty-four hours.

The most common form of communication for business purposes is still the written word. Contracts, business letters, progress reports and all manner of other correspondence are the mainstay of many businesses. Time-critical data is transmitted via tachyon link, much like faxes today, with the most sensitive material being scrambled. However, hardcopy of documents is still vital, and some information is just too sensitive to transmit over communications channels. Since the cost to transport paper and other organic materials through space is prohibitive, most documents are transported on data crystals: small, inexpensive light polymer crystals capable of being transported easily and very difficult to tamper with.

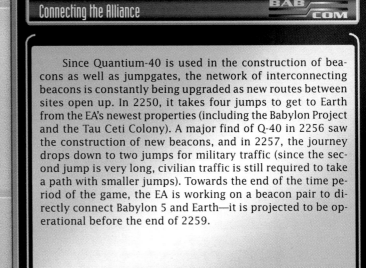

Connecting the Alliance

Since Quantium-40 is used in the construction of beacons as well as jumpgates, the network of interconnecting beacons is constantly being upgraded as new routes between sites open up. In 2250, it takes four jumps to get to Earth from the EA's newest properties (including the Babylon Project and the Tau Ceti Colony). A major find of Q-40 in 2256 saw the construction of new beacons, and in 2257, the journey drops down to two jumps for military traffic (since the second jump is very long, civilian traffic is still required to take a path with smaller jumps). Towards the end of the time period of the game, the EA is working on a beacon pair to directly connect Babylon 5 and Earth—it is projected to be operational before the end of 2259.

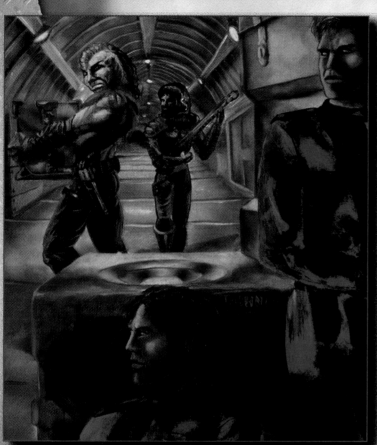

any publicly-available information can be found on the many common computer networks in the EA or among one of the alien races. Such networks are accessible from interstellar locations via tachyon transmissions, though again such direct communication is expensive. As with most public networks today, networked information systems are generally very user-friendly, and rarely require any particular skill to search for information (though a little expertise can often speed things up a bit). Military computers, in addition to access to public databases, have access to additional databases of secure information. Governmental computers tend to have the most information available, but access to them is the most restricted.

Computers are also used as design tools. From scientific research notebooks to virtual worlds for mechanical designs, the powerful data manipulation tools allow theoretical and practical design in many fields.

Automation and Labor

Computers handle many of the routine tasks of day to day life. The management of space traffic into and out of docking bays, for example, is one of the more complex tasks that computer automation performs. Operation of jumpgates is normally completely automated, and manufacturing and other industrial tasks are performed by computer controlled equipment. Additionally, remote operations and routine tasks in vacuum or other hazardous environments can be performed by semi-autonomous robots.

The most involved tasks, however, still require sentient beings at the controls. Jobs for talented construction workers in zero-gravity are hazardous, but well-paying. Dockers, shipping pilots and other groups are in high demand. Labor unions and other organizations still protect the interests of their members.

Data crystals are also the method of transfer most often used between different computer systems. Within the Alliance, most computer networks communicate with each other seamlessly, and unless the user is trying to access sensitive data, it is not easy for a layman to tell whether data is coming from the EA network, the WebNet, or one of thousands of corporate networks. With thousands of years of separate evolution, however, different races have developed different computer systems and this seamlessness is not available. Computer technicians who can translate data from one system to another are always in high demand. In some cases, though, the use of a data crystal is the only method of data transfer.

Data Analysis and Design

Computers are also used as instruments for data analysis and design tools. Almost

Military Technology

One thing common to every race in the galaxy is conflict. From Humanity's struggles through centuries of territorial conflict to the Centauri fight for survival against the Xon, every race has experienced some form of armed conflict and every race is familiar with ways of making war. Specific weaponry varies from race to race, but there are always early forms of clubs, then bladed weapons, and finally projectiles and then weapons of mass destruction. Defenses against these weapons, each of varying degrees of usefulness, are not far behind in a race's development.

While each race has its own form of destructive weaponry, the inherent dangers of space travel necessitated new weapons. The projectile and mass destruction weapons that work so well on the ground work even better in space: too well, in fact. In Earth's history, a simple terrorist holdup turned into the destruction of the first Mars Colony as a poorly placed grenade had much more effect than intended. Most races soon after settling space began to use energy weapons and hand-to-hand weapons instead of projectile weapons.

Many common personal weapons are covered in the next section.

Character Equipment

Characters in *The Babylon Project*, like all people, use a myriad of objects in their everyday lives. From domestic tasks like cooking, sleeping and cleaning to professional tasks like design and manufacturing, travel, and office work, Humans and aliens use all sorts of equipment in every aspect of their lives.

Some examples of these objects are used throughout this book, and others are simply assumed to be there. Clothing, for example, is not covered in detail here, but everybody wears something over his or her skin. Look through the art in this book for examples of clothing that typical characters might wear.

Common objects such as briefcases, clocks, barstools and so forth are much the same as they are today, and are a necessary part of the backdrop, but are not detailed here. When such objects become important to events in the game, use your common sense and imagination to deter-

Piracy in the Space Lanes

Hyperspace and hostile aliens aren't the only dangers to space travel. Heavily loaded cargo ships can be slow to accelerate and maneuver, making them easy prey for someone with a few weapons and total disregard for the law. Much as piracy on the seas terrorized mariners of old, groups of raiders can attack transports without warning. A thriving interstellar black market makes piracy a lucrative trade.

A favored raider trick is to wait in hyperspace near a jumpgate, emerge and attack a ship as it approaches the gate, then retreat back to hyperspace when pursued. Jumpgates are too numerous to be individually guarded, especially in systems with more than one gate. Earthforce and the militaries of other races constantly patrol for raiders—and many transports go armed—but the problem persists.

Raiders come from many different races, and usually operate in small groups with a few fighters to disable their prey and a light transport to retrieve the cargo. Raider bands are usually small, and often riddled with internal power struggles. However, to lone ships in the dark of space, raiders remain a constant threat.

mine whether items are present and how they might affect the characters or be used by them.

Use that same common sense when characters wish to purchase or locate specific items. Mundane equipment such as rope, flashlights, arc welders and such are generally as easy to obtain in the world of *The Babylon Project* as they are in our world. The EA Credit, the currency used throughout Human space, is roughly equivalent to today's U.S. Dollar. Thus, it may cost only a few credits for rope or a flashlight, while it could cost 500 EAcr or more for a good arc welder.

Some specialized equipment has very specific game effects. Characters cannot get from one star system to another without the use of a space ship, for example. A pressure suit is a necessity when working in the vacuum of space. Weapons and armor drastically affect combat. These objects, unlike more mundane items, need to be defined a little more precisely for game purposes. The following sections define the nature, capabilities, availability, and costs of such specialized equipment. Costs represent approximate retail prices in places where items are freely available—in small stations or outposts, alien systems, or other isolated locations, such items may be much more expensive or completely unavailable. Likewise, prices for restricted and Earthforce-issue items represent costs through legal channels—obtaining such equipment through the black market or other illicit sources might double or even triple costs.

Personal Weapons and Armor

The Weapons Table opposite lists game statistics and costs for many types of hand-to-hand weapons and firearms, some of which are described in more detail below. Obviously, there are many thousands of models of commercially-available weapons in known space, and only a few representatives are covered on this list.

The firepower and ammunition capacity of PPG weapons is variable and can be adjusted. The Damage listed on the table is standard, however, the cap (see the sidebar) can be "turned down" to extend capacity at a cost to firepower: every "notch" down reduces the Damage of all remaining shots by 2, while increasing the number of available shots by 1. The cap must still have at least half its ammunition capacity remaining, and once turned down to do less damage cannot be turned back up, until replaced with a new cap.

Generic weapons include clubs, knives, swords, staves, and even brass knuckles. They can vary dramatically in form and design, but need little explanation. Most are commonly available in one form or another almost anywhere. Generic weapons made and used by one race are generally about as effective as similar weapons used by others. Improvised weapons are similar in use, but may be slightly less effective, while specially-made weapons will often be a bit more effective. Use the listed information to estimate the effects of such non-standard weapons.

Armor from one race is tailored to fit the race that created it, and generally can't be worn by members of other races (in the case of very similar races, such as Humans and Centauri, armor can be worn, but at a cost of an additional point or two of Initiative Modifier). Armor hit by Phased Plasma damage must be discarded immediately; gear usually burns through in about five rounds, at which point it begins inflicting one level of damage per round.

Minbari Fighting Pike: This is a traditional Minbari weapon used only by those trained in the ancient Denn'na art. Pikes are usually handed down from one generation to the next, and are rare and hard to buy. Cost: when avaiable, they typically fetch a price in excess of 5,000 EAcr.

Coutari: This is the traditional Centauri dueling sword. It is used in the Morago dueling art, but is also used widely by the Guardsmen. Older Coutari belonging to the noble houses can be quite valuable. Cost:

Guns, Guns, Guns

The PPG is the standard type of firearm for Humans in space. "PPG" stands for Phased Plasma Gun, a type of weapon that shoots a burst of superheated helium plasma contained within a magnetic field. PPG shots are brightly visible when fired, but as they travel only slightly slower than bullets from traditional "slug" weapons, it is nearly impossible to dodge a well-aimed shot. The magnetic "container" holds together long enough to penetrate flesh, and hence damages the target through both kinetic energy transfer and extreme heat. Unlike a bullet, however, a PPG round cannot penetrate sturdy materials like spaceship hulls, and is much safer to use in hostile environments like colonies and stations. For this reason, Earthforce and most alien military forces have adopted PPG technology for all off-planet personal weaponry, and slug weapons are very highly restricted.

PPG weapons are powered by "caps." Caps are small battery-like devices that provide the power necessary to superheat the plasma and provide the magnetic field and propulsion. A cap is only good for a limited number of shots, and must be replaced when used up. Caps can be recharged, but since they are very inexpensive most people discard them when they are expended.

Although all legitimate gun purchases are subject to background checks and gun licenses are required everywhere in the EA, it is much easier to get a PPG, even on the black market, than any other type of firearm anywhere except on Earth itself. Traditional "slug throwers" are only used for some planetary private security firms and for hunting game. The transport of all weaponry is regulated, but slug throwers are the most restricted of all.

Weapons Table

Weapon	To-Hit Bonus	Dam. Bonus	Dam. Type	Shots per rnd	Ammo cap.	Cost (EAcr)	Notes
Hand-to-Hand Weapons							
Brass Knuckles	0	+2	Impact			20	generic
Club	+2	+3	Impact			20	generic
EF-issue Nightstick	+2	+4	Impact			50	EF issue
Staff	+2	+3	Impact			150	generic
Minbari Fighting Pike	+3	+3	Impact			5000	Minbari staff
Small Knife (slash)	+1	+1	Cut			40	generic
(stab)	+1	+2	Cut				
(thrown)	0	+2	Cut				
Large Knife (slash)	+1	+2	Cut			90	generic
(stab)	+1	+3	Cut				
Sword (slash)	+2	+4	Cut			300	generic
(stab)	+1	+4	Cut				
Coutari (slash)	+2	+4	Cut			300	Centauri sword
(stab)	+2	+5	Cut				
Katak (slash)	+3	+5	Cut			5000	Narn sword
(stab)	+1	+4	Cut				
Pistols							
W&G Model 10	0	14	PP	1	5	250	Human civilian PPG pistol
Auricon EF-7	+1	14	PP	1	15	450	EF issue PPG pistol
Kalat Avenger	+1	13	PP	1	10	300	Narn military issue PPG pistol
Tromo Handgun	0	14	PP	1	20	400	Cent. military issue PPG pistol
Sha'ann PP Weapon	+1	17	PP	1	n/a	4000	Min. military issue PPG pistol
Coleman .22	0	12	CS	1	10	150	Human civilian slug pistol
Coleman Magnum	0	14	CS	1	14	200	Human civilian slug pistol
U-Tech Stinger II	0	*	*	1	10	100	Human civilian stun gun
Longarms							
W&G Model 21	+1	16	PP	1	2	400	Human civilian PPG rifle
Auricon EF-PR	+2	17	PP	1	8	550	EF issue PPG rifle
Wesson Sportsman	+1	14	CS	1	7	300	Human civilian slug rifle
Shotgun	0	16	CS	1	2	400	generic Human
Bow	0	8	Cut	1/2	20	300	generic

* Does no serious damage, but causes a stun check as if hit with 14 Impact Damage.

Armor	Areas Covered	Init. Mod.	Dam. Mod.	Cost (EAcr)	Notes
Armor					
W&B Armored Jacket	2-7	-2	6	300	
Coleman EF Riot Jacket	2-7	-1	8	450	EF issue
Coleman EF Riot Helmet	1	0	9	240	EF issue
Talak Military Gear	2-9	-1	8	300	Narn military issue
Royal Guardsman Combat Jacket	2-7	-2	9	500	Centauri military issue
Minbari Military Caste Jacket	2-7	0	10	2000	Minbari military issue

300 EAcr (antiques may run 2,000 EAcr or more).

Katak: This is the Narn blade used in the fulfillment of justice oaths and in self-defense. All true Kataks are hand-made. It is a weapon of honor, and once drawn can- not be sheathed until it has drawn blood. Cost: 5,000 EAcr.

Westlake & Grumman Model 10: This is the most popular self-defense PPG weapon used by civilians in the Earth Alli- ance. It is a little unwieldy, but very dependable. It can be easily purchased with proper papers. Cost: 250 EAcr.

Auricon EF-7: This is the PPG issued by EarthForce. The workhorse weapon of the Alliance's official personnel, it is not legally available to the public, and is tightly controlled. Cost: 450 EAcr.

Kalat Avenger: This is the PPG smallarm that the Narn military uses in its peacekeeping missions and "reclamation" of territories. It is also available to civilian Narns, but is rarely sold outside the Regime. Cost: 300 EAcr.

Tromo Handgun: This is the standard sidearm of the Royal Centauri Guardsmen. It is light but deadly, with a good-sized cap. It is not generally given to civilians, but as with all things Centauri, can be obtained for the right price. Cost: 400 EAcr.

Sha'ann PP Weapon: This is the standard Minbari light firearm. Small and powerful, it has a lifetime energy supply and can be fired thousands of times without being recharged. It is used only by the Military Caste, and is completely restricted to the other castes and jealously guarded from other races. It can only be obtained on the black market at a very high cost. Cost: 4,000 EAcr (but likely to be sold for three times that amount, when available at all).

Coleman .22: This is a traditional "slug" pistol used on Earth for security firms and self-defense. Like all slug weapons, it is very tightly controlled off-planet. Cost: 150 EAcr.

Coleman Magnum: This is the weapon of choice for police forces on Earth. A heavy slug thrower, it packs a punch, and is easy to keep and maintain. Cost: 200 EAcr.

Universal Tech Stinger II: For non-lethal uses, the Stinger is the perfect choice. It stuns the victim without doing any permanent damage. It is heavily marketed and sold as an inexpensive, relatively safe weapon, and is a popular choice among those with families. Cost: 100 EAcr.

Westlake & Grumman Model 21: This is a moderately popular PPG rifle used by security professionals, particularly in colony domes. It packs quite a punch and its large profile can be a good deterrent. Cost: 400 EAcr.

Auricon EF-PR: This is the standard EarthForce combat PPG rifle. Like its smaller cousin, it is a highly dependable weapon only available legally to EarthForce personnel for official business. Cost: 550 EAcr.

Wesson Sportsman: This is a very common sport rifle used on Earth. Its PPG relatives are generally considered better for human targets, but PPG weapons often make for a messy kill in game hunting. Cost: 300 EAcr.

Miscellaneous Equipment

Even among those types of equipment that are commonly and directly used by adventurous characters, there are far too many items to detail. The following are some examples of equipment common or useful in the world of *The Babylon Project*. Most of these items are widely available, and representative of hundreds of similar models.

MTT Teleman Wrist Link: This tele-communications is device worn on the wrist and functions much like today's cellular phones. The Teleman communicates via a broadcast network that covers Earth and services most EA colonies and stations—but when outside of this network, the Teleman does not function. Service is metered, with monthly bills automatically withdrawn from the owner's bank account. The Teleman is an inexpensive, no-frills link, but many other models are made, including the lavish **Corpsman XL-200 Gold**, which offers a small video screen and even a short-range direct-broadcast feature that allows it to communicate with similar models without accessing the cellular net. Cost: Teleman: 35 EAcr (plus monthly fee, typically running around 20 EAcr for moderate usage); Corpsman: 380 EAcr (plus fees).

Corpsman Signal Devices Inc. Handlink Transceiver: This small device fits onto the back of the human hand, affixed by a special polymer, and functions as an audio transmitter and receiver. It is the standard Earthforce communication device for use on ships, stations, and colonies, and relies on the facility's computer network as a routing mechanism. Handlinks can also be set to private direct-broadcast channels much like walkie-talkies if no computer routing is available, but are very limited in range and features. Cost: 40 EAcr.

TransCom T1200 Terminal: The home (or office) terminal is the most common type of telecommunications device in Human society, and the TransCom is one of the most common models. A home terminal acts as both a computer and a vidphone in one. Like most such devices, the TransCom is installed in a wall panel or piece of furniture, and is not portable. It allows all the data processing, software capabilities, and network access of a computer as well as the communications connections of a vidphone. Many more powerful or widely-featured models are also available, as well as cheaper ones. Cost: 650 EAcr.

CommEx 400 Vidphone: This small console device allows face-to-face communication much like a current-day telephone but with a video screen as well. It can contact virtually any Human facility directly (via the tachyon/hyperspace telecommunications network), and seamlessly patch through communications to many alien planets, stations, and colonies as well. However, direct interstellar calls are very expensive, so the CommEx 400 and similar vidphones can also record messages, which are then transmitted to the recipient within a few hours when less expensive bandwidth becomes available. As with other consumer electronics, there are many alternative makes and models available, with a wide range of costs and features. Cost: 100 EAcr.

HoraComm Rascal PDA: There are many types of portable computers and computer-related devices; the Personal Data Assistant is the smallest and one of the most common. Though not true computers, many people use PDAs to keep track of personal information, appointments, and addresses, and to access the public net while on the go. No businessperson is without one. The

HoraComm OneNet is an upscale version that also functions as a portable vidphone. Cost: Rascal: 200 EAcr; OneNet: 650 EAcr.

HoraComm GoNote 3000: This is a notebook-sized computer for the person on the go. It can work alone with its internal software, or can connect to the net via a home terminal or public vidphone or over the airwaves. It is comparable in power and capability to a mid-range home terminal. Cost: 1800 EAcr.

Data Crystal: Used to transfer information and to back up computers, these cheap and plentiful data storage and transfer devices are comparable to today's computer floppy disks. Cost: 2 EAcr.

Corpsman Signal Devices Inc. Model 38 Tachyon Transceiver: A tachyon transciever allows direct live communication over interstellar distances. An expensive item, only the government, telecommunications companies, and some large corporations own them, and their use is highly regulated by the Earth Alliance since they rely on the jump gate/hyperspace beacon network to transmit data. Tachyon transceivers are also standard components on large ships, but many small civilian ships are not equipped with them. Cost: 992,800 EAcr.

MegaLan ML30 ImageCorder: The equivalent to today's video camcorder but with many more features, the imagecorder is a small device roughly five inches across that records audio and video images. Several hours of video imagery can be captured on a single data crystal, and still images can be taken from the video as desired. There are many other models of imagecorders available, including commercial models capable of hovering and maneuvering by remote. Cost: 500.

MedFirst Basic First Aid Kit: Basic first aid kits contain materials for medical aid for minor wounds. When used, add 1 to the Ability of the character administering the aid. Cost: 12 EAcr.

MedFirst Trauma Kit: This kit contains medical materials and pharaceuticals for immediate medical aid for all sorts of wounds and traumas. When used, add 1 to the Ability of the character administering the aid (3 if the character has the Medical, EMT skill and the victim is Human). This particular kit is specifically designed for Human medical requirements—obviously, other races have similar aid kits tailored towards their needs, with comparable effects and costs. Cost: 180 EAcr.

MedFirst Xeno-Trauma Kit: Human ships and stations that are commonly visited by aliens are often equipped with this kit, which contains medical materials and pharaceuticals for immediate medical aid to non-Humans. When used, add 1 to the Ability of the character administering the aid (2 if the character has the Medical, EMT skill). Cost: 180 EAcr.

InTech Poly-9 Forensics Analyzer: This powerful device is used to analyze materials and chemicals found at crime scenes, and is frequently issued to Earthforce investigators and other police and security personnel. Samples—liquids, gasses, or small particulates—can be placed within the analyzer, or "sniffed" through a small vacuum-like probe. The analyzer provides broad classifications of materials— "human blood," "animal or alien hair," "organic particulates," etc. If given a relatively pure sample and connected to a forensics database, it can provide specific chemical composition details, identify probable manufacturers or sources, and even identify DNA. Cost: 85,000 EAcr.

Breather Mask: This self-contained unit allows a character to breathe in many non-standard atmospheres for a limited amount of time (typically less than an hour between recharges). It does not protect the body against vacuum, radically different pressures, or corrosive or toxic gases, however. Cost: 140 EAcr.

Proxima Aerospace VS-A Pressure Suit: A pressure suit allows a person to survive and function in vacuum and other hostile atmospheric environments. The VS-A is a typical general-purpose model that is common equipment on commercial ships. It features a twelve-hour air supply, self-sealing membrane for protection from minor punctures, R-4 radiation protection, maneuver jets, and standard transciever. Cost: 3800 EAcr.

Ships

There are many types of ships plying the space lanes—far too many to cover in any detail here. Ship classes include shuttles and atmospheric shuttles, which are used to move people and cargo short distances (ship-to-ship, ship-to-station, or ground-to-orbit); transports and atmospheric transports, which generally move cargo and passengers within a single system or on short interstellar runs, and which are generally small enough to directly dock with other ships or enter station docking bays; and freighters and liners which make extended interstellar runs and which are too large to land or enter the docking bays of stations or outposts. For a more detailed example of a typical small civilian ship, check out the *No Strings Attached*, covered in the next chapter.

Chapter 4: The Campaign

Now you've read the rules and you're ready to gather a group of players together to play a game. This chapter is a lengthy adventure that lets you jump right in with little additional preparation. It contains ready-to-play characters, a compelling story, and descriptions of places they might visit and non-player characters they might meet, and can be used as a stand-alone adventure to introduce players to the game or the beginning of an ongoing story arc that you can build into an epic story. If used in that manner, it can serve as the Introduction and Identification Phases of the story arc (as discussed in chapter 2).

As with everything in this game, feel free to modify this adventure to fit the story you wish to tell. It's set up to occur as one connected series of events. However, the best way to personalize a story is to build your own ideas into it. Add more adventures between the chapters or as the characters travel around between the locales presented here, to customize the story to your own tastes, and to reflect interests and strengths of your players. Also, some of the scenes in this adventure are fairly rough and may require additional fleshing out. These scenes were deliberately left open to make the adventure easy to customize or expand into an epic story.

The outline for this adventure—a "Premise" section that explains the background and outlines the coming plot, followed by a series of "chapters," each broken into several "scenes" and a "Behind the Scenes" section—will be used for future published adventures. Unless otherwise specified, the term "chapter" herein generally refers to chapters within the adventure rather than other chapters in this book.

The Premise

This story takes place early in the time frame of the game, beginning in March of 2250. Babylon Station has begun construction, though most characters will only be aware of it as a passing news item, and the majority of the citizens of the Earth Alliance are still caught up in the aftermath of the Earth-Minbari War. But EarthGov knows that the current high morale will not last forever, and that the anti-alien sentiment

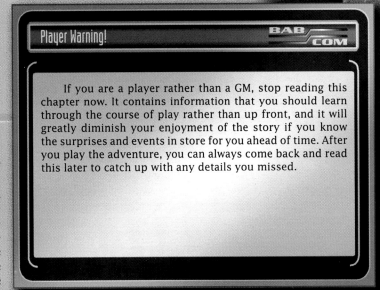

Player Warning!

If you are a player rather than a GM, stop reading this chapter now. It contains information that you should learn through the course of play rather than up front, and it will greatly diminish your enjoyment of the story if you know the surprises and events in store for you ahead of time. After you play the adventure, you can always come back and read this later to catch up with any details you missed.

that had begun to surface before the war will eventually return. To forestall problems, a small commission in Earthforce has set aside a meager budget for an investigative team of independent contractors. This team is the players characters' group. However, unbeknownst to the commission or to any of the members of the team, their first mission will be to survive a threat that comes from within Earthforce itself.

Homeguard, a subversive organization opposed to Human interaction with aliens, has sympathizers in positions throughout the Alliance, and the group has become aware of the formation of the characters' team. Even before the team comes together, plans were set in motion to sabotage the group and frame them for a major Homeguard terrorist action. As if that weren't enough, however, a second similar group, Earth First, will embroil the players in their own efforts. As these plans come to fruition, the players find themselves reacting to events before they have even had a chance to get to know one another.

The Background

The mystery behind this adventure centers around the destruction of Babylon Station and Babylon 2. The character team has been assembled to forestall isolationist actions. Unfortunately, the terrorists are one step ahead of Earthforce. Long before the team was assembled plans were set into motion to ensure that Babylon Station would be dead before it went online. The formation of the team was noted by these antagonists, and to prevent exposure the conspirators set the team up for a fall. It is into this political squeeze that the player characters stumble as the story begins.

The PCs begin the game ignorant of the forces at work against them. The two separate organizations involved, Earth First and Homeguard, are at first working at cross purposes. Both want to prevent the Babylon Project from coming to fruition, and have each independently planned to sabotage the effort. Coincidentally, their plans are set to go off almost simultaneously—but Earth First's effort will ultimately delay the effects Homeguard's plan. Earth First is the smaller of the two organizations, a vigi-

lante group set up by EA Senator James Sidhe. Working for him is a small group of well-placed family and friends who share his views, and who have arranged for the station to fail by shipping critically flawed building materials to the construction site. Their efforts culminate in the partial destruction of Babylon Station,

Homeguard's sabotage is much more subtle than Earth First's. They've already booby-trapped the station's fusion reactor almost undetectably. Their intent is to frame the Narns for the "bombing" of the station not only to destroy it, but also to widen the diplomatic gap between the races. To build on that cover, they've arranged for a ship to be destroyed in the explosion—a ship which, unknown to its pilot, is carrying crates of explosives and Narn uniforms. They've further arranged for that ship to be the one on which the PCs travel—posthumously framing the characters for working for the Narns becomes a convenient way to place the blame while getting rid of a potential enemy at the same time.

The Plot

Earth First's plan goes off first, and the station's infrastructure collapses before the reactor comes online. The sabotage to the reactor, while already completed by Homeguard, is not discovered since the reactor wasn't activated, and ultimately causes the explosion of the second station. Near the end of the adventure, the PCs gather clues that point toward an underground organization to whom Earth First is reporting. This organization, Homeguard, has a very cellular nature which makes it impossible to expose even over the course of this lengthy adventure. Earth First, however, is an ideal willing scapegoat for both acts of terror, and the PCs' investigation will bring Senator Sidhe's actions to an end.

The story takes place in seven chapters. The characters will largely be reacting to events during the first few chapters, taking a more proactive hand in things as the story progresses. They should experience chapters 1-3 in order. Following that, their actions will determine the order of the remaining chapters (see the Story Chart).

Chapters 1 and 2 introduce the characters to one another and set them into their first mission. A set of false orders brings them to the site of the Babylon Project just in time to witness the destruction of Babylon Station. Stuck at the site, in chapter 3 the characters are drawn into the investigation of the event—and find themselves the subject of suspicions.

In Chapters 4, 5 and 6 the PCs pursue their investigations to other star systems where key information can be found—Proxima and Sol. These chapters can be experienced in whatever order the group decides to take them.

Finally, by Chapter 7 the group has pieced together enough of the Earth First conspiracy to confront some of its key players. As they approach the close of this adventure, they find that Earth First is merely the tip of the iceberg, and that if they are to end the threat to the Babylon Project, their real task is still ahead of them.

If you decide to use this as part of an epic story arc for a longer campaign, you will need to work out a few details beyond those provided here. By the end of this adventure, the group will be entering the Preparation Phase of the story. They will need to get ready to face Homeguard, and the adventures you write from this point on will give them tools and opportunities to stop their opponent. This means that you will have to decide who in Homeguard they will face and how much power this antagonist has at his or her command. You may want to flesh out the details of the characters' base on Tau Ceti IV (or elsewhere if they choose another location). The Homeguard, and any specific antagonists, will also have bases of operations and other resources that will affect how they interact with the player characters and determine where they must go to beat the foe. And you may want to bring additional parties into the plot—alien organizations, for example, or other groups on either side of the issue. This story can provide a great conflict that both you and the players will enjoy, and using it as part of an epic story can be very rewarding.

The Cast

The players can take on any roles that would fit into the premise of an investigative team. The only requirement for this story is that they are open to the idea of Humans interacting with other races and that Earthforce would have no reason to doubt their loyalty. Have your players make up their own characters, or use some or all of the characters detailed at the end of this chapter.

The characters included here are representative of the wide variety of character types that might make up a team such as this. If you and your players want to make up your own characters, keep in mind the types of characters that a team of this nature needs. Since the team is a unit working for Earthforce, at least one military officer will be included. The team should also have someone trained in investigation, a medically trained member, and a technically savvy member. You may also wish to add other types of characters if you are planning to build on the story arc as presented.

The pre-generated team is initially made up of five different Human characters. Early in the story others have the op-

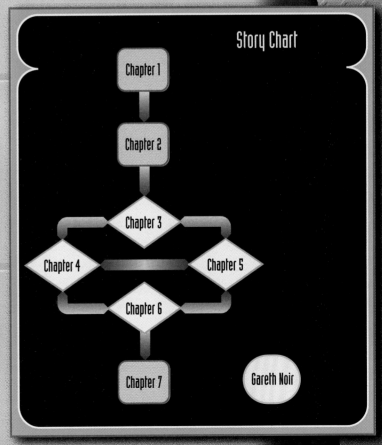

As noted in Integrating Character Concepts in chapter 2 (page 79), there are several ways to get the PCs together. Two methods are used in this example. The first is the team approach, which is used to include the five core members of the team. The second is the circumstantial approach, which brings both Gareth and So'Shal into the party. These characters have specific roles to play early in the story, but will afterward be free to do whatever they choose. If you have players who join the game late, or players who do not mind fulfilling a predetermined role early on, they might enjoy these characters. If you have players who want to play other aliens, you will have to find a similar way to bring them into the story.

portunity to join. You can use these opportunities as you see fit to accommodate other types of characters who would not fit into the team format described here. In total, there are six player characters presented here for you to use, and one NPC whose role is large enough that you may wish to use him as a player character. Character sheets for each are presented at the end of the chapter. The characters are:

Lt. James O'Conner: Lt. O'Conner is the Earthforce officer assigned to the group. He is a loyal, straight-laced officer with little sense of humor. He comes from a long line of police officers, including both his father and grandfather back on Earth. O'Conner is fresh out of the ground services, where he served during the Earth-Minbari War after being conscripted from his local police force.

Dr. Kaia Daryas: Dr. Daryas is a Human doctor with an interest in xenomedicine. Originally from London, as a youth she traveled extensively through Human space with her father, an EarthGov diplomat. Her interest in medicine grew from her father's few interactions with aliens.

April Vincent: Vincent is a Human computer programmer. Her twin loves are computers and music, and she is talented at both. She primarily makes a living as a software consultant for Earthforce, but still she loves to perform on stage now and again.

Alec Lichtopitis: Lichtopitis is a Human guard. Alec grew up as an orphan on the streets of Mars, learning fast and staying alive only by virtue of his strength and size. A line of jobs as bouncers and bodyguards led to his eventual employment with Earthforce.

Jacob Marin: Marin is a Human telepath. As a kid, Jacob was saved from a life of poverty by the emergence of his powers and the intervention of Psi-Corps, for which he owes the organization a great debt. He is a licensed commercial telepath, used to routine negotiations between private businessmen. The Corps has put him on temporary assignment to Earthforce.

So'Shal: So'Shal is a Narn citizen. After a youth spent in religious and physical training on Homeworld, So'Shal has set out into the galaxy. He is presented as a PC, but can be played as an NPC at the GM's discretion.

Gareth Noir: Noir is a shuttle pilot for hire. The players will encounter him early in the story, but he is a character with a checkered past and quite a few secrets to hide—he is in fact a Centauri. He accrued massive gambling debts with certain members of the Republic who would be "very disappointed" if he couldn't pay them back, and has been hiding for several years as a Human. Over that time, he has tried to learn as much about Humanity as possible (to further his disguise), and has seen how aliens are often treated. He believes that he will be turned in to the authorities if he were found out. The presence of a Narn in the party makes his fear even worse. If the PCs find out about his true bloodline, they will need to deal with both his reaction and theirs. Gareth is presented as an NPC, but he could be developed into a PC.

Chm: 3	Int: 5	Str: 3
Fin: 7	Ins: 4	Agl: 4
Pre: 6	Wit: 5	End: 4
Xen: 6	Per: 4	Cor: 6

Primary Skill: Piloting
Major Skills: Gambling
Hiding
Lang., English

There are two main groups of antagonists interacting with both the players and each other during the course of the story, both opposed to the influence of aliens on Human society. The first group is Earth First, a small, closely knit organization headed by EA Senator James Sidhe (see below). He runs his organization much like a family, initiating only those whom he trusts into his circle, and using his political influence to accomplish those things that can't usually be done by others within the group.

Homeguard is a larger organization that will factor into the story later on. As opposed to Earth First, Homeguard is not controlled by one person, but is a loose organization based around several "cell" groups that occasionally communicate. The sabotage of Babylon Station is the first big act in which several cells coordinate. Homeguard is always on the lookout for new members, and Earth First's sabotage of Babylon Station will draw Homeguard's eye.

The players' team will interact with several additional important people over the course of the adventure. These include:

Lt. Scott Sherman: Lt. Sherman is the aide to Commander Masters, the direct supervisor of the characters' group. O'Conner (or your group's Earthforce officer) is supposed to report to Masters periodically. However, during the crisis that arises from the collapse of Babylon Station, Cmdr. Masters is called back to Earth for a closed advisory session, and Lt. Sherman is the team's liaison. Sherman is a young officer nearing the end of his term of duty, looking forward to returning to Mars and getting a "regular job" in the private sector. He is willing to help the team as they request, but isn't particularly interested in the success or failure of the Babylon Project.

Chm: 7	Int: 5	Str: 4
Fin: 6	Ins: 6	Agl: 3
Pre: 4	Wit: 4	End: 3
Xen: 5	Per: 4	Cor: 6

Primary Skill: Physics: 5
Major Skills: Writing: 3
Mathematics: 3
Diplomacy: 4

Cmdr. Lionel Dawson: Cmdr. Dawson is the second-in-command at the Babylon Station construction site. The players first meet him in chapter 3. He is a career officer, more interested in his own advancement than the station itself, and when it collapses he knows that his service record is in jeopardy. He wants to close the case as quickly and simply as possible, with a minimum of fuss.

Chm: 6	Int: 6	Str: 3
Fin: 5	Ins: 5	Agl: 6
Pre: 4	Wit: 5	End: 4
Xen: 3	Per: 5	Cor: 5

Primary Skill: Tactics, Spc. Comb.: 5
Major Skills: Combat, Ranged: 3
Software Design: 3
Business: 3

Lt. Sandra S. Bookerman: Lt. Bookerman is a shipping clerk at Ganymede Outpost. She was the inspector on the "Earthforce shipment" sent to Babylon Station aboard the PCs' ship. The daughter of James Sidhe, she is in EF mainly because her father expected her to serve. She is in the middle of her tour of duty, anxiously awaiting her discharge when she will head back to Suffolk and start a family with her husband there. She did a favor for her father by passing his shipment along to the station, but she did not actually inspect them, and does not realize her part in a conspiracy. She is devoted to her father, however, and loyal to him.

Chm: 6	Int: 5	Str: 3
Fin: 6	Ins: 5	Agl: 6
Pre: 4	Wit: 3	End: 5
Xen: 4	Per: 4	Cor: 6

Primary Skill: Law: 4
Major Skills: Art: 4
Writing: 3
Software Design: 3

David Sidhe: Mr. Sidhe is the CEO of Daedalus Omicron, a small mining and manufacturing company based out of Proxima III. He is the brother of Senator James Sidhe, the organizer of Earth First. His views are not as polarized against aliens as those of his brother, but he does concur with many of James' principles. He pursued the contract for the station's infrastructure when his brother assured him that he could circumvent the inspection process. Later on, as the events in chapters 4 and 5 unfold, he is persuaded to let D.O. take the blame for the reactor explosion. David is very passionate about the future of his company and its employees, but he is also loyal to his brother—his only living relative besides his niece (Bookerman, above). He is also aware that his part in the conspiracy could cause him trouble, and is prepared to cover things as far as he can.

Chm: 8	Int: 5	Str: 3
Fin: 8	Ins: 5	Agl: 5
Pre: 4	Wit: 5	End: 3
Xen: 3	Per: 4	Cor: 5

Primary Skill: Business: 5
Major Skills: Diplomacy: 5
Savvy: 4
Mathematics: 3

Senator James Sidhe: James Sidhe is the EarthGov Senator for the United Kingdom. He is also the organizer of Earth First, an organization devoted to keeping the subversive influences of alien societies out of the EA. He formed the group after the death of his wife during her service as a fighter pilot in the Minbari War, and as head and functional center of the group is the only one who knows its complete plans. A powerful speaker on issues of defense. He was elected to the Senate after Sir Peter Ashton became President, but has always moderated his views on aliens in public. After his plan to sabotage Babylon Station succeeds, he is tracked down by Homeguard, and as the investigation begins to close in on him, he agrees to take a fall not just for his actions, but also to cover Homeguard when the reactor on Babylon 2 explodes. As a martyr, he hopes to be a savior of his people.

Chm: 7	Int: 5	Str: 4
Fin: 8	Ins: 5	Agl: 4
Pre: 4	Wit: 6	End: 4
Xen: 2	Per: 6	Cor: 5

Primary Skill: Diplomacy: 5

Major Skills: Business: 5
History: 4
Savvy: 5

Bill Mainer: Mainer is a shopkeeper on Proxima III (or Ganymede, depending on where you decide to play out chapter 6). He owns a small grocery store in the commercial district. He is also a member of Homeguard—not a leader, just a rank and file bigot loyal to the cause of a pure Earth.

Chm: 6	Int: 5	Str: 4
Fin: 7	Ins: 5	Agl: 4
Pre: 5	Wit: 5	End: 4
Xen: 3	Per: 4	Cor: 5

Primary Skill: Business: 4
Major Skills: Law: 3
Savvy: 3
Combat, Ranged: 3

Chapter 1: Touchdown and Takeoff

This Chapter begins at what is supposed to become the team's home base of Tau Ceti IV (detailed on page 187). It introduces the player characters to one another and sets them into their first mission.

Scene 1: Arrival

Each of the PCs in the Earthforce squad will have received notice and transport to Tau Ceti IV. In the case of civilians, this will be a contract requiring that they be to Tau Ceti IV by March 10, 2250 along with a travel voucher. EF officers will simply receive transfer orders around that time. The player characters can arrive over several days or all on the same day, however you or the players decide. The office that they report to is little more than a two-room suite with some chairs and a couple of desks, along with a non-functional vidphone. They will meet as they arrive, either on the shuttle or at the office, as you determine. Give them a little time to look around and introduce themselves to each other in character, but not much. The events that take place in the next scene will happen very quickly.

Scene 2: Plans in Motion

Before they get a chance to settle in, the player characters will be drawn into events around them. The very day the last team member arrives, two things happen: a raider attack on a Narn transport coincides with the arrival of their first mission orders.

The raider attack apparently occurred just after the last of the player characters arrived at Tau Ceti, and local ships carrying survivors begin arriving within hours. Over thirty Narns were killed in the attack on the *Ta'mazad*, which was passing through the Tau Ceti system on the way from Altair to Kotok IV. As the PCs are settling in, the dozen or so Narn survivors are ushered through to the colony's Medlab. In the sudden rush of medical emergencies, the party's doctor (if there is one) will be called upon to help, treating several Narns for minor wounds. Others on the team may be called upon to help move the wounded or clear debris. Among the wounded are So'Shal, who was aboard the transport.

The second event is the transmission of orders to the team from their Earthforce liaison on Ganymede:

> Orders To: Lt. James O'Conner, Earthforce Investigator
> From: Commander Samuel Masters, Ganymede Base
> Date: 10 Mar 50
> Report with team to the EA station at Epsilon Eridani III, Major Johnston, for standard training exercises. Passage has been booked aboard civilian transport *No Strings Attached*, for launch at 0500 hrs 11 Mar 50. Training orders await at Epsilon Eridani III.

Nothing about these orders seems out of the ordinary, and they can be verified with the commander's office on Ganymede (although the commander himself is not available for such routine inquiries). Epsilon III is the site of construction for Babylon Station, but characters may not realize this unless they look it up in the news.

The ship on which passage has been booked is the *No Strings Attached*, a private transport captained by Gareth Noir. The ship is scheduled to leave early in the morning, and cargo loading begins the night before. The ship itself is detailed on page 189.

Scene 3: Up and At'em

Gareth is a night person who feeds his passion for gambling as often as possible, and his last evening on a civilized colony before a long trip certainly qualifies as a time to play. At 0500 the next morning, the departure hour according to the orders, there is nobody at the ship waiting for the player characters. Gareth is still in bed in his hotel, having only just returned from the casino a few hours earlier.

The PCs will either have to wait or try to find and wake him. With a little ingenuity, they can track him down at the hotel and call his room or beat on the door. Unless they manage to wake him early, the ship will not get off the ground until 0900. The timing has no real effect on the adventure, but may be an opportunity for some interesting roleplaying and a little tension.

Behind the Scenes

This chapter seems very simple, but several elements in this chapter set the stage for later events. The antagonists have a head start, and their plan is already in motion.

Gareth was given a lucrative rate to take on the passengers along with his cargo, with a very strict deadline, and although suspicious, he takes the job because he owes a large payment on his ship—which he can't otherwise make. The cargo of the *No Strings Attached* consists of three shipping containers, each of which contains a separate lot of goods. Unknown to Gareth, two of these lots are false shipments from Homeguard.

The first is a lot of Earthforce "construction supplies" bound for the station at Epsilon III. In reality, this is a shipment of Narn military uniforms planted to implicate the Narns in the sabotage. The second shipment is a lot of "mining tools" being shipped for IPX, ostensibly to be transferred to an IPX corporate ship at Epsilon III. In these crates are military-grade explosives, planted to ensure the complete destruction of the *NSA* and scatter her cargo where it will easily be found. The third container holds a lot of food supplies from Habitat of Care bound for Centauri Beta 3, which is exactly what it appears to be.

These shipments are Homeguard's "evidence" of Narn involvement. The PCs' orders were also sent by Homeguard, to time their arrival with the activation of the reactor so that it would blow up with the *No Strings Attached* there. Homeguard is still unaware of Earth First and the fact that the station will collapse before the reactor becomes active, but their plan is in motion.

So'Shal is brought into the story in a less than friendly manner. The raider attack on the Narn transport was coincidental, but it did provide Homeguard with an additional opportunity. During the night, Homeguard thugs drug and kidnap So'Shal from his bed in the Medlab, and place his unconscious body in an extra crate in the Earthforce container aboard the *No Strings Attached.* His placement aboard the ship was afterthought to their primary plan, an effort to lend credence to Narn involvement—Narns often send someone along with smuggled goods to make sure that they are not used against the Regime.

Chapter 2: The Space Case

This chapter begins shortly after the first leaves off, an hour or two out from Tau Ceti IV. The jump gate is several hours away from the planet. The station is one jump away from Tau Ceti IV, with a travel time of just under two days.

Scene 1: An Unexpected Package

As everyone else is getting settled in for the ride after liftoff, Gareth heads to the hold to check that the cargo is secure for the trip through hyperspace. This is a routine check, and he doesn't bother locking the door behind him. While there, So'Shal, in the Earthforce crate, regains consciousness, finding himself unable to escape from the box. If both Gareth and So'Shal are NPCs, the scene plays out as follows: Gareth, hearing an odd noise, opens the crate. So'Shal, bursts out, knocking Gareth unconscious with the lid. So'Shal knows he's been shanghaied and recognizes that he is on a strange ship, so he appropriates Gareth's PPG and takes him hostage, guarding the door and waiting for action from the unknown crew. The first indication the PCs have that anything is wrong will not be until later.

If either Gareth, So'Shal, or both are player characters, or if a PC goes along with Gareth, adapt the events to the reactions of your players. So'Shal may fight or flee, or other characters may flee and alert the rest of the party to his presence. If any of the characters interacted with him in chapter 1, they might try to talk to him and calm him down. In any event, the PCs must come to terms with a panicked Narn who is extremely capable of defending himself.

Scene 2: Into the Gate?

While Gareth is engaged with So'Shal in the hold, the ship itself continues on course toward the jumpgate. As the ship approaches the gate, its computer begins preparations to enter hyperspace. This process requires a pilot at the seat to confirm the operation. If Gareth is missing, an alarm will sound, which may be the player characters' first warning that anything is amiss in the cargo hold. From that point, they will have to figure out a way to deal with So'Shal. How this unfolds relies largely on the players' actions.

Life Aboard the No Strings Attached

BAB/COM

Life aboard a small ship like the *NSA* is pretty boring. Gareth has a few gambling games programmed into the ship's computer, and the kitchen facilities have a storage closet with equipment for isometric exercises, but other than that it is largely a matter of being cooped up in unpredictable gravity for a few days with very little to do other than hang around (literally) in the bunks. Experienced space travelers may have prepared for this, but not everyone will necessarily realize how long the experience will seem. If you wish, encourage a little roleplaying and give the players a chance to let the characters interact. Although he prefers to be alone in the cockpit, Gareth can be convinced to allow someone to occupy the single copilot seat at times.

Once the dust has settled, Gareth will want to continue on to their destination. He has a cargo deadline to meet, and isn't about to let a mere stowaway turn him back.

Scene 3: Alas, Babylon

The rest of the trip goes uneventfully (unless you decide to add adventures along the way), and this scene begins shortly before the *No Strings Attached* opens the jump gate at Epsilon III. Due to the late start and the discovery of So'Shal in the cargo hold, the ship is running about twelve hours late, and Gareth is in danger of losing his fee.

Instructing everyone to strap in, he returns to the cockpit and activates the jump gate sequence. Through the gate, there is no problem. The approach to the station's Construction Habitat (the temporary station) is set to take about three hours. Gareth is playing the comm chatter over the intercom during the approach.

Two hours into the approach, Gareth and anyone with an audio or vid feed to the cockpit is witness to the destruction of Babylon Station. The event is preceded by the following comm conversation:

An official-sounding voice over comm audio: *"Construction control to Bravo 7."*

Gareth's voice: *"Bravo 7 reads."*

C&C: *"Please initiate holding pattern delta. Ship traffic is to be delayed for two hours."*

Gareth: *"Roger that, control. What's the delay?"*

C&C: *"Station operations, Bravo 7. The computer guys are starting the gravity spinup. They want traffic clear."*

Gareth: *"Any chance we can get in under the wire? We've been out here floating around a few days and we're looking for a good walk."*

C&C: *"Sorry, Bravo 7. No exceptions."*

Gareth: *"Can I at least get my cargo marked received?"*

C&C: *"Hold on Bravo 7, we'll check."* Pause.

A third voice: *"Look out!! It's—what's happening?!?"*

Gareth: *"Great m— my god!"*

Jumpgate Procedures

As a ship approaches a jumpgate, certain procedures are standard. Most ships' computers are perfectly capable of carrying out those procedures, though the presence of a pilot, as in all but the most routine maneuvers, is standard. In most cases, the computer will take certain standard steps until Human intervention occurs. The pilot need only issue a confirmation to open the jumpgate. In a routine trip, that confirmation serves only to ensure that the pilot is at the controls as the ship begins the more tricky procedure of locking onto a beacon once in hyperspace.

Aboard the *No Strings Attached*, if no confirmation is given for the jump gate activation sequence, five minutes before the scheduled activation a klaxon sounds within the ship to call the pilot to the cockpit. If no jump confirmation is given by the time the jump sequence is to begin, the ship automatically aborts the jump program and veers off course, clearing the gate. After five more minutes, it begins transmitting a preprogrammed distress signal.

C&C: *"Clear channels. All ships clear channels!"*

Voice: *"Mayday! Mayday! The station is—"*

The conversation is overtaken by a loud burst of static. Anyone in the cockpit, or with a video feed to their flight station, can follow events from that point visually. Babylon Station is a mere speck at first, but Gareth quickly increases the screen magnification. For the first few moments, the lanky skeleton of the giant space station looks perfectly normal—a straight spine with a series of spindly rings around it. In almost slow motion, that spine begins to bend. Three joints appear along the central column, each near one of the rings, and the whole structure begins to fold in upon itself. Smaller ships flee the area, like tiny insects next to the huge crumbling station.

Within moments it is over. Comm comes back online, and all ships are instructed to remain in the area. Departure access to the jump gate will be restricted indefinitely. After a short wait, the *No Strings Attached* is granted access to dock in the Construction Habitat.

Behind the Scenes

The PCs have now seen the first act of sabotage come to fruition, although they do not yet know it. The collapse of the station was Earth First's success, and although it will be called an accident, the PCs will come to discover otherwise. Homeguard, caught off guard by this event, now begins to put a few political clues together back home and will soon discover who was behind the collapse (though they won't learn all of the details until Senator Sidhe joins their ranks).

As for So'Shal, he is an innocent. He has no knowledge of where he is, how he got there or why. He doesn't remember anything about his abduction and can provide no answers to the party as to what his part in this is. Outside of a few bruises and the narcotic effects that quickly wear off, he is unwounded.

Chapter 3: Searches and Suspicions

This chapter takes place aboard the Babylon Station Construction Habitat during the aftermath of the collapse of the main station. Once on the Habitat, the player characters immediately become the target of suspicion, especially when So'Shal is discovered. Once the PCs clear themselves, without jumpgate access they are stuck at the Habitat with no official guidance. Their orders are suspicious, but with wounded coming and no explanation for the collapse they should be able to occupy themselves. After scene 1, let them encounter the scenes here in the order their actions take them.

Scene 1: Colors of Suspicion

The player characters were not expected at Epsilon III, and the timing of their arrival arouses suspicion. As soon as the *No Strings Attached* completes docking, the PCs are met by armed guards and ordered to surrender their weapons. O'Conner or anyone in EF uniform can present their orders, but all others will be commanded to remain aboard the ship for the time being.

Major Johnston, the commander at the site to whom the characters were to report, was aboard the station with the technical crews when it collapsed and is severely injured. The senior officer on the Habitat is now Commander Dawson, the major's aide. It is to him that the PCs must report.

Their orders were not received by the station personnel until the morning of their arrival, even though they should have been filed upon their departure from Tau Ceti. Verification of the PCs' paperwork with Tau Ceti IV will show it as authentic, which will, after some tense negotiation with a suspicious Cmdr. Dawson, prompt him to release the party from their house arrest. However, the commander has no idea what "routine training exercises" the PCs were supposed to perform, and has other issues on his mind now. He suggests that they check with their CO back on Ganymede, and that they "stay out of his hair."

Scene 2: Lending a Hand

If the PCs wish to lend a hand to the wounded coming onto the station, they can do so much as they did back on Tau Ceti IV, with those able to lend medical assistance doing so and others helping to move and clean up damaged ships. The wounded will be coming in for several hours, in various degrees of injury, and the need for helping hands is great.

In the confusion, word of their arrival with a Narn gets around, and rumors about the player characters spread. Even if So'Shal tries to help, he and any with him will be treated with suspicion. The confusion can help the PCs in their investigation, though, as they pick up rumors and converse with personnel. They might, for example, be treating one of the technicians from the station when she says in a delerium, "there wasn't anything wrong with my readout!" Or they might overhear a worker talking to his buddy, "Man, I'm glad I wasn't on duty when it happened. They say the longitudinal just gave way! Zack was lucky to get out before it ripped his suit open."

It will be some hours before anything like normal operation resumes aboard the Habitat, and construction timetables will take another several days to straighten out. Until then, the Habitat will be full of chaos.

Scene 3: Fishy Orders

In accordance with Dawson's suggestion, the PCs will probably want to check with Cmdr. Masters on Ganymede regarding their orders. Masters' office has no record of these orders, and the personnel there are surprised to learn that the PCs are at Epsilon and not Tau Ceti. After a little effort on their end, they can confirm that the computer did transmit a copy of the bogus orders to Epsilon III that morning, but there is no record of who originated the orders or when. Any further in-depth research on the computer records requires that the researcher be at Ganymede—but Masters' office does not have the manpower to devote to further investigation.

In the absence of real orders in the meantime, the player characters are on their own. After two days, if they haven't taken any initiative, orders will come from Masters' office that they are to investigate and follow up all leads to determine the cause and nature of the loss of Babylon Station.

Scene 4: Investigations

If the party requests it, they will be given a temporary meeting room aboard the Construction Habitat from which to conduct their investigation. Here at the site of the accident, a wealth of information is available—but not all of the answers. The team's first steps will probably be to seek out technical details surrounding the incident. They might interview various technical crew members around the Habitat, or search the computer logs if one of the characters can interpret the complex engineering data. Information that they might uncover includes:

• The collapse of the station was directly caused by structural failure in the spine. Miraculously, the damage is far less severe than it looks, and is restricted to the central support structure and the couplings on the habitat sections that the workers were attempting to spin up. The only casualties were those who were in the operations center on the station, directly monitoring the spinup.

• Investigation may turn up some or all of these details. The computer programs that controlled spinup were not tampered with, and the software was working per-

179

fectly. There are no reliable reports of workers acting in a suspicious manner, and the computer technicians noticed nothing amiss until the collapse began. The records of shipment indicate that the station's construction materials were built in various locations throughout EA space, and were thoroughly inspected before shipment to Epsilon III. With some effort, the PCs can track down the fact that the sections that failed were all constructed in the Proxima system. Deeper research will reveal that the company that made them was a private concern called Daedalus Omicron, Inc., located in the Proxima asteroid belt. No further information about this will be available unless the characters go to Proxima.

• The cargo aboard the ship is incriminating (see the "Behind the Scenes" section of chapter 1). Furthermore, as mentioned below, Gareth will attempt to shuffle the contents, which will probably muddy those waters. Investigating the cargo will yield the following further information:

The explosives are military-grade, although without detonators are not particularly volatile. According to the manifest, the container originated from IPX shipping offices on Proxima III and should contain "tools." It was transferred aboard the *NSA* by dockworkers on Tau Ceti IV.

The Narn uniforms are military, most likely stolen or purchased on the black market, although there is really no way to trace them back that far. The container originated at the Earthforce outpost on Ganymede, and is listed as containing "construction supplies." It was also transferred aboard the *NSA* by Tau Ceti dockworkers.

• Cmdr. Dawson doesn't seem very interested in the success of the PCs' investigation. Although he does provide access and information that they request, within reason, he is often slow to respond and provides only minimal resources. He complains several times about their "unsubstantiated allegations" (if they report suspicions of sabotage) and attempts to "stir things up." Unfortunately, Earthforce seems to agree with him: within just a few days, an Earthforce investigator back on Earth accepts Dawson's report that the event was an accident, without even visiting the site.

Since investigation at the Habitat will yield a lot more questions than answers, the player characters will need to travel elsewhere to follow up the investigation. They will likely wish to travel to Proxima, Ganymede or Tau Ceti. In fact, if they have any loose ends when they report to Cmdr. Masters, he will suggest they leave Epsilon III to follow those leads up. While it will not be difficult for them to arrange jump gate access, they might find it difficult to book passage. The military ships in the area that have been put on alert will not be leaving for a while, and there is very little non-military traffic due to that same alert status. The only private ship available is the *No Strings Attached*, so the PCs will need to commission its services again.

In any case, once it becomes clear that structural failure was the cause of the collapse (and that there is no proof of sabotage), the military ships in the area will be ordered down from extreme alert to standing watch, and orders will come from Earth-Gov to begin the construction of Babylon 2 (see chapter 3 of this book for more details). The players may have suspicions, but with-

Investigative Authority

The player characters' team, being a part of EarthForce, has a fairly broad spectrum of investigative powers. They are effectively a Federal police unit, and can question people all they like, as well as gain full access to EF records and computers. Additionally, they can contact Ganymede for paperwork such as subpoenas and search warrants if they have proper evidence to support those measures.

They also have their wits and equipment. Lt. O'Conner was issued a forensics analyzer (see page 168) as part of his post, which he should have brought with him to Epsilon III. It is a powerful device, but it is also expensive, and he is responsible for seeing that it is not damaged. The forensics analyzer can be a valuable tool in some aspects of this adventure. Among other functions, if connected to a tachyon link, it can communicate with the EF databases at the Ganymede Outpost.

out proof they cannot stop the construction, so they will need to get that proof elsewhere in Human space.

Behind the Scenes

Once the characters leave the station, if So'Shal is an NPC he will want to look for the first passage back to Narn. If he is a PC, he will probably be more adventurous, though, and may stick with the party.

As mentioned above, Gareth will do a little behind-the-scenes snooping around the cargo early in this chapter (if he's an NPC—if he's a player character, he may not react to events in this manner). After their arrival, Gareth learns that there is no recipient for his cargo. In a panic (fearing that he won't receive the desperately-needed payment for the trip), he takes the first opportunity when alone on the ship to examine the cargo. He discovers what is really in the containers in his holds. Being Centauri, he is particularly spooked by the Narn uniforms. There's nowhere on the ship to hide so many of them, so he comes up with the best plan he can think of: hide the uniforms in the other shipment. He takes the Narn uniforms and hides them under the explosives, splitting the shipments so that in both the IPX and EF containers, every crate has explosives on top and uniforms underneath. His hope is that the containers won't be searched until he's long gone—not a great plan, but the best his panicked mind can produce. As a part-time smuggler he knows how to reseal the crates and containers to prevent detection, so only the most perceptive of searchers later will notice the tampering.

As already mentioned, the other characters' orders were faked by Homeguard in order to draw them and the *No Strings Attached* to Epsilon III in time for the reactor explosion, which was of course preempted by the collapse.

While the PCs are active, Homeguard and Earth First are in action, as the former seeks out the latter. Senator Sidhe joins Homeguard, making Earth First a Homeguard cell.

Though the PCs might come to suspect him, Dawson is no Homeguard sympathizer—just a career-minded officer keen to

---

Framed!

The Homeguard's plan was to have the PCs on the station when the fusion reactor explodes. The Narn uniforms (and a Narn body) are part of Homeguard's plan to blame the Narns for the explosion. Both of these pieces of evidence do not actually have a place in the collapse of Babylon Station, but in what was to have happened—the reactor explosion that Homeguard had rigged. That disaster will now befall Babylon 2, and the player characters (and their phony cargo) will probably be nowhere near.

The PCs will not be aware of why the cargo was planted, who planted it, or why they were picked to carry it. Furthermore, if Gareth has been tampering with the cargo and the PCs use their forensics analyzer in their investigation, they might discover Centauri DNA all over the suspect containers, providing yet another confounding factor. If he has had time to shuffle the cargo before it is discovered, they will have to figure out which cargo originated where. When the clues are finally sorted out, they will have to travel to both Ganymede and Proxima to actually find the links to Earth First, although there may be much speculation among them as to how the pieces of the puzzle fit.

---

put the collapse behind him before it blights his record. His report, though a shallow investigation, contains no falsehoods. And he's in luck—Homeguard has members in the investigative team back on Earth, who are delighted to accept the findings of such a poor investigative effort. As a result, the only true EF investigation is being carried out be the PCs.

As the PCs' investigation begins to bear fruit, Homeguard realizes that the truth about their own sabotage—which will now take effect sometime in the future—could still be discovered before they can eliminate the PC group and discredit their work. They arrange to have Earth First and Senator Sidhe take the blame for the coming reactor explosion by altering the shipping records to indicate that Daedalus Omicron, the company owned by the Senator's brother, was responsible for the construction of the fusion reactor for the station and altering those on the IPX shipment of explosives to point to Daedalus Omicron as their origin.

Chapter 4: IPX

This chapter takes place on Proxima III, home of the IPX shipping office that originated the shipment of explosives. It takes about a week of travel to get to Proxima from the Station or Tau Ceti, and a little over one day to get there from Earth. The characters could have traveled here directly from one of the other chapters, or could have had adventures along the way.

Scene 1: Into IPX

Once they get to Proxima Colony, the player characters will have to figure out how to get to the information that they need. Checking the shipping records for the IPX container aboard the *No Strings Attached* at the docks will yield no information that couldn't be obtained from Epsilon III. More accurate and detailed records only exist at the IPX offices.

There are a few different ways to try to get this information. The PCs might try to talk one of the receptionists at IPX into giving them the information. The records of IPX shipments are not public , so it will take negotiation or subterfuge access them. The possible approaches to this are limitless.

Another approach they might take is to hack into the IPX computer to get the information. Getting into the records from a computer terminal outside of IPX is a Next to Impossible task, and the hacker attempting it will be caught or traced unless he or she gets a Significant success or better—even if the information is found. If the player characters can access a terminal inside IPX, getting the information is a Basic task (unless there are time constraints).

If the player characters manage to get the information in the computer records one way or another, they will find that the "supplies" were assembled and shipped by a subcontractor, a company called Daedalus Omicron, Inc., whose base office is here at Proxima III Colony. They may also find out that the shipment was originally scheduled to go directly to Epsilon III, but was diverted to Tau Ceti by the cancellation of a regular shipping run due to engine failure on the shuttle.

Scene 2: Daedalus Omicron

If the PCs find out about Daedalus, they will probably want to learn more about the company. By checking public records or visiting the corporate office, they can find out that Daedalus Omicron is a small mining company and foundry operating from Proxima, whose main operation is the mining of the nearby asteroids for Quantium-40 and other metals. As a sideline, it also builds custom construction supplies for some government contracts. It's owned by David Sidhe, a businessman on Earth who holds stock in several mining companies. Some of the PCs might recognize that last name: for those characters who are Proficient or better in a skill relating to EarthGov politics, perform a Difficult Task Resolution to see if they connect it with that of Senator Sidhe.

Again, by negotiation or subterfuge the characters can get a bit more information out of the company. The only parts that relate to the story, however, are that the shipment for IPX isn't in the Daedalus records, and the construction beams for the station were double-checked before they left and after they arrived at Sol by Earthforce inspectors.

Behind the Scenes

Proxima III is an industrial colony, bustling with activity. The PCs are just another annoyance to the people who work in the offices of IPX and D.O. Most of the people involved in the companies, including the receptionists with whom the players interact, aren't involved in any sort of conspiracy. Talk of Babylon Station's collapse is met with disinterest, as by the time the PCs arrive at Proxima it's old news.

The explosives and Narn uniforms were actually shipped from the IPX facility, by Homeguard sympathizers within the company, and never had anything to do with Deadalus Omicron. The links to D.O. in the records result from tampering that has already been done to set up Sidhe and Earth First for the Babylon Project disaster.

Chapter 5: The Home Front

This act takes place in the Sol system, at the Earthforce administrative offices on Ganymede. It takes about a week of travel to get to Sol from the Station or Tau Ceti, and a little over one day to get there from Proxima. The characters could have traveled here directly from one of the other chapters, or could have had adventures along the way.

The Earthforce office on Ganymede is the main transfer point for low-sensitivity EF shipments. It is a standard military base, consisting of one small dome with the official buildings, one for barracks (including quarters for those with families), and one for commercial areas.

Commander Masters, the PCs' supervisor, has his office on this base. After the destruction of Babylon Station he was called to Earth. His assistant, Lt. Sherman, will help the players as much as possible, but the lieutenant is not in a position to do much more than the team's leader. However, with the powers of EF investigators, there is little that they cannot find out in pursuing Earthforce matters.

Computer records indicate that the IPX "construction supplies" were routed from another department within Earthforce (which is unaware of the shipment), and were inspected by Lt. Sandra S. Bookerman.

Lt. Bookerman is still stationed on Ganymede and is easy to find. If asked, she will lie about the shipment, stating that the shipment contained various tools and raw materials for work on the station, just as stated on the computer record. A telepath attempting a surface scan of her will probably know that she is lying, though Bookerman won't concede to a scan, and an unauthorized scan is both illegal and inadmissable as evidence. A Significant or better success by a telepath might also yield results that she was thinking about her father during their questions. Her records reflect her family connection to Senator Sidhe, but are sealed and require a warrant (or some sneaking or hacking) for access.

Behind the Scenes

While the players are on "home ground" as it were, things are somewhat easier. Ganymede is familiar to most military personnel, and it's very easy for them to find out information and to go from place to place with little interference. Homeguard and Earth First play no direct part in this chapter, but that will soon change.

Chapter 6: The Missing Link

As the player characters pursue their investigation on Ganymede, Proxima or both, Homeguard catches wind of their activities. The PCs are starting to become a dangerous threat, and Homeguard is running out of time for subtleties. They will try to put an end to the PCs' efforts at their next port of call.

Scene 1: Ambush!

Homeguard's plan is to have local thugs ambush and kill the PCs. They might go about this in any of several ways, depending on what the characters do, where they go, and how careful they are. Homeguard might ambush the PCs when they are leaving the *No Strings Attached*, for example, when they are returning to the ship, or when they are some other relatively isolated area in the dome. They will wait for the best opportunity, when the PCs' guard is down.

The hangar bay is one good location to play out the ambush, giving lots of cover to both PCs and NPCs. Three Homeguard thug NPCs (see the sidebar) are led by Bill Mainer. All are armed with PPGs and knives. Their orders are to kill the PCs or hurt them badly enough to end their mission. They will flee if their leader goes down, but otherwise they will not disengage from combat. Security will not arrive for at least five minutes, plenty of time for a good fight.

Assuming the PCs defeat their attackers, they find only standard ID cards, showing that the thugs were all local residents with spotty criminal pasts. Bill Mainer is the owner of a small grocery store, with no criminal record. Nothing in any of the attackers' records indicate anything important to the PCs' investigation.

Scene 2: The Scene of the Criminal

If the PCs check out Mainer's store, they will find an unremarkable grocery, with a teenager behind the counter who is totally uninvolved in anything illegal. Searching the store yields only one clue, a note in the cashbox. The message is anonymous and untraceable, but clearly linked to the case:

> B— Good work on the IPX records, esp. the power plant. Our mutual friend has another task for you. Some curious cats are due into port on a ship called No Strings Attached. We think they know about D.O. and the "family business." Educate them before they invite outsiders into our midst. —P

Scene 3: Boom Today

This scene takes place about the time that the characters collect the last pieces of the puzzle, and is more a narrative scene than one in which they participate actively. The characters will probably have experienced chapters 4 through 6, although they can still pick up information in those chapters after this scene if they have not exhausted all possibilities.

If you are presenting this adventure as the first part of an ongoing campaign, this is the point where the story turns from the Identification Phase to the Preparation Phase. Time this event to maximize the dramatic impact, especially if the characters have figured out that there is something fishy about the station's fusion reactor.

The travel time between Epsilon and the systems near Sol is about one week for civilian vessels, and between Sol and Proxima is another day, not to mention any time the PCs spend involved in the different chapters. In the weeks of their investigation, new construction supplies were leaving various ports of call around the Earth Alliance, and Babylon 2 has been under construction.

As mentioned in chapter 3 of this book, since the only things seriously damaged in the collapse of Babylon Station were the support beams, the rebuilding process has gone fairly quickly. Eleven days after the PCs leave the station, the fusion reactor is brought online as part of the new Babylon 2. The sabotaged reactor goes critical and explodes three hours after activation, killing over 200 construction personnel and disabling the EAS *Pennsylvania*, injuring several on board. The Construction Habitat is also destroyed with all hands when a flying piece of debris knocks it off axis and sends it flying apart under the strain.

The reactor "accident" immediately gets picked up by ISN and becomes the top story for the next two days.

Behind the Scenes

The ambush is a straightforward attempt to kill or scare off the player characters, and there is little additional going on behind the scenes. If the PCs thwart the ambush too easily, Homeguard might try again with a larger force.

There are two important clues in the letter found at Mainer's store. The first is the phrase "D.O. and the family business," referring to Daedalus Omicron and the fact that the Senator's relatives are the ones who have been pulling the strings. If they haven't figured out the relations yet, this should help. The second clue—the comment about power plant—is a bit more vague, but may give the PCs a little more insight into the story arc. It is a reference to the sabotage of the Babylon Station reactor. They can check Earthforce's records to find that Daedalus Omicron is the company who built the fusion reactor for Babylon Station. But those records are faked, part of the phony paper trail intended to divert suspicion to Earth First. If the PCs have developed any familiarity with D.O. through their research, they should quickly realize that the company has no production facilities for manufacturing such a reactor.

Chapter 7: The Case for Sabotage

This chapter takes place before and during the explosion of Babylon 2. The explosion is obviously not an accident, and the PCs, having been the only ones continuing an investigation between the two incidents, are the furthest ahead, and will hopefully pick up the ball and solve the case.

This chapter involves questioning David Sidhe and Sandra Bookerman in order to fill in the last holes in the investigation. Neither is fully informed of Earth First's plans, and until presented with evidence that convinces them that they are conspirators to murder, they will be very uncooperative.

Scene 1: Book Her, Man

Lt. Bookerman, unaware of her part in the destruction of Babylon Station (and completely uninvolved in the loss of Babylon 2), makes no attempt to run or hide from the law, and the PCs will be able to find her on duty even after the explosion. If they manage to convince her that she could lose her job over her involvement with the false shipment, she will try to get in touch with her father for protection. If they manage to convince her that she could go to prison, she will tell them what she did, honestly claiming that she did not know what was in the shipment that she examined and that she thought she was doing a small favor for her father. She is not a hero, and her loyalty to her father does not extend to going to prison for him.

Scene 2: Sidhe's Choice

David Sidhe knows that there is more to this than just the Senator. Though not a part of Earth First, he supports the actions that the group has taken. He will only reluctantly talk to the PCs, who can meet him in his office—is a large, plush affair on the second floor of the D.O. building with a real wood desk and a view down the central street of the dome.

Sidhe cares very much about his company and people who work for him—which accounts in part for his opposition to aliens in Human space, who might take Human jobs. Like his brother, he is passionate about the cause. Unlike his brother, however, he is not willing to be a martyr. He's made a contingency plans in case things get rough, with a good stash of money in hidden bank accounts and a new identity set up on Delphi IV.

If the PCs can convince him that they have enough information to close Daedalus Omicron down, he will try to put his plan into motion. Talking long enough to distract the PCs, he calls in security guards using a hidden switch under his desk. While he waits, he will admit his part in things to the PCs and tell them what little he knows about Homeguard (mainly just their name and that they are very well placed all over the Alliance) to stall them before his escape.

After a few moments, three security guards burst in suddenly, with two more just a few paces behind them (use the com-

---

The thugs that Mainer hires to ambush the PCs are of the standard type—big, mean low-lifes common to the underworlds of all cities. They get paid and do what they're told, asking no questions and not caring about legalities or cause. They're not interested in idealism or aliens, they just want to make a few bucks.

Assume that Mainer's thugs have the following combat stats:

Strength:	6
Toughness:	0
Initiative:	4
Ranged Combat:	8 (total Ability)
Unarmed Combat:	8 (total Ability)
Armed Combat:	7 (total Ability)

bat Abilities listed for the thugs on page 185, though these personnel are somewhat more reputable in appearance). Sidhe hits the floor behind the desk as soon as they enter, yelling at the guards to "stop them!" The guards draw their weapons, and the PCs will have to defend themselves.

While the PCs are busy with the fray, Sidhe makes his escape. He jumps from beneath his desk and through the plate-glass window behind him. In the lighter gravity of Proxima III, the three-meter fall is hardly fatal, and one or more of the PCs will have to chase him through the streets if they wish to capture him.

As the PCs pursue, have them perform Contested Agility and Endurance tasks against David. The more the PCs succeed against him, the closer they get. It is suggested that six normal successes over David will allow a PCs that follows quickly to catch up with him.

With the confessions of the two accomplices and the computer records and other evidence gathered by the PCs, the investigation of the collapse of Babylon Station is complete and case is strong enough to prosecute those involved. All that's left is to wrap it up and report to Cmdr. Masters.

Behind the Scenes

During this act all of the cards are on the table, and the PCs follow the trail to the end, finally getting enough evidence to pinpoint D.O. as the guilty company in the destruction of Babylon Station and Babylon 2 and Earth First as the conspirator. Further, they have begun to get their first hard evidence that Homeguard is out there, and have struck a hard blow against this enemy by incriminating D.O. and Senator Sidhe.

Epilogue: The Spin Doctors

Once the characters report the investigation to Cmdr. Masters, their evidence will be transferred to his office, where the Earthforce Attorney General's office will take the case for prosecution.

Unfortunately, the case is buried. Daedalus Omicron goes into bankruptcy, Lt. Bookerman is dishonorably discharged and Senator Sidhe resigns for "health reasons," but other than any evidence that the PCs may have kept, the case disappears, and is greeted publicly like a crackpot conspiracy theory. The PCs know the truth, however, and it looks like their real job is just beginning...

This is the end of this sample story. From here, should you choose to continue this as an epic story, the PCs must begin to prepare for the fight against Homeguard by both repelling subversive attacks against them and trying to figure out exactly who they are fighting, building toward an epic showdown with Homeguard down the road.

Settings

This adventure takes the player characters to a variety of locations. Some of the more important locales are detailed here.

DAVID SIDHE'S OFFICE
Daedelus Omicrom, Proxima

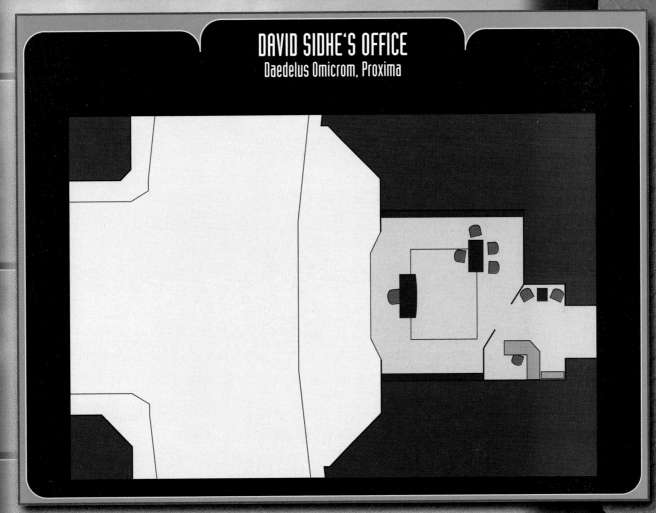

David Sidhe's Office

David Sidhe's office is a reminder of times past. Rather than the modern greys and blues of most offices, it is an early twentieth-century design—wood paneling shipped in from Earth along with solid chairs and a beautiful oak desk. Off to one side are a small couch and a coffee table, with wingback chairs, suitable for his less formal meetings. The centerpiece of the office is a picturesque view through the window behind the desk of one of the busier streets in the Proxima III dome.

Tau Ceti IV

The colony on Tau Ceti IV is brand new, with the feel of a frontier town where the law is still more in the hands of the citizens than the local police. The supplies are second-hand, the scant supply runs supplemented by a little alien traffic, and the single dome is dusty and fragile, even creaking in the wind during some of the fierce storms that batter the hostile planetscape outside.

The PCs do not actually get a chance to set up their field office at the beginning of the adventure—that will come in time. But some may have a few hours to explore while they're there. The important public areas are a shopping district, a casino/bar and a small public park. They also have access to the Police Office and the Hangar Bay, both of which are restricted to EF personnel and local police.

Earth Alliance Registered Ship
No Strings Attached

COMPARTMENTAL LAYOUT

NO STRINGS ATTACHED

EA Class D Registry NR-983E-14
Non-Atmospheric Mixed-Cargo Transport with Passenger Capacity
Owner of Record: G. Noir Transport Co., Ceti Station
Captain of Record: Gareth Noir Lic. No. 48-957338-A
Port of Registry: Ceti Station
Special Transport Permits: None

SPECIFICATIONS

Tonnage: 800 Tons gross cargo capacity
Passenger Capacity: 6, with amenities for 144 hrs.
Crew: 1 or 2
Environment Control: Life support rated at 120 man-days
Propulsion: 2xPratt-Allison Model 400 plasma-jet drives
Power: 2xPratt-Allison Model T-11 fusion reactors

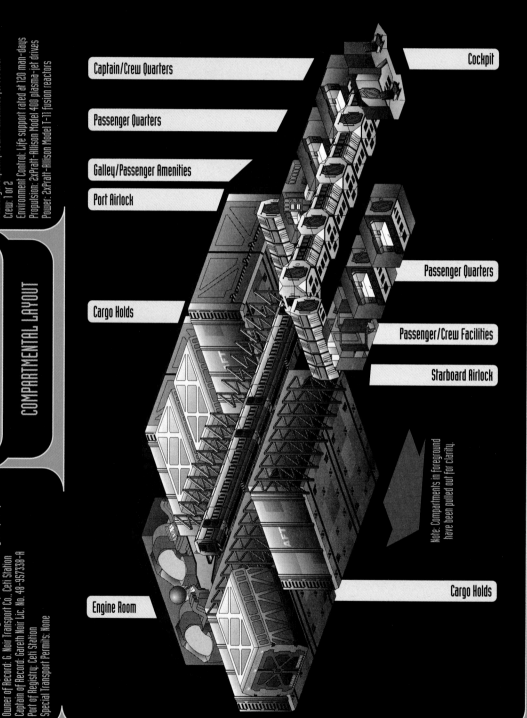

Captain/Crew Quarters

Passenger Quarters

Galley/Passenger Amenities

Port Airlock

Cargo Holds

Engine Room

Cockpit

Passenger Quarters

Passenger/Crew Facilities

Starboard Airlock

Cargo Holds

Note: Compartments in foreground have been pulled out for clarity.

No Strings Attached

The *No Strings Attached* (*NSA*) is a medium cargo transport with room for a few passengers. She will be the PCs' home for most of the adventure. The layout of the ship is very simple and spartan: a cockpit; three staterooms each capable of holding 2 passengers; the captain's quarters; the galley/crew room; personal facilities; four cargo holds; and an engine room (see the map opposite). There are no real amenities other than a library of electronic gambling games, and the ship does not spin for gravity.

The cockpit has a seat for a pilot and copilot, with a great view through the front screen. Gareth is used to flying alone, and as such prefers to be alone in the cockpit, but can be talked into allowing someone to sit in the copilot's seat at times. The ship's cockpit contains all of the flight and communications avionics, as well as rudimentary access to engineering functions (the engine room is not normally manned). It also contains the flight recorders and sensor screens for video images from outside the ship. As is standard on most ships of this size, an audio or vid feed of cockpit com and screen imagery can be accessed from most flight stations. Also, all cockpit telemetry, including vid screen imagery, is recorded, though the record is usually overwritten after a few days' flight time.

The captain's quarters is Gareth's permanent room. He will not share this room, even if it means overloading the other rooms with more passengers than they can handle. The reason for this is Gareth's secret: a roommate might discover his true race, or otherwise snoop into his affairs.

The other quarters have two bunks each, spacious enclosed compartments that also serve as flight stations. Passengers are expected to spend most of their time in their bunks, especially when the ship is maneuvering, docking, or entering or exiting jump gates. Each bunk has a comm panel which can be linked to the ship's computer (for entertainment purposes) or to the cockpit audio or vid feed (to keep tabs on what's going on). The quarters also each feature a hook-in for a third temporary restraint—a much less comfortable position with no comm panel. Finally, each of the quarters also has a false back to one or more storage lockers, for any light smuggling that Gareth might do. They are closed and empty for this trip.

The cargo bays are pressurized and heated during the initial trip, since one of the cargo lots is food supplies that require moderate conditions to prevent perishing.

Babylon Construction Habitat

The Habitat is a rotating station that provides workers with a place to live and a base of operations while building Babylon Station. A mobile structure, it can travel under its own power between projects. Mostly just a set of barracks with a few amenities and engineering facilities, the Habitat is home to over 2,000 construction workers and engineers. Conditions are spartan but liveable, with workers generally sleeping six to a room and relying on a single Medlab, an Earthforce PX and a small collection of bars and lounges. The Habitat also features offices for the many contract construction companies, a number of machine shops and engineering facilities, and a low-G hangar bay that services supply ships and the many scores of construction vehicles that work the site.

Lt. James O'Conner

Race: Human Profession: EF officer
Age: 34 Gender: Male
Archetype: Straight-laced cop
Home: Chicago (US), Earth

Characteristics:

Haunted: Was stranded on dead ship during the war. Still has nightmares and dislikes space travel.
Allies: Former CO, Chief Robert Jones, is now Assistant Chief of Security for Solos Planum dome on Mars.
Authority: In charge of PC party, as far as EF is concerned.

Attributes:

Charm:	4	Intel.:	4	Strength:	4
Finesse:	5	Insight:	6	Agility:	5
Presence:	6	Wits:	5	Endur.:	5
Xeno:	3	Percep.:	5	Coord.:	5

Skills and Specialties:

Investigation	4	Forensics	Case Mgt
Law	3	EA Civil	EA Criminal
Comb., Rgd.	3	Handgun	Longarm
Comb., Armed	3	Strike	Parry
Comb., Unarm.	2	Strike	
Acumen	2	Veracity	
Athletics	2	Running	
Geography	2	Mars Colony	
Medical, EMT	1	Human	
Acrobatics	1	Zero-G Maneuvering	
Diplomacy	1	Inquiry	
Sleight-of-Hnd	1	Pick-pocketing	

Equipment:

EF-7 PPG
Handlink
Forensic analyzer

Kaia Daryas

Race: Human Profession: Physician
Age: 28 Gender: Female
Archetype: Diplomat's kid turned Doctor
Home: Menchester (UK), Earth

Characteristics:

Dedicated: Pacifist. Will do no harm if at all possible, and will heal whenever able.
Allies: First medical instructor, Dr. Eileen White, works in London. A premier xeno-pyshician, White is influencial in Earthgov xenorelations committees.
Assets: Supported by a modest trust fund, and stands to inherit a large estate from parents.

Attributes:

Charm:	5	Intel.:	7	Strength:	3
Finesse:	4	Insight:	5	Agility:	6
Presence:	3	Wits:	5	Endur.:	4
Xeno:	5	Percep.:	4	Coord.:	6

Skills and Specialties:

Medical, Surg.	4	Human	Narn
		Centauri	
Medical, EMT	3	Human	Narn
		Centauri	Minbari
Medical, Diag.	3	Human	Centauri
Lang., Minbari	3	Comprehension	
Lang., Cent.	1	Comprehension	
Lang., Narn	1	Comprehension	
Diplomacy	2	Minbari Protocol	
Mathematics	2	Statistics	
Art	2	Photography Drawing	

Equipment:

Handlink
Military-grade first aid kit

April Vincent ("Nebula")

Race: Human   Profession: Computer Analyst
Age: 30   Gender: Female
Archetype: Computer Hacker/Musician
Home: Proxima III Colony

Attributes:

Charm:	6	Intel.:	6	Strength:	3
Finesse:	4	Insight:	7	Agility:	5
Presence:	4	Wits:	5	Endur.:	4
Xeno:	5	Percep.:	5	Coord.:	3

Skills and Specialties:

Software Des.	4	Authoring	Repair
		Hacking	
Music	3	Vocal Perf.	Jazz Comp.
		Piano Performance	
Enginr., Elec.	3	Device Applications	
		System Applications	
Enginr., Mech.	3	Mech. Apps.	Robotics
Gambling	2	Craps	
Medical, EMT	2	Human	
Piloting	2	Shuttle	
Nav., Aerosp.	2	Insystem	
Comb., Rgd.	1	Handgun	
Comb., Unarm.	1	Grapple	

Equipment:

Portable computer (state of the art, prized possession)
Handlink

Characteristics:

Stubborn: Once she sets her mind to something, it *will* get done.
Allies: An ex-lover (still a friend) works as a lead programmer at Earthdawn Technologies back on Proxima III.
Assets: Owns a top-of-the-line portable computer which she lovingly maintains; has a wide investment portfolio.

Alec Lichtopitis

Race: Human   Profession: Bodyguard
Age: 20   Gender: Male
Archetype: Straightlaced cop
Home: Syria Planum, Mars Colony

Attributes:

Charm:	6	Intel.:	4	Strength:	6
Finesse:	6	Insight:	4	Agility:	6
Presence:	4	Wits:	4	Endur.:	5
Xeno:	3	Percep.:	5	Coord.:	4

Skills and Specialties:

Comb., Unarm.	4	Grapple	Strike
		Dodge	
Comb., Armed	3	Strike	Parry
Acumen	3	Attitude	Emotion
Tracking	3	Urban	Desert
Art	2	Drawing	Painting
Hiding	2	Shadowing	Sneaking
Savvy	2	Underworld	
Diplomacy	2	Obfuscation	
Comb., Rgd.	1	Handgun	

Equipment:

EF-7 PPG
Handlink

Characteristics:

Missing Basic Skills: Illiterate (having never attended school). Tries to keep illiteracy a secret.
Proud: Believes he is doing good; doesn't want to be thought of as street trash.
Impulsive: Wants to be seen as decisive, so rarely pauses to think things through.

Jacob Marin

Race: Human   Profession: Comm. Telepath
Age: 27   Gender: Male
Archetype: Psi-Corp loyal member
Home: Psi-Corp Center, New York (US), Earth

Attributes:

Charm:	6	Intel.:	5	Strength:	4
Finesse:	6	Insight:	6	Agility:	5
Presence:	4	Wits:	4	Endur.:	5
Xeno:	4	Percep.:	4	Coord.:	4
		Psionic:	4		

Characteristics:

Dedicated: Loyal to the Corps which rescued him from a life of poverty.
Proud: Very proud of his accomplishments as a telepath, and considers himself a good person because of what the Corps has let him achieve.

Skills and Specialties:

Telepathy	4	Scanning	Blocking
Law	3	EA Civil	EA Criminal
Med., Psych.	3	Human	Centauri
Acting	3	Theater	Voice
History	2	EA	Telepaths
Writing	2	Prose	

Equipment:

Handlink

So' Shal

Race: Narn   Profession: Soldier
Age: 18   Gender: Male
Archetype: Wandering Adventure Seeker
Home: Narn Homeworld

Attributes:

Charm:	3	Intel.:	4	Strength:	8
Finesse:	3	Insight:	3	Agility:	7
Presence:	5	Wits:	4	Endur.:	7
Xeno:	3	Percep.:	5	Coord.:	5

Characteristics:

Dedicated: Dedicated to the code of ethics taught by his Katek'eth master. Will not fight unless there is no other choice, and will defend the weak and innocent.
Allies: A member of the 7th circle of the Kha' Ri.
Curious: Feels he is on an odyssey, and wants to explore the galaxy.
Assets: An ancient Katak, which he is honor-bound to care for.

Skills and Specialties:

Comb., Armed	4	Strike	Parry
Religion	3	Book of G'Quan	
		G'Quan Ceremonies	
Comb., Unarm.	3	Strike	Dodge
MA: Katek'eth	3		
Acrobatics	2	Contortion	Gymnastics
Metalworking	2	Construction/Repair	
		Ornamentation	
Hiding	2	Concealment	Sneaking
Lang., English	2	Comprehension	

Equipment:

Katak with scabbard
Small sum of EAcr.

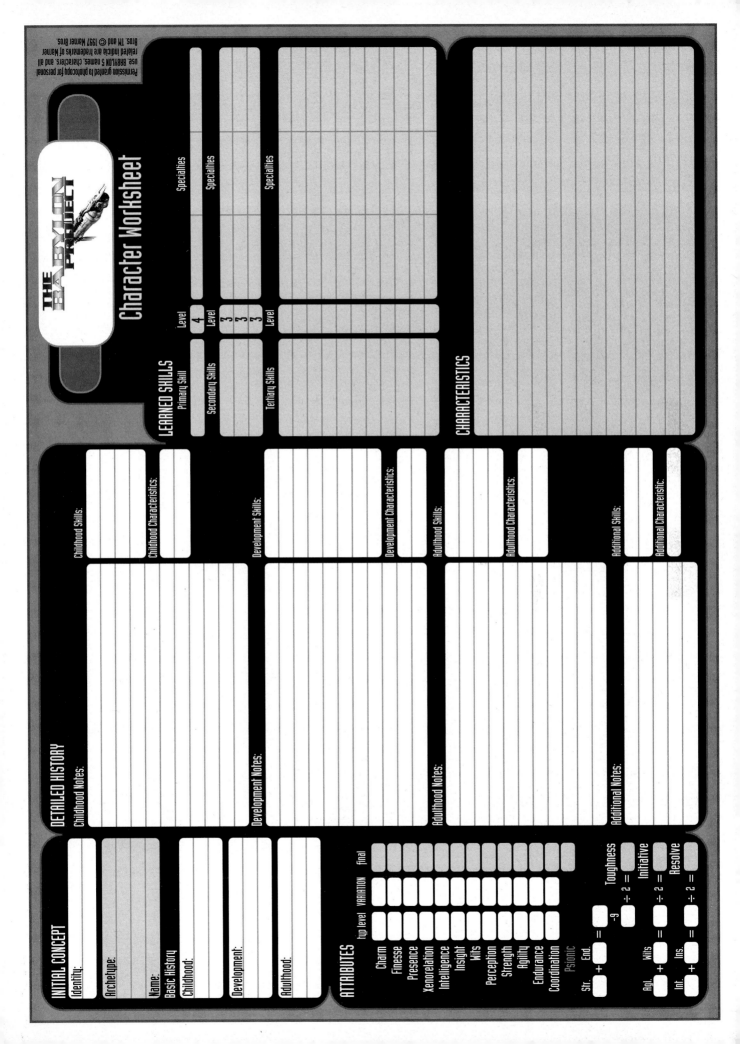

THE BABYLON PROJECT

Character Worksheet

LEARNED SKILLS

Primary Skill — Level 4 — Specialties

Secondary Skills — Level 3 / Level 3 / Level 3 — Specialties

Tertiary Skills — Level — Specialties

CHARACTERISTICS

INITIAL CONCEPT

Identity:

Archetype:

DETAILED HISTORY

Childhood Skills:

Childhood Characteristics:

Childhood Notes:

Development Skills:

Development Characteristics:

Development Notes:

Adulthood Skills:

Adulthood Characteristics:

Adulthood Notes:

Additional Skills:

Additional Characteristic:

Additional Notes:

Name:

Basic History

Childhood:

Development:

Adulthood:

ATTRIBUTES

Typ. level | VARIATION | final

Charm
Finesse
Presence
Xenorelation
Intelligence
Insight
Wits
Perception
Strength
Agility
Endurance
Coordination
Psionic

Str. + End. = ÷ 2 = −9 = Toughness

Agl. + Wits = ÷ 2 = Initiative

Int. + Ins. = ÷ 2 = Resolve

Character Worksheet

SKILL LIST (with Specialties)

Acrobatics: Climbing, Contortion, Gymnastics, Zero-G Maneuvering.
Acting: Theater, Film, Voice.
Acumen: Veracity, Attitude, Emotion.
Anthropology: Archaeology, and by individual culture.
Athletics: Jumping, Running, Swimming, Throwing, and by specific sports.
Art: Graphic Design, and by specific media.
Biology: by Kingdoms within a particular biosphere.
Business: Economics, Management, Marketing, Operations, Ethics.
Combat, Armed: Strike, Parry.
Combat, Martial Arts (specify one school): varies.
Combat, Ranged: Handgun, Longarm, Autofire
Combat, Unarmed: Block, Dodge, Grapple, Strike.
Cooking: by types of cuisine.
Dancing: by types of dance.
Diplomacy: Dulcification, Ingratiation, Inquiry, Obfuscation, Persuasion , and Protocol by Culture.
Driving: Cars, Trucks, Motorcycles.
Engineering, Aerospace: Aerodynamics, Structural Design, Plasma Engine Design, Jump Engine Design.
Engineering, Chemical: Alloys, Ceramics, Explosives, Fuels, Plastics, Applications.
Engineering, Civil: Urban Design, Planetary Structures, Orbital Structures, Applications.
Engineering, Electrical: Device Design, Systems Design, Power Systems Design, Computer Systems Design, Device Applications, System Applications.
Engineering, Mechanical: Internal Combustion Engines, Robotics, Mechanical Applications.
Gambling: by game.
Geography: Interstellar, Star System, Planetary, Region.
Geology: by planet type and regional type.
Hiding: Disguise, Concealment, Shadowing, Sneaking.
History: by area, culture and time period.
Instruction: by Race.
Investigation: Research, Forensics, Case Management.

Language (specify one language): Comprehension, Speech, Writing.
Law: by legal system.
Mathematics: Geometry, Trigonometry, Statistics, Calculus.
Medical, Biotech: by Race.
Medical, Diagnostic: by Race.
Medical, EMT: by Race.
Medical, Pharmaceutical: by Race.
Medical, Psychiatry: by Race.
Medical, Surgery: by Race.
Metalworking: Structural Design, Construction/Repair, Ornamentation.
Music: Composition by style, Performance by instrument.
Navigation, Aerospatial: Atmospheric, Insystem, Hyperspace.
Navigation, Planetary: Ground, Water.
Philosophy: by school of thought.
Physics: Quantum, Mechanical, Optical, Nuclear, Hyperspatial.
Piloting: Atmospheric Fighter, Atmospheric Shuttle, Atmospheric Transport, Fighter, Shuttle, Transport/Escort.
Religion: Texts by sect, Ceremonies by sect.
Savvy: Underworld, Politics by Culture, High Society, other specific subcultures.
Sculpture: by medium.
Shiphandling: Freighter/Liner, Escort, Capital Ship.
Sleight-of-Hand: Juggling, Prestidigitation, Pick-Pocketing.
Software Design: Authoring, Repair, Hacking.
Survival: Life Support by environment, Foraging by environment.
Tactics, Troop: by military doctrine.
Tactics, Space Combat: by military doctrine.
Telepathy: Scanning, Blocking, Broadcasting.
Tracking: by environment.
Weapons Systems: Ship, Planetary, Orbital, Vehicular.
Writing: Expository, Poetry, Prose.

CHARACTERISTIC LIST

Contentious: The character can be difficult to get along with.
Curious: The character has an insatiable desire to figure things out.
Dedicated: The character is highly devoted to a particular goal or ideal, which is held above all other priorities.
[Fan]atical: The character firmly believes that his or her most passionate viewpoints are the only possible correct ones.
Heartless: The character has a cruel, or at least a cold, side.
Impulsive: The character acts first and thinks later.
Proud: The character thinks highly of him or herself.
Selfish: The character always puts him or herself ahead of everyone else.
Stubborn: The character is difficult to sway once he or she has reached a conclusion or developed and opinion.
Addicted: The character is addicted to a substance.
Amnesiac: The character's past, or parts of his or her past, cannot be remembered.
Fragile: The character extremely sensitive to personal confrontation, stress, or violence.
Haunted: The character is dogged by regretful or horrifying memories of a trauma in the past.
Insomniac: The character has a great deal of trouble getting sleep, or staying asleep for any length of time.
Paranoid: The character believes that no-one can be trusted and that others are out to exploit, hurt, or kill him or her.
[Pho]bic: The character is completely afraid of a particular situation or object.
Ambidextrous: The character is equally apt with both the right and left hand.

Attractive: The character's physical appearance is pleasing to those who appreciate members of his or her race.
Handicapped: The character suffers a significant permanent disability.
Assets: The character owns one or more items of value.
Death Dream: (Centauri only). The character has forseen his or her own death through a dream.
Gift of Prophecy: (Female Centauri only). The character has the ability to see events that are yet to come.
Missing Basic Skills: The character is missing some of the basic skills of his or her society.
Ally: The character is associated with a person of value to the character.
Authority: The character is in a position of rank or authority.
Dependent: The character has ties to someone or something for which he or she must care.
Enemies: Through some course of action or twist of fate, the character has acquired one or more enemies.
Famous: The character is well-known, either to the public at large or to some subset of society.
Justice Oath: The character is the subject or issuer of a Narn judicial oath.
Latent Telepath: (Human only). The character has unknown and undiscovered telepathic abilities.
Rogue Telepath: The character has psychic abilities and is on the run from Psi-Corps or his or her race's equivalent.
Sleeper: The character is a Human telepath who has opted out of the capability.

THE BABYLON PROJECT

Character Record

NAME

Race

Archetype

Profession

Age

Gender

Home

CULTURAL ATTRIBUTES
- Charm
- Finesse
- Presence
- Xenorelation

MENTAL ATTRIBUTES
- Intelligence
- Insight
- Wits
- Perception
- Psionic

PHYSICAL ATTRIBUTES
- Strength
- Agility
- Endurance
- Coordination

DERIVED ATTRIBUTES
- Toughness
- Initiative
- Resolve

CHARACTERISTICS

Marginal Success (−2 Dam)

Normal Success

• Significant Success

• Critical Success (+2 Dam)

FORTUNE POINTS

EPs

Equipment Notes

Wounds	Dam Type	Dam	Imp

SKILLS	Level	Specialties

Task Difficulty Levels

Trivial	2
Easy	3
Basic	5
Average	7
Tricky	9
Difficult	11
Very Difficult	15
Next to Impossible	17
Miraculous	25

GM Reference Sheet

Task Resolution Interpretations

roll failed by 6 or more	Critical Failure
roll failed by 4 or 5	Significant Failure
roll failed by 2 or 3	Normal Failure
roll failed by 1	Marginal Failure
roll made by 0 or 1	Marginal Success
roll made by 2 or 3	Normal Success
roll made by 4 or 5	Significant Success
roll made by 6 or more	Critical Success

Permission granted to photocopy for personal use. BABYLON 5 names, characters, and all related indicia are trademarks of Warner Bros. TM and © 1997 Warner Bros.

Hit Diagram

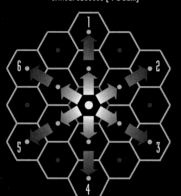

- ▨ Marginal Success (-2 Dam)
- ◸ Normal Success
- ● Significant Success
- ◉ Critical Success (+2 Dam)

Body Map

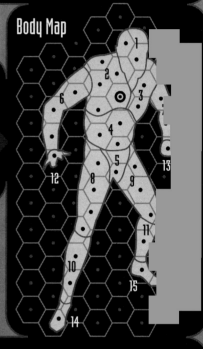

Immediate Effects Table

Top Result ▶ Stun Number
Bottom Result ▶ Imm. Impair.

Damage ▶ Location ▼	1-6	7-10	11-13	14-15	16+
Head (1)	2 / 0	4 / 2	6 / 4		
Torso or Thigh (2, 3, 8, or 9)	— / 0	-2 / 2	2 / 2	2 / 4	
Vitals or Groin (4 or 5)	— / 0	2 / 2	4 /		
Arm or Leg (6, 7, 10, or 11)	— / 0	— / 0	0 / 2	0 / 4	0 / 4
Hand or Foot (12, 13, 14, or 15)	— / 0	— / 0	-2 / 2	-2 / 4	-2 / 4

Final Effects Table

Damage ▶ Location ▼		1	2	3	4	5	6	7	8	9	10	11	12	13	14	15+
						▼ Secondary Effects ▼										
Head (1)	2								240	180	120	80 B	60	35 E	15	12
Torso (2 or3)	0											240 B	130	70	25 E	4
Vitals/Groin (4 or 5)	2									200 B	120	70	45	20 E	8	4
Arm (6 or 7)	-1											200 B	80	16	M	
Thigh (8 or 9)	0											240 B	160	80	40	
Leg (10 or 11)	0											200 B	100	12	M	
Hand/Foot (12, 13, 14, 15)	-2										240 B	160	25	M		

◀ Damage Modifier

▼ Dam. Type ▼ Final Impairment ▼

		1	2	3	4	5	6	7	8	9	10	11	12	13	14	15+
Impact	-3	0	0	0	0	0	1	1	1	1	1	2	3	3	5	6
Cut	0	1	1	1	1	1	1	2	2	2	3	3	4	4	5	6
Burn	-5	1	1	1	1	1	1	2	2	2	3	3	4	5	6	6
CS	3	1	1	1	1	2	2	2	3	3	3	4	4	5	6	6
PP	-1	1	1	1	2	2	3	3	4	4	4	5	5	6	6	6

◀ Bleed Shift

	1	2	3	4	5	6	7	8	9	10	11	12	13	14	15+
Heal Time ▶	1	1	1	1	1	1	2	2	2	2	3	3	4	6	8
Decline Time ▶													10	4	1